T0339841

The World's Richest Neighborhood

THE WORLD'S RICHEST NEIGHBORHOOD

How Pittsburgh's East Enders Forged
American Industry

QUENTIN R. SKRABEC, JR.

Algora Publishing
New York

Library of Congress Cataloging-in-Publication Data —

Skrabec, Quentin R., Jr.
    The world's richiest neighborhood: how Pittsburgh's East Enders forged American
industry / Quentin R. Skrabec, Jr.
        p. cm.
    Includes bibliographical references and index.
    ISBN 978-0-87586-795-3 (soft cover: alk. paper) — ISBN 978-0-87586-796-0 (hbk.: alk.
paper) — ISBN 978-0-87586-797-7 (ebook) 1. Industrialists—Pennsylvania—Pittsburgh.
2. Industrialization—Pennsylvania—Pittsburgh. 3. Pittsburgh (Pa.)—History. I. Title.
    HC108.P7S57 2010
    338.092'274886—dc22

                                2010019774

Printed in the United States

To Our Lady of Snows and my sister, Marilyn

TABLE OF CONTENTS

PROLOGUE

The research for this book and my Pantheon of Capitalism has taken me many places, but the gods of my research could all be found in the East End of Pittsburgh. I grew up literally in Frick's backyard. I played and learned in Frick Park for days on end in my youth. My home in Swisshlem Park was built on the location where troops camped during the Homestead Strike and the mills dumped generations of steel slag into man-made mountains. Across the street from my home on a steep cliff was a panoramic view of Homestead where my grandfather worked. My grandfather Skrabec also worked for Frick's Union Railway, and my great grandfather Rechinger was one of Carnegie's engineers. I owe my education to the generosity of robber barons such as Carnegie and Frick. My inspiration for writing was rooted in my first trips to the Carnegie Library. My grandparents lived in Swissvale near where the Frick family often picnicked. I know the very footsteps of most of the East Enders well. I collected fossils from the same rock formations as Childs Frick. My family had many steelworkers, and given my fascination with steel I earned a metallurgical engineering degree from the University of Michigan.

I worked for years as a manager of a steel melt shop. I loved the nightglow of the steel city of Pittsburgh. As a manager, I came to know the Duquesne Club, University Club, and Pittsburgh Athletic Club. I could envision my pantheon of steel masters there. Unfortunately, my days in the steel industry and industry in general were days of decline for these once great enterprises. For Pittsburgh, industry was like the army was for Sparta. Its decline went to the heart of a people. Yet these men were also known for excesses and control. Some, like Henry Clay Frick, remain symbols of union busting. Their giving back to society in the form of libraries, hospitals, social services, museums, and schools is the other side of the same story. The residents of the East End represented this strange dichotomy; and for decades, the East End was a fortress against the press and general public.

INTRODUCTION

For thirty years I have been researching and writing a literary pantheon of American industrialists. These industrial "gods" have included George Westinghouse, Henry Clay Frick, William McGuffey, H. J. Heinz, William McKinley, Edward D. Libbey, Andrew Carnegie, Michael Owens, and others. As I filled these seats with biographies, a number of issues and questions arose. They were not saints but had the same human faults as all of us that money only magnified. They were often much like us; still, they stood out among the robber barons of the Gilded Age (some might say the best of the worst). This Pantheon of greatness was, however, meant to be an example of the best of capitalism and social responsibility for the students at the university. The marriage of the two makes the pantheon uniquely American. They were not the scammers of today, so often seen on the news. They were not financial men but manufacturers who profited from the making of things. An in-depth look at their lives reveals the complexity that would make sitting in the judgment seat a difficult task. They professed strong beliefs and ideals, whatever their shortcomings. As I searched for these ideals, a high percentage of these men were coming from one Pittsburgh suburb — the East End. What did they have in common? A number of factors emerged. Many were Scotch–Irish, and certainly Scotch–Irish values are a common thread even among those of non-Scotch–Irish backgrounds. These values included a thrifty style of living, an assumed responsibility to give back to the community, and a disciplined life. With a few exceptions, they rose from rags to riches. Many were Freemasons, as was common among the Scotch–Irish, and many were Presbyterians. Most believed in the Presbyterian and Scotch–Irish concept of the absolute property rights of individuals. All or most all were Whigs or Republicans. Most were from abolitionist families. Still, the factor that seems most dominant among these self-made men was a geographical location; and that location was Pittsburgh's East End. Geography can account for almost all of the other factors.

3

There was, however, a connecting network on several planes. Ethically and morally, many of these men were raised on the *McGuffey Reader* in one-room schoolhouses and had a deep love and appreciation of education. The *McGuffey Reader* worldview was imparted to them in their earliest days. Even the First Readers (kindergarten and first grade) in the McGuffey series highlighted the Scotch–Irish message of property rights, hard work, thrifty living, and giving to the less fortunate. McGuffey and his Scotch–Irish worldview evolved out of the frontier Scotch–Irish communities of Western Pennsylvania, not far from Pittsburgh's East End. The McGuffey worldview was a philosophy of an area more than that of one man or religion. The *McGuffey Readers* promoted giving to the poor, property rights, patriotism, competition, democracy, republican rule, and self-improvement. These beliefs were a natural fit with Presbyterianism, Freemasonry, capitalism, and philanthropy. Many of their beliefs about economic freedom were embodied in the planks of the early Republican and Whig parties. Again that is not so surprising when the birth of the Republican Party was in Pittsburgh, and the area voted Republican in every presidential election from Lincoln to Hoover. They were extremely patriotic, putting nation above money making.

The political views of these industrialists were, of course, formed by their manufacturing bias and industry-based needs. Most were immigrants or sons of immigrants with a deep hatred of slavery; and the reason most of their fathers initially joined the Republican Party had more to do with their opposition of slavery than economic factors. But the single principle that unites all of them was their belief in putting America first and a worldview centered on American democracy and industry. That view started with Abe Lincoln and would reach its peak during the administration of William McKinley (1896 to 1901). It's not surprising that every Republican president from Lincoln to Hoover made the pilgrimage to Pittsburgh's East End to receive the crown of industry. Pittsburgh and Allegheny County never went for a Democrat from 1860 to 1928. Ohio's McKinley, a Scotch–Irish mason born of Western Pennsylvania stock, would become the politician of Pittsburgh's East End. And in turn, the bronze busts of the East Enders would be immortalized at the McKinley Presidential Library in Niles, Ohio. McKinley and East Ender George Westinghouse made railroads safe through air brake laws. The great McKinley Tariffs of the 1880s and 1890s would create a boom for three of the East End's favorite products — steel, glass, and pickles. McKinley's presidential and even Ohio congressional campaigns were financed from Pittsburgh's East End. Not surprisingly, one of the last trips made by the Zeus of the East End — Henry Clay Frick — would be to Niles, Ohio, for some quiet moments of remembrance. Likewise years earlier, the great trustbuster Teddy Roosevelt would make a trip to the Frick mansion in the East End to pay homage to its industrialists.

The East Enders, while not monolithic, had some other shared beliefs and interests. They all found character in Napoleon and listed him as one of their heroes. Other heroes were George Washington, Henry Clay, Daniel Webster, Ben Franklin, poet Robert Burns, Robert Wallace ("Brave Heart"), and Alexander Hamilton. Not surprisingly, these were also common heroes in the *McGuffey Readers*, and their busts were found in the East End homes and parks. Several, such as Carnegie and Mellon, were followers of Herbert Spencer and his social Darwinism. All of the East Enders were patriotic to an extreme. Capitalism, to them, was not based on free trade but the dominance of American-made products and ideas. Most, like Westinghouse and Heinz, owned America's first international corporations, but country always came first. Only God and country would be allowed to stop their passion to earn money. During World War I they donated money to buy guns and tanks. Henry Clay Frick personally purchased tanks for the army. Frick and Heinz led the nation in buying "victory bonds." Veterans were given every advantage in their employment and were honored employees. Frick, Westinghouse, and Heinz guaranteed their employment upon their return. Second-generation sons such as William Thaw joined Pittsburgh's "Iron Division" in World War I.

For many people today, the biggest question about them is in regard to greed. Many have labeled these men's creed as the "Gospel of Greed," or in Carnegie's own words, the "Gospel of Wealth." However, evaluating greed requires perspective. Compared to the million-dollar weeklong parties of the New York wealthy, the East Enders were a sober bunch. When wealthy East Enders joined the Astors and Vanderbilts on New York's Fifth Avenue, they stood out. They tended to live quietly in their pursuit of art and philosophy. They were at the same time great philanthropists and "robber barons." The East Enders, in most cases, had first generation wealth, which affects people far differently than inherited wealth such as that of the "aristocracy" of New York. Most had come from the lowest level of immigrant society. Many had been in ghetto gangs in their youth. To these East End capitalists, money marked their success in distancing themselves from that past.

The question of how they obtained their wealth is just as complicated. Generally, they played by the rules that were in place at the time. One author generalized one perspective by categorizing Henry Clay Frick as a "master of honorable tricks."[1] They made their money producing things and employing many. Generally, they disliked old money and New York bankers. They clearly accumulated excess wealth, which for those with a socialist perspective, makes them suspect. They often set childhood goals of making millions such as Henry Clay Frick and Andrew Carnegie; others such as George Westinghouse wanted to be a famous inventor. They all seemed to turn money making into a type of sport. Yet like Olympic athletes, they gave up much and trained hard. The existence of industrial ghettos such as Braddock and Homestead within miles of their mansions makes one question the fairness of the distribution of money. Their anti-union bias also makes them suspect. Still, the workers did not want to take them down so much as to emulate them. The workers saw nothing wrong with the skewed distribution of wealth as long as the system to obtain wealth was fair and open to all. Both East Ender and worker believed strongly in Lincoln's "right to upward mobility." Most East Enders knew well the path from poverty to wealth. Several such as George Westinghouse and H. J. Heinz pioneered the welfare of workers. With the possible exception of Carnegie, they claimed no divine rights. Most often they listed their job types as "capitalist."

---

1 Samuel A. Schreiner, *Henry Clay Frick*, (New York: St. Martin Press, 1995). p. x

Critics point to Carnegie and Frick's hatred of unions as a sign of oppression of the poor. Even Westinghouse and Heinz, who ran employee-driven companies, were against unions. In fact, the general population of Pittsburgh was anti-union. The reason for the hatred is complex. It appears to be more one of control versus oppression. The unions of the period did not represent the unskilled and poorest of the workers but the skilled worker. Many of the titanic battles were over control of the workplace, not improved wages. Crafts unions were fighting the new industrial management system. The immigrants in Pittsburgh feared the Marxist unions of Europe, which many had fled. Further, the public had turned against the unions when Pittsburgh was left in ruins after the Great Railroad Strike of 1877. In general, the Pittsburgh immigrants had come to the factories to make money and dreamed of becoming wealthy themselves. The worker and the East Enders believed the key was the ability to rise in society. While lacking property, these immigrants cherished the property rights they lacked in Europe and hoped that they would gain property someday. This complex, ambiguous issue will be looked at in Carnegie's and Frick's roles in the Homestead Strike.

Judgment of their lives becomes more complicated the more one researches them. Even in the case of Frick, who for many is the Devil of Capitalism, it would be hard to throw the first stone. He was a caring family man who anonymously gave over $70 million to poor children and families. Judgment becomes difficult as one sees the breadth and extent of this giving. These capitalists built most of Pittsburgh's hospitals, schools, and social institutions. They built the only social services and organizations of the time prior to government taking on this role. The Carnegie libraries, universities, and foundations continue to give to American families to this day. Carnegie was far from alone, as many others helped build the University of Pittsburgh and Carnegie Institute of Technology. Carnegie spent most of his life giving away over $300 million that he had earned. He refused to create a dynasty such as those of New York's wealthy by passing the wealth on to family. Like Carnegie, most feared what they saw in second generation wealth.

Even the term "robber baron" did not really apply to the East Enders. Generally they worked hard for their fortunes and sacrificed much. They disliked most of the eastern bankers who, they believed, did not earn their money. Their fortunes were made by making things versus the stock manipulations of the New York crowd. Even the Mellon family of bankers invested in America's core industries of coal, steel, and aluminum. They abhorred inherited wealth. They avoided the press when it came to their wealth and lived quiet lives in their woodland suburb. Their belief systems, politics, attitudes, and religion were initially not much different than those of the workers they managed. Upward mobility was more important than wealth distribution in itself.

They believed in the Scotch–Irish principle that education must be free to all members, and fairness was in distribution of education more so than distribution of wealth. Education was the equalizer and offered the class mobility they believed in. Like the early Scotch–Irish immigrants, they believed that the wealthy class of Europe controlled their status by restricting education to the upper class. By contrast, they gave generously to schools of all types. In a way, they felt that paying low wages was balanced by the education that was freely given to the workers to improve themselves. It was a deep-rooted Scotch-Irish concept, and it had been reinforced in their education from the *McGuffey Readers* of the period. In turn, it can be seen in their philanthropy to schools of all levels, free libraries, free museums, free admission to observatories, and the development of parks. At the time, the approach was criticized, but in the long run it created generations of successful citizens from the immigrant workers of the period.

Another part of the East Enders' legacy was how they were impacted by and how they impacted industrial Pittsburgh. Pittsburgh worker society was different than the immigrant worker societies of cities like Chicago. People like Henry Frick saw Westinghouse's and Heinz's paternal capitalism as a form of socialism; and today, socialist parties indeed aim to bring better conditions to all of society, not only to a certain group of employees. However in the 19th century socialists were lumped together with anarchists and were considered anti-establishment — against capitalists, government, and religion. Radical socialists and anarchists could not gain a foothold in Pittsburgh. Even after the bloody Homestead Strike when popular opinion turned against Frick and the East Enders, it was quickly regained a few days later when an anarchist tried to assassinate Frick. The East Enders and the workers reflected this anti-socialism at all levels. It was reflected in the very nature of the Pittsburgh unions which favored the amalgamated crafts union versus the trade unionism of the more popular national Knights of Labor. Like capitalism, the crafts union promoted a steep wage distribution with a high paid hierarchy of skilled craftsmen. The eight-hour day was actually opposed by most Pittsburgh unions because they wanted to earn as much as they could. Pittsburgh workers wanted mobility more than protection. For many, the East End was not an example of unfair accumulation of wealth but a goal of what could be obtained through hard work.

CHAPTER 1. THE WORLD'S RICHEST NEIGHBORHOOD

By 1900, Pittsburgh's East End neighborhood was the world's richest. It was the rich suburb of what had become America's fifth largest city and the world's manufacturing metropolis. In a short walk, one might run into a member of the Carnegie family, Henry Clay Frick, George Westinghouse, H. J. Heinz, or one of the Mellon family. You would surely run into one of the 36 millionaire partners of Andrew Carnegie and at least a major city bank president. It would be likely that you would meet an executive of the Pennsylvania Railroad. You would probably run into a U.S. senator or congressman. Mail was delivered seven times a day to keep America's greatest capitalists in touch with their factories, banks, and markets. The residents of Pittsburgh's East End controlled as much as 60 percent of America's assets. Three major corporations — Standard Oil, ALCOA, and Gulf Oil — were formed in East End homes. It was the first neighborhood to adopt the telephone with direct lines from the homes to Pittsburgh's biggest banks. The neighborhood had its own private station of the Pennsylvania Railroad and the world's first AC power plant. This wealthy burgh commanded visits from American presidents and future Presidents such as James Monroe, Andrew Jackson, John Q. Adams, Zachary Taylor, William Harrison, Rutherford Hayes, William McKinley, Teddy Roosevelt, William Taft, Calvin Coolidge, and Herbert Hoover. Colonel George Washington led the Virginia militia through the East End on his way to Fort Duquesne. James Monroe stayed several days at the East End mansion of Pittsburgh's glass manufacturer, Benjamin Bakewell. No other suburban neighborhood can claim so many presidential visits. They visited the East End with good reason. Up to four of these presidents owe their presidency to neighborhood "nomination" meetings and fund drives.

President William McKinley had several dinner stops and stayed over at the Westinghouse mansion "Solitude." Teddy Roosevelt stopped over at the Frick mansion for lunch and took a nap in the upper room. William Taft had dinner and gave a speech in 1910 at the East End mansion of steel baron Henry Laughlin. The weekly neighborhood poker game was often a political war room. Pittsburgh's East End was the home of U.S. Senator Philander Knox, who often joined in the weekly poker game at Frick's mansion. The game included the Mellon brothers and the Carnegie brothers. Out of this poker game would come an Attorney General (Philander Knox under President McKinley) and Secretary of the Treasury (Andrew Mellon under President Hoover). With Frick, Mellon, Carnegie, Knox, and Westinghouse at the table, it must have been the most prestigious poker game in history, and the table talk may well have changed the world.

Even prior to 1890, the East End had a long pedigree of national politicians such as a U.S. senator (James Ross), U.S. representatives (Henry Baldwin and William Wilkins), Cabinet secretaries and assistants (William Wilkins and Thomas Scott), two Supreme Court judges (Henry Baldwin and William Wilkins), and an ambassador in William Wilkins. Judge Wilkins Sr. was a brother-in-law of an American vice-president. Even General Lafayette stopped in the East End on his 1825 trip back to the United States, visiting glassmaker Benjamin Bakewell. Another early famous resident was painter James Audubon, who married into the Bakewell family.

America's first industrial millionaire, James O'Hara, was the founder of the neighborhood and owned much of the East End. Judge Wilkins's cobblestone mansion known as "Dumplin Hall" was at Hay and Kelly Streets in then McNairstown (later renamed Wilkinsburg) and entertained many famous Americans.

Eight blocks of Pittsburgh's East End had enough major art pieces to rival any American or European museum. There were more Egyptian artifacts and Native American artifacts than in most of the world's museums. There were more conservatories per square foot than anywhere in the world as well as some of the most rare and exotic flowers. It was here that Westinghouse conceived of the AC power grid; Captain Hunt planned the first commercial aluminum production plant; Tom Carnegie persuaded his brother to get into the steel business; Charles Lockhart co-founded the world's largest oil company; and Heinz created his "57 varieties." Its famous Hotel Schenley was a corporate gathering place of some of the world's greatest industrialists, politicians, bankers, art collectors, and philanthropists. It was the first to use natural gas and had one of the world's first natural gas wells. The neighborhood was the first to have a telephone switching station; the first to be electrified; the first to use aluminum in homes; and the first to have a gas station. In 1905, the neighborhood had more telephones, automobiles, and dollars per capita than any community in the world.

The East End of Pittsburgh was described by New York reporter Theodore Dreiser as: "Never in my life was the vast gap which divides the rich from the poor in America so vividly and forcefully brought home to me . . . Never did the mere possession of wealth impress me so keenly . . . Even the street lamps were of a better design than elsewhere." It was truly the center of opulent wealth of the Victorian era. Besides the more famous mentioned, other millionaires abounded. Frick's closest neighbors were the Mellon brothers, Andrew and Richard, George Westinghouse, and H.J. Heinz. By 1900 more millionaires lived in Pittsburgh's East End than anywhere on the planet.

In Pittsburgh in the 1890s, there lived Thomas Armstrong, the founder of Armstrong Cork and Sons; Philander Knox who would be a U.S. Senator and Attorney General under President McKinley and Teddy Roosevelt; and Thomas Howe, a banking and copper magnate, who served two terms as a U.S. Senator from the Whig Party. Andrew Carnegie's mother lived on the southern edge of the neighborhood as well as Tom Carnegie in the 1880s. At one point, all of Carnegie's partners and many of their sons lived in the neighborhood over the years. Some of these partners were Francis Lovejoy, William Coleman, Latham Abbott, Lawrence Phipps who would become a U.S. Senator, Henry Curry, John Scott, David Stewart, John Vandevort, George Lauder (Carnegie's cousin), Alexander Peacock, Daniel Clemson, and the Borntraeger brothers — William and Carl. Charles Schwab, the first president of United States Steel, lived on the East End's "Millionaire Row" on Fifth Avenue. Other industrialists included George Mesta, founder of Mesta Machine Company; Jacob Vandergrift, partner of Rockefeller in Standard Oil; Thomas Mellon, founder of Mellon Banks; Charles Lockhart, co-founder of Standard Oil with Rockefeller; Alfred Hunt, founder of ALCOA Aluminum; Sylvester Marvin, founder of National Biscuit Company (Nabisco); James McCrea, president of the Pennsylvania Railroad; Robert Pitcairn, vice-president of Pennsylvania Railroad and industrial investor; John Pitcairn, president of Pittsburgh Plate Glass; Oswald Werner, developer of dry-cleaning; William Lash, president of Carbon Steel and co-founder of ALCOA; Willis McCook, co-founder of Pittsburgh Steel; Wallace Rowe, co-founder of Pittsburgh steel; Alexander King, glass magnate; David Stewart, president of Pittsburgh Locomotive; Henry Hillard, president of Alcania; Henry Laughlin, Jones and Laughlin Steel; Alexander Bradley, stove manufacturer; Benjamin Thaw, railroad magnate; James Guffey, oil and gas magnate and co-founder of Gulf Oil; Julian Kennedy, world blast furnace expert; George Macbeth, founder of Macbeth–Evans Glass; Daniel Clemson, a Carnegie partner; Benjamin and Thomas Bakewell, Pittsburgh's famous glassmaking family; Thomas Messler, president of the New York and Erie Railroad; Lillian Russell, national theater star; and Joseph Woodwell, hardware baron and artist. Others included Durbin Horne, president of Joseph Horne Department store; Alexander Moore, newspaper baron (as well as Ambassador to Spain); James McClelland, famous homeopathic physician; Arthur Braun, publisher and banker; Thomas Howe, president of the Exchange National Bank of Pittsburgh; George Berry, president of Citizen's National Bank; Rueben Miller, president of Fidelity Trust Company; August Succop, banking executive; James Callery, president of Pittsburgh Railways; and bank president John Holmes. After 1900, the list slowed but added people like Charles Schwab, first president of United States Steel, and many United States Steel executives.

In the 1880s and 1890s, the East End was a tight knit neighborhood. Sundays were days of picnics and walks. Frick often met with the Mellon brothers and Joseph Woodwell to discuss art. Early Sunday morning they would meet in Frick's library, and later in the day they moved to Woodwell's home studio. On Saturdays, Frick often walked over to his friend and lawyer, Philander Knox, with his daughter, Helen Frick. Mrs. Frick often walked the gardens of H. J. Heinz. There were many neighborhood flower shows in which the Fricks participated. Often Frick would offer a small prize for the best flower.

Frick and Heinz opened their conservatories to the public. H. J. Heinz maintained a public museum on the fourth floor of his mansion. Westinghouse was one of the first to institute the company picnic for his employees. Mr. and Mrs. Westinghouse were best known for their informal East End dinner parties. Westinghouse often included his neighbors to dine with a visiting scientist, artist, royalty, or politician such as Nikola Tesla, Lord Kelvin, or William McKinley. The period from 1880 to 1895 was the peak of these informal days. As the close of the century neared, many of the neighbors had summer and winter homes elsewhere. But when they were in town, Sundays were special days for the East End. The tradition of a leisurely Sunday with picnics went back to one of the area's founders and Pittsburgh's first industrialist, James O'Hara. In the winter, neighbors might enjoy ice skating at the Casino dance pavilion (at the time the world's largest), now the site of the Frick Fine Arts Building.

Probably more typical of the dominant race of East End Scotch–Irish was that of the Mellon family. The family mustered the members for Sunday services at East Liberty Presbyterian Church. Service was followed by a "long, silent lunch."[1] Meals were said to be eaten in silence unless business was talked about. By all accounts, it was a boring lunch except when the men met afterward for a whiskey and cigars. The Mellons, like many of the Scotch–Irish, did not mix in social settings or parties. The Scotch–Irish, much like their German neighbors, suppressed emotions in public. They were serious people who believed in hard work six days a week. Sunday was to remain free for relaxation, a belief they had imposed on the area until the 1880s when Andrew Carnegie found it necessary to make his steel mills run seven days a week. Henry Clay Frick's friend and son of Judge Thomas Mellon, Andrew, was a bit of an exception. The only social schedule of the Mellons was family driven, and included events such as the Judge's birthday, Thanksgiving, and New Year. They joined with only a handful of non-family members such as Thomas Alexander, the Negley family, and James Ross. Judge Mellon had named one of his sons James Ross Mellon, and these families were Scotch–Irish Presbyterian and founding families of Pittsburgh. The Mellons had a dislike and distrust for the social elite of eastern cities.

H. J. Heinz and his family would take a carriage drive to services at Sharpsburg Methodist Church on Sundays. Heinz would also stay to teach Sunday school. They would return to a picnic or walk their St. Bernard, "Homewood Don," around the neighborhood. Heinz would ride his horses and saddle his ponies for the children. He would not share a glass of whiskey with a neighbor as he was a leader of the temperance movement. Heinz was even known to remove his ketchup from saloons and bars. Church and neighborhood picnics were always supplied with ample supplies of pickles. Heinz, in fact, supplied pickles to churches throughout the Pittsburgh area. While most neighbors attended one of the area's Presbyterian Churches, the Pitcairns belonged to the Swedenborgian movement with Andrew Carnegie. Frick attended Calvary Especial, but most Scotch–Irish and

---

1 David Cannadine, *Mellon*, (New York: Alfred Knopf, 2006), p. 125

Germans belonged to the Presbyterian Church; and East Liberty Presbyterian was known as the "cathedral of capitalism."

East Liberty was about six miles from downtown Pittsburgh. Telegram offices and telephones came to the area in the 1860s and 1870s. The first telephone in Allegheny County was installed at the East Liberty home of Thomas David (president of the local telegraph company) in 1877. H.J. Heinz was one of the first to use a telephone for his business in 1879. Frick added several phones to Clayton in 1883. Pittsburgh's first telephone switching station was built in East Liberty and manned by operators twenty-four hours a day. The system was needed because of the network set up by East End bankers. The area had a special flag station for the Pennsylvania Railroad which allowed men like George Westinghouse to take the daily train to his factories, east of Pittsburgh in the Turtle Creek Valley. The Fifth Avenue Car System and Citizens Passenger Railways, which were both horse drawn trolley systems, serviced East Liberty in the 1870s.

Many of the neighbors invested in Westinghouse's Pittsburgh Traction Company, which installed a new cable car system in 1889; but the first trolley line was that of Citizens Traction Company. Westinghouse had built one of the first electric train systems on his East End estate, including his own power plant. Frick and Andrew Mellon were investment partners in the Citizens Traction Company with the Republican machine bosses, Christopher Magee and William Flinn. The cable car was the first "rapid" transit system, reducing the hour and half trip to Pittsburgh to one hour. In 1890, an electric trolley serviced the area, cutting the commute time to Pittsburgh to thirty minutes. George Westinghouse had also installed an experimental electric trolley around his mansion. The Pennsylvania Railroad had its only long distance non-stop train, the "*Pittsburgher*" and the "*Iron City Express*," which went directly from the East End to the New York financial district. Westinghouse built his own railroad station in the 1870s along with an underground tunnel to his mansion. He had his own special Pullman railcar maintained at the station. The car included an engineering drafting room for Westinghouse. Similarly, his neighbor Henry Clay Frick had his own Pullman.

Neighbors such as Robert Pitcairn helped build a Pennsylvania Railroad to a mountain resort for summer vacations. The Cresson area included a mountain inn, exclusive cottages, and a club of East Enders. Andrew Carnegie built a cottage-style mansion for family and friends. Many of the neighbors were founding members in an exclusive club in the mountains around Johnstown, Pennsylvania. The organization was known as the South Fork Fishing and Hunting Club, which would be mired in the famous Johnstown Flood of 1889. The resort had a special railroad station for the man-made mountain top lake. A dam on a small mountaintop created a lake for fishing and sailing. It became known by Carnegie as the "glorious mountain," and reporters talked of sailboats on a mountain. The faulty dam that was built would burst in May of 1889, creating a terrible disaster. The Johnstown Flood had an official death count of 2,209 with hundreds missing. Wherever the blame belonged, the press pinned it on the wealthy members of the club in the East End, and the name of Frick was the most prominent. The night after the flood, East End neighbors held a meeting. Of the club members, Frick gave $5,000, Andrew Mellon gave

$1,000, and Carnegie gave $10,000 to help the victims. Still, the Johnstown Flood would forever be linked to the wealthy of Pittsburgh's East End.

These same neighbors became partners in the commercial development of Pittsburgh's East End and Oakland area. Men like Andrew Mellon and Henry Clay Frick had been buying land in the East End for years, seeing its growth potential. Entrepreneur Franklin Nikola believed in the future of Oakland as a cultural center for the Pittsburgh area. Nikola formed Bellefield Company to develop the Oakland area. He was able to enlist Frick as an investor as well as H. J. Heinz, Andrew Carnegie, George Westinghouse, and Andrew Mellon. The first project was a first class hotel — the Hotel Schenley. H. J. Heinz and United States Steel would move their annual company meetings to the Hotel Schenley. Built in 1898, the hotel would have guests such as William Howard Taft and Teddy Roosevelt. Known as the "Waldorf of Pittsburgh," it was the host to the "Millionaire's Dinner" that hailed the formation of United States Steel in 1901. Carnegie built his new museum across the street, and a few blocks further, his university — the Carnegie Institute of Technology (Carnegie Mellon University). In 1909 the University of Pittsburgh moved to Oakland at "Frick Acres," followed by Forbes Field and the Pittsburgh Pirates. University of Pittsburgh's Cathedral of Learning is located on "Frick Acres." The register included President William Taft, Andrew Carnegie, J. P. Morgan, President Harding, President Teddy Roosevelt, British royalty, Babe Ruth, Ty Cobb, and Roger Hornsby. Today the Hotel Schenley is part of the University of Pittsburgh (William Pitt Union).

These neighbors had difficult schedules and auxiliary homes elsewhere such as in New York. Many such as Philander Knox, Joseph Woodwell, Henry Clay Frick, Andrew Carnegie, Benjamin Thaw, and Robert Pitcairn were members of the South Fork Fishing and Hunting Club. Henry Clay Frick was one of the founders of the Schenley Riding Club and participated in races at their track on Brunots Island. In 1899 Heinz was introduced to a new game — golf. In 1899 Pittsburgh's first golf course was built in the East End Homewood neighborhood. Belmar was a six-hole course. Later, Henry Clay Frick built an exclusive golf course in Schenley Park. Frick and Howard Heinz also became interested in automobiles, as the first races were held in nearby Schenley Park. Howard Heinz would also become an attendee and racer. It was a neighborhood of greenhouses. The greenhouses supported some personal plant experiments as well as plants from around the world, inspired by the nearby Phipps Conservatory which had opened to the public in 1899. The Phipps Conservatory was considered the second largest in the world. H. J. Heinz opened his conservatory to the public. He had over ten greenhouses where he was testing new vegetables and flowers. Heinz's fall chrysanthemum show became a favorite with the people of Pittsburgh. In 1915 he put much of the grounds into war victory gardens. Frick had his own conservatory as part of Clayton and took up the hobby of raising orchids and other flowers. It was a life-long hobby he shared with his wife, and Frick also was happy to take visitors through the conservatory. Often there was an informal competition between neighbors. Frick opened his conservatory to the public in 1915. In New York, Frick entered flower shows and financially supported them. He was also known for raising mushrooms. He became a charter member of the International Garden Club in 1914.

H. J. Heinz was within a block of Frick, and his mansion became a public attraction. Heinz continued to expand his "Greenlawn" mansion in the late 1890s with a billiard room, conservatory, bowling alley, tennis court, additional greenhouses, an expanded library, and an expanded museum. Eventually, his mansion would have ten specialized green houses. Heinz's sisters, Mary and Henrietta, lived there and acted as hostesses for Heinz. Heinz, like Frick, had trees brought in from the world over including cuttings from the Vatican. In 1897, Heinz added a pedigree St. Bernard dog known as "Homewood Don." Dogs were extremely popular in the neighborhood. Helen Frick had a dog named "Fido." Heinz's private museum on the fourth floor had caught the imagination of the local and national press in 1897 and was opened on a limited basis. Heinz had hired Professor Samuel Harper, a local scientist, to maintain and catalog the museum. The collections included the pre-Indian mound people of the Pittsburgh area, a collection of footwear from around the world, carved ivories, oriental rugs, a complete armor collection, art pieces, and endless curios. Heinz's curios were much different than the classic art of Frick's Clayton and the Mellon mansion. Heinz loved to collect, and his passion took him in many different directions. He often took his salesmen and customers as well as hundreds of social guests and local school children through the museum.

The East End of Pittsburgh was about more than money. Money was merely the motivator and a measure of success. The neighborhood was not a testimony to a new American aristocracy such as the mansion on New York's Fifth Avenue, but a testimony to American invention and industry. East Enders invented the railroad air brake, oil distillation, preservative-free ketchup, the kerosene lamp, gas meters, tinplate rolling mills, cast steam engines, steamboats, new glass making systems, natural gas and electrical distribution, commercial aluminum production, and endless iron and steel processes. Westinghouse's alternating electrical current was tried first in the East End and revolutionized electrical power distribution. That power distribution led to the development of commercial aluminum by other East Enders. The modern spark plug evolved in the East End.

The East End was one of America's first true suburbs. The beautiful mansions were in a rural setting. A deep wooded ravine cut by Nine-Mile Run ran several miles from the back of Clayton to the Monongahela River (today it is still a nature preserve known as Frick Park). Not far was the hilly nature preserve known as Highland Park. Highland Park was a 436-acre park created in 1889 with the help of East End resident and Pittsburgh political boss, William Flinn. Frick Park and Schenley Park were popular horse riding paths. Helen Frick was fond of riding her mare called "Patricia" on these wooded trails. Even the mansion owners such as H. J. Heinz brought in large trees to plant on their grounds, keeping the rural nature of the area to this day. The Fricks loved to picnic in nearby Swissvale on the Monongahela side. More than anyone in the family, Helen came to love walking in the woods and neighborhood. Childs Frick, who developed his love for nature and fossil collecting in the wooded East End ravines and parks, left for Princeton in 1901 to become a famous paleontologist.

Henry Clay Frick was also spending more time in New York where United States Steel was headquartered. Like many of his neighbors, he had his own railroad car — *The*

Westmoreland — on the Pennsylvania Railroad, allowing him to go to New York in luxury and take the family on vacation. Henry had rented an apartment in New York's Sherry's Hotel; and the family often vacationed at the Breakers Hotel in Palm Beach, Florida. In fact, the development of Palm Beach, Florida, was a result of East End investors. East Enders Henry Clay Frick and Philander Knox built summer homes at Eagle Rock on Boston's North Shore. Neighbors included William Taft, Henry Cabot Lodge, Louis Comfort Tiffany, Theodore Roosevelt, and Justice Oliver Wendell Holmes. Helen Frick, however, preferred Clayton to these other homes, which seemed to pull the Frick family back to Pittsburgh. The family never sold their mansion; it just passed from the family in the 1990s to a public trust. Frick's Eagle Rock home was not far from President Taft's summer home, and Taft and Frick became good friends and golfing buddies. Thomas Bakewell of the East End was a close friend of Taft and would often visit him there. They were members of the exclusive Myopia Hunt Club. The Myopia had the nation's first polo field for Childs Frick to learn the game, and one of the most famous golf courses, which hosted the U.S. Open in 1898, 1901, 1905, and 1908. Frick would golf with Taft and take part in his famous "automobile parties." They also competed in the Myopia Club's horse shows in which Frick often won medals for his horses. At Eagle Rock, one of Frick's first visitors was George Westinghouse and his wife, who had a summer home in the Berkshires.

Frick, Westinghouse, Mellon, and Heinz and their neighbors drew many of the world's most powerful men to this Pittsburgh suburb. Presidents, princes, artists, politicians, and scientists came routinely to visit the residents of Pittsburgh's East End. Frick's neighbor, George Westinghouse, invited a constant stream of famous scientists to dinner such as Nikola Tesla, Lord Kelvin, and Benjamin Lamme. When Nikola Tesla worked in Pittsburgh for Westinghouse, he was often an overnight guest at the Westinghouse mansion. Many presidents before, during, and after their presidencies — George Washington, James Monroe, Rutherford B. Hayes, Grover Cleveland, William McKinley, Teddy Roosevelt, Warren Harding, William Howard Taft, Herbert Hoover, and Calvin Coolidge — made stops at the neighborhood. Probably the most famous visit was that of Teddy Roosevelt to Clayton in 1902. The affair was on the Fourth of July and included the U.S. Marine Corps Band. Roosevelt came to pay tribute to the East End capitalists, who were nervous over his progressive views. The guests were some of Pittsburgh's top businessmen. Frick sat at the head of the table with Roosevelt to the right and friend and Attorney General Philander Knox to the left. Others included Henry W. Oliver (steel "aristocrat"), Andrew Mellon, George Laughlin (steel "aristocrat"), James McCrea (President, Pennsylvania Railroad), General John P. Penny, George Oliver, George Cortelyou (President's secretary), John Wylie, James Brown, Charles Speer, Calvin Wells (President, Pittsburgh Forge), Henry Porter (Pittsburgh locomotive manufacturer), William McConway (iron manufacturer), W. C. Latin, John Urie, Albert Barr (Pittsburgh editor), J. O. Brown (banker), J. O. Jones (military guard — Sheridan troop), and Albert Logan.[1]

---

1 *Pittsburgh Times*, July 4, 1902

After lunch a number of Pittsburgh businessmen stopped by, as well as some major politicians such as William Flinn, Christopher Magee, and B.F. Jones (head of local Republicans). Over 600 American Beauty roses were used in the rooms as well as special Frick-grown roses and orchids. Twelve waiters served a luncheon from New York's Waldorf-Astoria Hotel, with salmon, mayonnaise, melon, tomato aspic, sweetbreads, filet of beef, roast duck, new potatoes, Heinz pickles, asparagus, peas, and cheese. The dessert included ice cream, cake, coffee, and fruit. In addition, tents in the back were used to serve the troops. After lunch Roosevelt took a nap in the guest room. That evening he would head for the Schenley Hotel in Oakland for a large dinner meeting. While a major contributor to Roosevelt, Frick was not a huge fan, but Frick would be involved with Roosevelt in a number of future trust cases as well as being an envoy for J. P. Morgan. Roosevelt intended for this visit to win over Frick. Roosevelt had become president after the assassination of William McKinley in the fall of 1901. Frick, a lifelong Republican, cared little for the progressive wing of the party that Roosevelt represented.

Frick had given Roosevelt a Frits Thaulow painting known as *Smoky City*. It was obviously a symbol of the industrial might of Pittsburgh. Roosevelt needed to calm the Pittsburgh industrialists as his rhetoric about "trust busting" heated up. Roosevelt had kept Frick's neighbor, Philander Knox, as Attorney General to help assuage their fears. Roosevelt would also need Frick's support to win in 1904, so the visit was to build an alliance and a relationship, which both men would draw on in the future. While young Childs Frick may have been a fan of President McKinley, Helen Frick took to Roosevelt more than her father. Martha Frick Symington Sanger suggests that it was the environmental policies of Roosevelt that inspired Helen to ask her father to establish Frick Park as a wilderness perverse.[1]

Henry Clay Frick, however, never warmed up to Roosevelt, calling him the "damned cowboy." He did realize that Roosevelt was the only Republican for 1904. After Roosevelt became president with the 1901 assassination of McKinley, Roosevelt went after some big trusts, which worried capitalists like Frick. Philander Knox, Attorney General and Frick friend, convinced Frick that Roosevelt's actions were necessary. Frick, however, had deep philosophical differences with Roosevelt and the progressive wing of the Republican Party. Frick became a financial supporter of Roosevelt in 1904, donating $50,000, while other board members such as Morgan and Rogers donated $150,000. Frick actively supported Roosevelt in financial circles. After Roosevelt's victory, however, Frick thought Roosevelt owed him a favor. Frick would, of course, call in the marker to allow the formation of United States Steel without trust review. Before that, however, Roosevelt appointed Frick to the popular Isthmian Canal Commission (Panama).

The Thomas Mellon home was the first in Pittsburgh to have running water in 1857. The East End was one of the first neighborhoods in the world to have natural gas and then

---

1   Martha Frick Symington Sanger, *Helen Clay Frick*, (Pittsburgh: University of Pittsburgh Press, 2008), p. 83

electric lighting, thanks to George Westinghouse. The first electric light of the Westing-house system was installed at the home of James Ross Mellon at 401 Negley Avenue.

Westinghouse also hired geologists to explore the grounds at Solitude near Thomas Boulevard. By the end of 1883, Westinghouse had started to drill for gas on his property. He beamed with enthusiasm and spent nights designing drilling tools to amuse himself. He encouraged the drilling crew and spent hours talking and taking notes on drilling. One night the well came in, with a major explosion, and a hurricane-like hiss disturbed the once peaceful residential neighborhood. To test the well, it was lit, producing a huge col-umn of bright light that could be seen for many miles. The brightness was described thus: "The gas lamps of the city dwindled to a little points of light, and persons in the street not less than a mile away were able to read distinctly the finest newspaper print by the light of gigantic natural flambeau on the heights of Solitude." The Pittsburgh fire department had to be summoned to hose down the mansion to prevent it from burning. The tremen-dous pressure at the wellhead was obvious, and the first step was to design and make a stopcock to cap the well. Westinghouse handled this task personally as the neighborhood awaited some relief. By 1885, Westinghouse was supplying Pittsburgh's industry natural gas and the East End gas lighting. Westinghouse owned the Philadelphia Gas Company that supplied the East End, and Frick served as a director. Westinghouse converted his neighbors, H. J. Heinz and Frick, to natural gas first. Frick's home was converted to natu-ral gas in 1884 and then to electric with the help of George Westinghouse in 1890.

The neighborhood received commercial electric service in 1886 with the formation of the East End Electric Light Company. East End was the first residential neighborhood in the world to be electrified. The company started as a direct current arc company for East End street lighting. In 1887 it converted to the Westinghouse system of alternating cur-rent, which allowed for home lighting. The new alternating current generating station on Penn Avenue was the world's largest in 1887, servicing a nine-mile circuit. This distribu-tion area was considered a limit for alternating, but it was much better than the Edison direct current system, which needed a power station every two-city blocks. The houses of George Westinghouse, Herman Westinghouse (George's brother), and Henry Frick Clay were the first on the circuit. While George and Frick were neighbors, Herman's house was four miles away in Edgewood. The company used 1,000 volts of pressure to distrib-ute power and then stepped it down to 110 volts for incandescent lighting; however, to reach Herman's house in Edgewood required a pressure of 2,000 volts. By 1889 Johnstown, Pennsylvania, almost 100 miles away, was being supplied from the East End station of George Westinghouse. Allegheny County Light Company took over the East End in 1896. Westinghouse even built a private street car line around his mansion to test new motors, and that experiment would lead to Pittsburgh Railways with the Mellon family investing in the company, which would serve the entire Pittsburgh region.

Another technology that developed in Pittsburgh's East was the automobile. The East End would foretell how the American automobile linked suburbs. Frick had taken his first auto trip in a Mercedes while in France in 1904. That same year he purchased a Mercedes, one of Pittsburgh's earliest cars; Frick had it shipped over but could not find a driver, so he had to import a French chauffeur. Frick's neighbor and son of H. J. Heinz, Howard Heinz, had another of the first cars in Pittsburgh at his East End Mansion. It was an imported Panhard-Levassor with a German Daimler engine. The Heinz car reached a speed of forty miles an hour and became known by East End residents as the "Red Devil." Today it can be seen in the Frick Museum at Clayton. H. J. Heinz preferred his chauffeured Pierce Arrow, while his neighbor Thomas Hartley had two Stanley Steamers and an electric automobile in 1902.

East End neighbors Louis and Charles Clarke started an automobile company in 1897, Autocar Company, years before Henry Ford. They produced a small car called the "Pitts-burgher." The Clarke brothers first patented the spark plug. The sparkplug rights were later sold to Champion. In 1904, the East End had 2,000 cars. This was years before Henry Ford released his first Model T. It is not surprising that many believe the nation's first au-tomobile accident occurred in the East End. By 1906, there were 3,000 cars in Pittsburgh, and 2,000 of them were in the East End. Pittsburgh's first traffic light was at Penn and Highland Avenues in the East End.

In the early 1900s the East End had an unbelievable array of steamers, diesel, electric, and gasoline cars. The first automobile club in Pennsylvania was formed in the East End and was known as the Wilkinsburg Automobile Club. The Wilkinsburg Club arranged horseless carriage caravans to "tour" weekly. Beechwood Boulevard was used for short races in the first years of the century and had to rebuild in 1903 by Fredrick Olmstead. Thomas Hartley (Vandergrift family) was one of the nation's most famous auto enthusi-asts with steamers, electrics, and gas-driven autos. In 1905, Carnegie partners and East Enders, Francis Lovejoy and Alexander Peacock, had over 12 automobiles each. There were 12 dealerships in the East End in 1906, two of them selling all electric cars. For a brief period from 1898 to 1905, Pittsburgh became the "Motor City" with 20 carmakers includ-ing the Penn, the Keystone, the Brush, and the Artzberger. Pittsburgh Motor Company opened in 1907 in the East End to fix and manufacture electric cars, and George West-inghouse was a minor investor. Because of the demand in 1906 and before Henry Ford opened his first assembly-line operation, Ford Motor had a small hand assembly operation in the neighborhood. George Westinghouse, Frick's neighbor, had one of the nation's first electric cars but preferred the railroad to car trips. Frick was one of the first of the Pitts-burgh capitalists to fully embrace the automobile. In 1907 Frick took an automobile tour of Europe. Gulf Oil of Pittsburgh (founded in the East End) built the first drive-through gas station in Pittsburgh's East End.

In the late 1890s, Frick was introduced to a new game, golf, which had gained popular-ity in the East End. The East End Belmar Golf course was a six-hole course. Frick would often see H. J. Heinz at Belmar but preferred the nine- or eighteen-hole courses. Most of the neighborhood including Frick belonged to the exclusive Oakmont and Pittsburgh Coun-try Clubs. Pittsburgh Country Club was on Beechwood Avenue, and members included Henry Clay Frick, H. J. Heinz, Andrew Carnegie, Charles Schwab, and most of Carnegie's partners. Frick also financed the building of a private golf course in Pittsburgh's East End Schenley Park. He also used the clubs for business entertaining. Frick became one of the

East End's most avid golfers. He would have some very distinguished golf partners such as President William Taft, and he played on the world's greatest courses. He appeared to have played almost daily in his later years. Frick and H. J. Heinz also loved winter golf trips to Palm Beach with their neighbors. Frick, Heinz, and Mellon became major investors in Florida resort and golf areas.

The East End was full of beautiful churches, parks, and other recreational facilities. The dominant church was that of the Scotch-Irish Presbyterians. The most famous church was the East Liberty Presbyterian Church known as the "cathedral of capitalism," built in 1819 at Highland and Penn Avenues by some of the founding families of Pittsburgh such as the Negleys and the Mellons. East Liberty Church was the church of the Mellon family and a long line of Pittsburgh industrialists including George Westinghouse and H. J. Heinz. East Liberty Presbyterian Church is considered the mother church of Shadyside and Point Breeze. Frick was never a regular churchgoer; he preferred the ritual of Calvary Episcopal Church as well as its active social outreach programs such as the Kingsley Association. Calvary Episcopal, a beautiful Gothic church with a 220-foot spire, was redesigned in 1906 by a donation from Frick.

Recreation was always a big part of life in the East End. East Liberty had the beautiful Highland, Schenley, and Frick Parks on its borders. Political boss, neighbor, and Frick business partner, William Magee, opened a zoological garden in 1898 and later opened a zoo at Highland Park. The zoo was one of the delights of East End children such as Childs Frick and Howard Heinz. The Carnegie Museum and Art Institute was also in the East End and was another of Childs Frick's favorites. The world's first collection of huge dinosaurs not far from Clayton clearly inspired his career in paleontology. In addition, the Natural History Museum housed many of then-Colonel Teddy Roosevelt's many big game trophies. Years later, stuffed animals of both Roosevelt and Childs Frick would be exhibited together. Carnegie's Art Museum was also built in 1895 and was the nation's first modern art museum. The Tavern of Shakespeare Gardens at Penn and Shady Streets in the 1840s may well have been one of the country's first night clubs with its floor show.

Pittsburgh's East End had become a cultural center and included some outstanding schools. Shadyside Academy was built in 1883 and designed to be a college preparatory high school for the sons of East End's wealthy such as Childs Frick, Howard Heinz, and George Westinghouse III. For the daughters there was Pennsylvania Female College, now Chatham College. Pennsylvania Female College became a pioneer in offering hard science degrees to women by having the money to equip large biological and chemical laboratories. Frick believed in the education of women and was a donor to the Pennsylvania Female College. Both schools reaped the rewards of being in the world's wealthiest suburb with guest speakers such as President William Howard Taft. Taft visited both Frick and Bakewell before and after his presidency. Of course, the East End was the home of two great universities. The University of Pittsburgh was built on "Frick Acres" with donations from Frick, Carnegie, Mellon, and Heinz. In neighboring Oakland, Carnegie Tech (Carnegie-Mellon) was built in 1905 on the city land of Chris Magee and William Flinn, with Carnegie providing the funds for the buildings.

The formation of United States Steel created an emigration of Carnegie executives such as Charles Schwab and Henry Clay Frick. Frick had started his move to New York with the formation of United States Steel in 1901 as USS headquarters were moved to New York. Still, Frick loved Pittsburgh as did his daughter, Helen, and the move was a gradual one. More motivation came in the sulfurous smoky atmosphere of Pittsburgh. Often the city experienced daylight for only a few hours each day. Mill dust was everywhere and the sulfur in the air was highly corrosive. Silverware had to be polished weekly because of the sulfurous air. The atmospheric attack on Frick's beloved paintings became obvious. Frick had been planning for years to build an art museum on nearby Gunn's Hill, which overlooked the great Homestead Works. Pittsburgh's sulfurous air changed Frick's mind. In 1905, Frick leased a Vanderbilt mansion on New York's Fifth Avenue. It was considered one of America's most beautiful homes. It was the house that a young struggling Frick had visited on his way to Europe and had never forgotten. Frick moved about half of his paintings at Clayton to New York. The move appeared to affect Helen Frick the most, but Frick had always planned to return to his daughter (Martha died at Clayton as a young child) at Homewood Cemetery in death. Mrs. Westinghouse would only wear black in Pittsburgh because of the soot and smoke, and the Heinz women often complained about the effect of the darkness on outdoor gardens.

Even as these great industrialists were pulled to New York, they maintained their old homes and ties in the neighborhood. Henry Clay Frick would always remain a legal resident of Pennsylvania and maintained an office in the Frick Building. Helen Frick had a deep love of Clayton and often wanted to return. In fact, it would be Helen who returned later in life to maintain Clayton until her death in 1984. Helen continued her high school education in New York but refused to have a debutante party in New York. She clashed with her father, who wanted to use the beautiful art gallery of their Fifth Avenue home as a backdrop. Frick would relent and allow for a Clayton début. The neighborhood was happy to see Helen Frick's beautiful party. Because Frick had been an original and major supporter of the orchestra, a 22-member group from the Pittsburgh Orchestra played on the porch. As was typical, flowers were everywhere, many grown in the Frick greenhouse. The Mellons lived their entire lives in the East End as did H. J. Heinz who remained until his death at his East End mansion "Greenlawn".

Like Hollywood of today, the East End would have its sex scandals and national crime cases. One of Helen Frick's best friends and neighbor was Henrietta Thaw, the daughter of railroad and coal magnate, Benjamin Thaw. It was Henrietta's uncle who would make the headlines in the O. J. Simpson-type trial of the 1900s. In 1905 Harry Kendall Thaw married a chorus girl, Evelyn Nesbit, who had been in relationships with architect Stanford White and actor John Barrymore. Harry took his wife to the New York Theater in 1906. Seeing her old boyfriend there, Harry casually went over and shot him. What followed was one of the most sensational trials ever held in America, as the case turned into a racy scandal. Thaw's mother hired America's most famous lawyer in Delphin, Michael Delmas, for $100,000. The trial evolved into stories of immorality, sex parties, torture, child molestation, and drugs on a scale never heard of in America. The nation's newspapers followed every detail; and it was the first time sex was discussed in an open court in America. Andrew Mellon and Frick used their influence to limit Pittsburgh press coverage, and East End Pennsylvania Railroad executives even blocked incoming New York papers. Mrs. Thaw even paid boys to buy up incoming newspapers at all Western Pennsylvania railroad stations. While the trial was in New York, Mrs. Thaw was pulling the strings from Pittsburgh's East End and bringing the limelight to the neighborhood. Mrs. Thaw allegedly paid Evelyn $200,000 to testify for her husband. The first trial ended in a hung jury; the second found him not guilty, but sentenced him to an asylum. His mother and family helped him escape to Canada, and a third trial found him not guilty and sane. He returned to Pittsburgh to a hero's welcome only to be convicted two years later of whipping a young boy in a hotel room.

There were lesser scandals as well that never made the Pittsburgh papers. Clifford Heinz, the youngest son of H. J. Heinz, became an expert equestrian and often traveled to horse shows and competitions. Clifford liked the social life of his position and was followed by the New York press. Many of his love affairs made the social pages of national newspapers but rarely were noted in Pittsburgh. On November 7, 1907, he "ran away" to marry a nurse. H. J. found out about the marriage through the *New York Times*.[1] H. J. traveled to New York, dragged his son home and had the marriage annulled. H. J. Heinz seemed much more forgiving of Clifford than his oldest son, Clarence, who failed to develop the necessary business skills to run the company.

By 1900 East End residents had developed "Pittsburgh chapters" in New York and Florida. Residents such as Benjamin Thaw and Louis Clarke were early developers of Florida's Palm Beach in the 1890s. Clarke bought the "Coconut Grove House" hotel there. East Enders such as Frick, Knox, and Harvey went there for the winter season. A lot of the Old South Fork Club members found their way to the new Florida resort. Frick loved the golf there, with many friendly wagers. Frick also loved fishing for sheephead and bluefish. Mrs. Frick was particularly fond of the tea and card parties, which resembled her Thursday parties. In the winter of 1904, the Fricks took one of their longer trips to Palm Beach, enjoying more of the ten-week season.

The story of Pittsburgh's East End is the story of America's industrial heritage, the Gilded Age, and Victorian living. It is local, regional, national, and international history all in one. It is a history of American industrialization. It contrasts the best and the worst of Victorian capitalism. It was at the center of major historical events such as the Johnstown Flood, the Homestead Strike, the Great Railroad Strike of 1877, the use of AC electric current for home lighting, and the formation of America's first billion-dollar corporation. The neighborhood played a major role in America's political systems and in the careers of many of America's presidents such as Lincoln, McKinley, Taft, Harding, and Roosevelt. It is a truly a cross-section of our nation's history.

---

1 "C. S. Heinz Maybe Husband of Nurse," *New York Times*, November 5, 1907

CHAPTER 2. PRELUDE

Pittsburgh's East End history starts with its position at the end point of America's last glacier. It was here at the edge of civilization about 12,000 years ago that a prehistoric people lived. Little is known of these prehistoric Americans known locally as the mound builders or Monongahela People. Their origin remains under debate, but fifty miles south of the area is one of the oldest human sites in America. The East End has several mounds in the Squirrel Hill area made by these mysterious people. The early German farmers in the area found many small mounds in the East End. East Ender and ketchup king, H. J. Heinz, would become a great collector of mound builder artifacts in the late 1890s and early 1900s. Sometime prior to 1500, the Monongahela People disappeared, leaving the area unoccupied.

For several centuries, the ownership of the Western Pennsylvania was disputed, with the ground being neutral for different Indian tribes to hunt. The area had an abundance of large game such as elk, deer, bear, and the now-extinct wood buffalo. Smaller game such as squirrel, fox, wolf, otter, and beaver were abundant also. Game birds such as turkeys and passenger pigeons covered the fields and darkened the skies. Passenger pigeons often traveled in flocks fifty miles long and a mile wide. Other birds included the bald eagle, Carolina parakeet (extinct), golden eagles, and vultures. Interestingly, some of the most common birds in the area today such as ravens, crows, and starlings didn't come to the area until after extensive settlements. The birds thrived at the three rivers which were rich in perch, pike, sturgeon, and bullhead. The game made the area popular with both white and Indian hunters. Other natural resources included hardwoods such as oak, maple, hickory, and chestnut. While little used in the 1700s, coal could be found in seams across the area. Its confluence of the Allegheny River and Monongahela River to form the Ohio River made Pittsburgh a natural transportation and trade center. For three centuries the area was contended for by nations such as the Delaware, Shawnee, Erie, Iroquois six nations, France, England, Spain, and the Americans as well three states — Virginia, Pennsylvania, and Connecticut.

When George Washington visited the area in the 1750s for the Governor of Virginia, he had to meet with many of these Indian tribes and George Croghan, the "King of Traders." George Croghan ran his Scotch–Irish trading network from the east side of the Allegheny very near to today's East End. Croghan's trading network moved furs from Western Pennsylvania to the Scottish trade centers of Europe. Croghan played a balancing act throughout the 1750s in Monongahela country. While Croghan started out as a Pennsylvania agent, he was soon drawn to his Scottish brethren in Virginia and Governor Dinwiddie who governed from 1751 to 1757. Dinwiddie was a Scotchman, and Virginia had argued early on that the Monongahela Valley and west was outside the Pennsylvania charter. Dinwiddie was from the Glasgow trading district that had supported the Scottish Act of Union in 1707 and was the fur trading center of the world. Many believe Glasgow of the 1700s to be the birthplace of capitalism, with its extended network reaching the Scotch–Irish traders of Western Pennsylvania. Clearly, this trading network inspired Glasgow resident, Adam Smith, and his basic ideas of capitalism. Prior to Dinwiddie's arrival, a group of Virginians including Lawrence Washington and Thomas Lee, had formed the Ohio Company to settle western Pennsylvania and develop trade with the Indians. Upon his arrival, Dinwiddie became a major shareholder, seeing it as a means of participating in the lucrative Scottish fur trade. He already had financial interests to Glasgow banking, warehousing, and shipping. Croghan also saw the Ohio Company as a means of getting military support as the aggressive French traders were moving into the Allegheny, Ohio, and Monongahela valleys in the 1750s. George Washington and Croghan both were shareholders in the Ohio Company.

The early influx of whites into Western Pennsylvania was led by the "Scotch–Irish." The "Scotch–Irish" or "Scots–Irish" defined early American beliefs, philosophy, and its economic success. The term Scotch–Irish consisted of a loose amalgamation of the Ulster Scotch–Irish, lowland Scotch, Presbyterians, and a mix of Protestant Scotch and Irish in America.[1] The Ulster Scots had been sent to colonize Ireland but then moved on to America to escape British oppression. Even some early Irish Catholics took to calling themselves Scotch–Irish to avoid discrimination. The hills of Western Pennsylvania were said to be reminiscent of those of Scotland. The Scotch–Irish dominated the colonial frontier and the formation of the American System in all aspects. Fifteen American presidents have claimed Scotch–Irish ancestry including three of pure Ulster Presbyterian lineage: Andrew Jackson, James Buchanan, and Chester Arthur. Philosophers and leaders included Alexander Hamilton, Patrick Henry, James Madison, John Calhoun, Daniel Boone, Sam Houston, and twenty-one signers of the Declaration of Independence. The Scotch–Irish excelled in all phases of trade and American industry, claiming the Pittsburgh East Enders of Thomas Mellon, Andrew Mellon, Willis McCook, Andrew Carnegie, James O'Hara,

---

1 The term Scotch-Irish is the most inclusive, while the Scots-Irish is specifically the Ulster Presbyterian Scots.

Isaac Craig, and Ebenezer Denny. They started and dominated industries such as pig iron, steel, whiskey, and wool. Especially in business, these Scotch–Irish had an informal clan of Scottish reciprocity going back to frontier days. The Scotch–Irish dominated the Western Pennsylvania trade distribution of furs, tobacco, cotton, ginseng, and pig iron. Few realize that Glasgow, not London, controlled colonial trade. This forgotten American race, more than any other immigrant group, is responsible for the capitalism that would flourish in Pittsburgh's East End.

The conflict with the French came to a head in 1752 as the French pushed south into the Allegheny River Valley, overrunning many of Croghan's trading posts as well as other Scotch–Irish traders such as John Fraser and John Findlay. Croghan had his headquarters near today's Pittsburgh east side. Croghan lost posts and employees throughout the Allegheny and Ohio valleys as well as in Kentucky. John Fraser retreated to his home on the confluence of Turtle Creek and the Monongahela River while Croghan reinforced his headquarters on the lower Allegheny..By the summer of 1753, the Scotch–Irish fur trade was shutdown. This threat to the Scotch–Irish trading empire would change the world. Virginia's Governor Dinwiddie immediately realized the threat to the Scottish and British fur trade by the French advance. He dispatched a twenty-one-year-old George Washington to take a letter of concern to the French in western Pennsylvania, along with frontiersman Christopher Gist, in late 1753. On November 23, Washington met with Scotch–Irish traders at Fraser's Turtle Creek home and later with Croghan at Logstown. After delivering the letter, Washington returned to Williamsburg to inform Virginia Governor Dinwiddie of the French defiance. Dinwiddie dispatched a regiment of forty-one Virginians to build a fort at the confluence of the Allegheny and Monongahela where the Ohio River formed. The Virginians teamed up with local Scotch–Irish to build the first encampment, as suggested by John Fraser and George Croghan in the 1740s, at the site of today's Pittsburgh.

By 1750, the Indians, Scotch–Irish, and lowland Scots formed a powerful fur trade empire including an extensive shipping business and the world's warehouses for distribution in Scotland. In 1752, over 50 percent of Pennsylvania exports to London were furs.[1] Even in the agricultural states such as South Carolina, fur was 10 to 15 percent of the exports. The Scots and Scotch–Irish controlled the fur trade and the supply chain logistics to Europe. The Scotch–Irish hunted and traded with the Indians for furs. The Scotch Presbyterians reinforced the supply chain with a string of settlements across Pennsylvania that could move furs from the west. The furs were assembled and transported to the seaports by trading networks of Scotch–Irish, such as George Croghan, who had wagon trains and riverboats throughout the colonies. Croghan utilized the many Scotch settlements to get his wagon trains across the Appalachian Mountains. Croghan represented the major logistics chain from the fur country to American ports, with Scots also controlling the ports. Men like Croghan and Daniel Boone expanded into the ginseng trade through the fur trade network. At the time, ginseng was common throughout the Pittsburgh area.

---

1 Jane Merritt, *At The Crossroads*, (Chapel Hill: University of North Carolina Press, 2003)

The Scots had the largest fleet of trading vessels in the 1700s. Early in the 1700s, they became the carriers of colonial tobacco with 386 ships engaged in the trade. In fact, by 1745 the Scottish imports of tobacco from America exceeded that of London and all English ports. Scotch shipping dominated the ports of New York, Philadelphia, Alexandria, and Baltimore. The control of tobacco shipping was well over 50 percent, giving the Scots domination of the Virginia colony. Scotland sent agents to Western Pennsylvania to monitor and control trade. The success of the Western Pennsylvania and Ohio Valley Scotch–Irish created a tension between the British, Indians, and French; all of them wanted to control the area for trade. The French and Indians challenged the British by building Fort Duquesne at Pittsburgh. This French move would result in what we call the French and Indian Wars.

During the French and Indian Wars, England and the colonies would unite, and England would send an army. Then England sent General Edward Braddock and two "Irish" regiments — Sir Peter Halket's 44th Foot and Thomas Dunbar's 48th Foot. These regiments had a mixed make-up, probably the majority being Scotch highlanders and Scotch–Irish. Officially, the 48th was listed as 40 percent English, 10 percent Scot, 34 percent Irish, and 16 percent American.[1] With Roman Catholics being banned from the army, the listed Irish had to be Scotch–Irish, Protestant Irish-English, and a considerable number of undeclared Roman Catholics. The poor conditions in the Scottish highlands in the 1750s made it a recruiting gold mine for the stretched British Empire. Once in America, many of these would desert to blend in the Scotch–Irish population. Washington's Virginians and the Carolina Americans would join Braddock's 44th and 48th. It should be noted that these units were considered the British's poorest as opposed to the famous Highlander regiments such as the "Black Watch." Yet the riflemen of Scotch–Irish Daniel Morgan demonstrated a new approach to frontier fighting that would be applied with success in the future Revolutionary War.

The road that Braddock built followed a wide trail developed for decades by Scotch–Irish immigrants through the Cumberland Valley (originally an Indian path) and would eventually be extended through Pittsburgh's East End (Fifth Avenue). On July 9, 1755, with Halket's 44th, Braddock crossed the Monongahela at Fraser's trading post on Turtle Creek (one of Croghan's trading posts). The French and Indians ambushed the force, and the result was the bloodiest defeat of the British on American soil. The field that day would have more future generals than any other known fight including George Washington, Thomas Gage, Horatio Gates, Daniel Morgan, Charles Lee, John St. Clair, Adam Stephen, James Craik, and James Burd. Others included Pontiac, the father of Chief Tecumseh, Daniel Boone, George Croghan, Christopher Gist, and William Shirley. Sir Peter Halket, who died that day, was a distant cousin of Scotsman Andrew Carnegie, who would build his first steel mill on this very site over one hundred years later. General Braddock also died in this defeat, and the town of Braddock honors him. Queen Aliquippa of

1 Stephen Brumwell, *Redcoats*, (Cambridge: Cambridge University Press, 2002)

the Seneca escaped, following another old Indian trail known as the "Great Trail" (today's Fifth Avenue) through today's East End.

Braddock's defeat caused many of the frontiersmen to leave in fear, with only the Scotch-Irish remaining at their reinforced trading posts. It changed British army recruiting as well. Lord Loudon was appointed commander of American forces after the death of Braddock, and General Forbes mustered a force to retake Western Pennsylvania. He listened to Washington and Croghan, forming light ranger units of American frontiersmen. He rebuilt the British regiments with pure Scottish highlanders in place of lowlanders, poor Irish, and English. The Highlanders would lead England and General Wolfe to a major victory at Montreal and General Forbes to victory in Western Pennsylvania. Forbes's troops followed the Indian Nemacolin Trail (Beechwood Boulevard) through the East End to capture Fort Duquesne (Pittsburgh) back from the French in 1758. George Washington and George Croghan advanced with over 3,000 men that captured a deserted Fort Duquesne. George Croghan and his company became the proprietors of the Indian and fur trade. With a shaky peace with the Indians and British security and frontier lack of taxes, the Scotch-Irish started to settle in the area. At the fort they became tailors, merchants, and started light industries such as blacksmithing. Letters from soldiers and frontiersmen brought more Scottish immigrants to Fort Pitt and the Monongahela region. The area east of Fort Pitt was declared free grazing land known as "the East Liberties," thus the name East Liberty. It was George Croghan who owned most of this grazing land. By 1760, Fort Pitt was the nation's western gateway and trading center. The fort covered 18 acres, and above it was a village of about 500 people with over 140 houses.

To understand the birth of capitalism in America, one needs to understand the Scotch-Irish who brought the system to our shores. The Scotch-Irish pushed the frontier lead by traders such as John Campbell and George Croghan. By the 1750s, Croghan had formed an extensive and lucrative trading network stretching into the Great Lakes. The British invested and supported this Scotch-Irish network because it competed directly with the French in the new world. The great trade warehouses of Glasgow, Scotland, were a major distributor of furs to Europe. This trade network would bring the founder of the Pig Iron Aristocracy, James O'Hara, to Fort Pitt. George Washington would learn his military skills from the Scotch-Irish as well.

The Scotch-Irish developed frontier industries around their trade network such as iron making and whiskey production. As these industries grew, Germans often moved in to help. The Scotch-Irish first developed these industries in the Cumberland Valley of Maryland and then moved to western Pennsylvania and in the early 1800s to Ohio. They built large charcoal iron furnaces to manufacture a variety of frontier products. These smaller Scotch-Irish iron furnaces would compete with the larger iron plantations of central and eastern Pennsylvania. As the Scotch-Irish moved down the Monongahela River Valley towards Ohio, they established America's whiskey industry. Wagon roads were lined with Scotch-Irish blacksmiths to repair wagons and shoe horses. These early rest stops also produced and sold rye whiskey. This "Monongahela Rye" won international acclaim as it was shipped to Europe via the Scotch-Irish trade network. It was the Scotch-

Irish whose village became today's Pittsburgh; and even today the linguistic accent of Pittsburghers is the mark of the Scotch-Irish. The small Scotch-Irish stills were soon supported by German crops and German gristmills, creating larger corporate distilleries. German farmers were not only the world's best farmers but also highly skilled mechanics and craftsmen. They built farming equipment which made American farming the most productive in the world.

The Scotch-Irish were best represented by the immigrants of Presbyterian Ulster Scots, who a hundred years earlier had migrated to Ulster, Ireland. The west coast of Scotland was about 30 miles away. Western Pennsylvania today remains the best linguist legacy of the Scotch-Irish with a strong accent of the population and the unique vocabulary such as hollows, burghs, and runs. The accent of western Pennsylvania combines the burr of the Scots with the brogue of the Irish and adds the gutturals of Germany. Many words and expressions remain in the local language such as "yinz" or "younz" for you or you people. Other words include "redd up" for clean up and "slippy" for slippery and "still" for steel. Street names of the area still include the Scottish word "diamond" for town squares. Pittsburgh's center today has a Diamond Street.

During one of the most trying periods of the Revolutionary War, George Washington noted: "Should it come to the worst, I will fall back into the mountain region of Pennsylvania and make my stand among the Scotch-Irish there." Washington had worked with the Scotch-Irish of the Ohio Company and knew well their toughness and perseverance. Interestingly, many of the British generals such as General Cornwallis had been given land rights to build plantations in Western Pennsylvania, assuming the British won the war. These British Generals with land promises for the area included the infamous Cornwallis. In those same trying years, General Washington depended on the patriotic Army Chaplin, a Scotch Irishman from Western Pennsylvania, Henry Brackenridge, to hold the army together. A volunteer group of 130 Scotch-Irish was the first to come to the relief of the Continental Army at Boston in 1775. Perhaps more importantly, it was the charcoal iron furnaces of the Scotch-Irish that supplied cannonball to the revolutionary army. The Scotch-Irish loved freedom and independence, which arose from their natural and long hatred of British control and taxes, more than their other American counterparts.

In the 1790s, the new American nation experienced the backbone of the Scotch-Irish in their resistance to a federal tax on whiskey. By the 1770s, the Scotch-Irish of western Pennsylvania had prospered, owning farms and dominating the little village of Pittsburgh. As one floated down the Monongahela River in 1790, the smoke of stills filled the surrounding hills (an estimated twelve thousand stills!). Whiskey production was an old Scottish art that now flourished in America. Monongahela rye had gained a reputation on a par with Scotch whiskey. As you floated to the confluence of the Monongahela and Allegheny, you could often run into flotilla of keelboats taking Monongahela rye to the port of New Orleans. From there, Monongahela rye was shipped to the East coast and into the European trading network via Scotland.

By 1790, this Presbyterian Scotch-Irish dominated the trade and agriculture of western Pennsylvania. By the revolution, the Scotch-Irish dominated the politics and were the earliest recruits to the Continental Army. Driven from the deep belief in Calvinistic destiny, the Scotch-Irish were the nation builders and capitalists. They had an inherent hatred of the British and taxation going back to their days in Ulster. They represented the extreme of beliefs. They traded and worked hard to create personal wealth. Drinking was considered a human right, while any work on Sunday was a major sin. On the Ohio frontier both the industrial elite and the hillbilly lower class were predominantly Scotch-Irish. The new American government soon learned their hatred for taxes in the 1790 Whiskey Rebellion, which was the first challenge to the federal government. The Scotch-Irish were fiercely independent which naturally drew them to the wild frontier areas. While many left for Kentucky and Tennessee from the Monongahela Valley, many stayed and built banking and manufacturing empires. The Whiskey Rebellion actually created a political rift within the Scotch-Irish with a group of Federalists and capitalists supporting a strong federal government. The values of the Presbyterian Ulster Irish would constraint Pittsburgh business into the 1870s by not allowing Sunday work. The capitalism that would be the root of the world's richest neighborhood was a blend of Scotch-Irish economics and German manufacturing. Moving into the nineteenth century, over 50 percent of Western Pennsylvania was Scotch-Irish and another 15 to 20 percent were German.

The most unusual thing about the Scotch-Irish Presbyterians was their fierce belief in education. John Knox's 1560 *Book of Disciplines* called for a national system of education through the church. Knox wanted every boy and girl to be able to read the bible. In 1696 in Scotland, the government Kirk passed the "School Setting Act." The Act required each parish to establish a school. The Act so established that a parish had to pay a minimum established salary to a parish schoolteacher. The education was to be free to all in the parish. The education supplied was extremely basic but achieved outstanding results. By 1720, Scotland had the highest literacy rate in Europe at 55 percent.[1] Many believe that the real root of the American education system of public schools can be found in the Scottish "School Setting Act." The motivation to read became explosive, and by 1750 every town in Scotland had a lending library. The Presbyterian Church brought this highly successful system to Western Pennsylvania and America in the early 1700s. Scotch-Irish farmers often pooled their money to hire a teacher and build a log cabin school on the Pennsylvania frontier. It was the Scotch-Irish who brought free libraries to America.

The Scotch-Irish focused on self-reliance and ethics in their education. East End capitalism was a reflection of this Scotch-Irish heritage. A belief in property rights, thrift, common schools, moralistic education, politically free education, hatred of taxes, state-rights, charity, and giving are directly traceable to Scotch-Irish heritage. This Scotch-Irish success would auger the textbooks of William McGuffey (from nearby Washington County) and the free library of the Scotch American, Andrew Carnegie. The Germans also set up or joined the Scotch-Irish. The Scotch-Irish set up "business colleges" such as Duff's Mercantile College in Pittsburgh. While Duff's was officially organized in 1840,

---

1 Arthur Herman, *How the Scots Invented the Modern World*, (New York: Three Rivers Press, 2001)

its roots go much further back. East Enders Henry Clay Frick, Andrew Carnegie, Tom Carnegie, George Westinghouse, and Thomas Mellon all took classes at Pittsburgh's Duff College — one of the first frontier Scotch-Irish colleges — as did hundreds of management employees of the area's businesses. By 1830, Western Pennsylvania's literacy rate was higher than that of Europe, thanks to the Scotch-Irish. The high literacy rate was a key factor in the development of American capitalism in the area.

The Scotch-Irish and Germans forged a unique form of capitalism. It was based on a heritage of giving back, much different than the stream of capitalism evolving in Europe and the American east coast from aristocratic traders and bankers. Property ownership was considered a basic right, but giving was a responsibility of property owners. It still allowed for greed, but it fostered giving. O'Hara's and the tradition of the Pennsylvania frontier required helping the community. The workers of the time were considered craftsmen versus hands of the future. It would be the root of the capitalism of the East Enders which became known as paternalism. Still, it could not prevent the greed of some second-generation capitalists as they moved further from their frontier roots and heritage.

CHAPTER 3. AMERICA'S FIRST CAPITALIST AND NEIGHBORHOOD FOUNDER

James O'Hara (1754–1819) was the first lord of East End capitalism and America's first "Captain of Industry." He was the leader of America's great Scotch–Irish capitalists. Prior to O'Hara, no industrialist in America had ever amassed such a fortune. O'Hara would set a lasting example of industrial philanthropy and community giving. By 1810, O'Hara literally owned Pittsburgh including its land and industries. O'Hara owned all of what would become Pittsburgh's East End as well as downtown, Southside, and a number of river islands that no longer exist. He was America's richest industrialist; and in adjusted dollars, he would still rank as one of America's richest capitalists. He was the first American millionaire to earn his own fortune, yet he had his share of failures. His bank branch and glass company would be two of those failures; but even in personal failure, he spread his frontier capitalism. O'Hara's money was to become the lifeblood of America's industrialization. O'Hara's financial, business, and family ties were an octopus that controlled Western Pennsylvania. O'Hara was bigger and richer but would be overshadowed by Andrew Carnegie and Henry Clay Frick decades later. O'Hara was not only the area's major industrialist, but also its banker. Most of the money that built Pittsburgh's early industries came from local bankers of which O'Hara was the most prominent.[1] The *Niles Register* of 1814 predicted Pittsburgh would soon become "the world's greatest manufacturing center." While O'Hara was never a politician, he was the key supporter of the Federalist Party with men like Senator James Ross. James Ross would become the area's first U.S. Senator in 1809, and with Henry Clay, would champion the protection of American industry. James Ross, Henry Clay of Kentucky, and James O'Hara were the earliest proponents of

---

1   Richard Wade, *The Urban Frontier*, (Urbana: University of Illinois Press, 1996), p. 45

Alexander Hamilton's national banking system. It was O'Hara who laid the groundwork and built the infrastructure for America's iron, steel, glass, oil, and coal industries.

O'Hara was a Scotch–Irishman with trading ties in Liverpool, England. In Scotland he had developed ties with the vast Scotch–Irish trading network in America. Trade capitalism became the teacher of a young O'Hara. In the 1700s, most of America's tobacco, furs, whiskey, and iron first passed through the trading warehouses of Scotland. It was through the study of this vast Scottish trading system that Adam Smith conceived the basic principles of capitalism with the publication of his book, *Wealth of Nations*, in 1776. Like Adam Smith, James O'Hara learned the principles of capitalism and money making from the great British trading networks. James O'Hara may well have been America's first true capitalist. His endeavors used capital for making more money from real estate, iron making, shipbuilding, salt production, shipping, retailing, glass making, banking, and brick making. Like the great Scottish traders of the 1700s, he had no real specialty other than the application of capital to make money. O'Hara would be the ideal for the future quintessential American capitalist and East End magnate Henry Clay Frick, who would emulate O'Hara by making money in a wide range of endeavors including iron, steel, banking, coal, real estate, and transportation.

O'Hara migrated in the 1770s to work as a trader. He worked with several of the Scotch–Irish fur trading companies such as James Campbell's trading firm of Philadelphia, using to great advantage his ties back in Liverpool and Glasgow. O'Hara built strong ties as an Indian trader for the Ohio Company of Virginia, which operated in Pittsburgh and the Ohio Valley. He fought in the Revolutionary War. He was appointed a presidential elector in 1788 and cast his vote for George Washington. From 1792 to 1794, O'Hara served as Quartermaster General; he was responsible for supplying the Army of Anthony Wayne and General St. Clair's western campaign against the Indians from Fort Pitt. O'Hara made his fortune early on, supplying the army of the United States. As a key officer in the 1790s Indian wars, he was a signer of the Treaty of Greenville in 1795. O'Hara set up and built a trading network of ships and wagons to bring salt from New York to Pittsburgh. He started a distillery business in the 1790s in Pittsburgh. He is also considered the founder of the influential First Presbyterian Church in Pittsburgh. O'Hara's 1800 land holdings cover most of today's downtown Pittsburgh and the north side. In 1800, O'Hara was one of America's wealthy men with land holdings and manufacturing in several states. He was a key powerful political broker in the then "west." Politically he was a Federalist and supporter of Washington, and during the Whiskey Rebellion, he was called on to lead the Pittsburgh militia against the whiskey rebels, creating a split among the local Scotch–Irish.

One of O'Hara's earliest projects was the building of a transportation network to bring salt from New York to Pittsburgh. He was a logistics genius. The network included river transportation companies and wagon trains to potage between rivers. O'Hara invested in shipbuilding, which may be considered Pittsburgh's oldest industry. During the Revolutionary War, Pittsburgh had been designated a government boatyard. O'Hara expanded into keelboats in the 1790s. Lewis and Clark had their famous keelboat built in Pittsburgh. Keelboats moved massive amounts of trade between Pittsburgh, St. Louis, Louisville, and

New Orleans. O'Hara built a trading empire which moved goods between Pittsburgh, New Orleans, and English ports. He even built sea-going ships in his Pittsburgh shipyards such as the famous "President Adams," "Pittsburgh," and "Senator Ross," which saw action against France in 1799. The boat launches were major social events in Pittsburgh featuring great dinners with imported wine. The parties often lasted days. These events were the social events for Pittsburgh elite. O'Hara put his old deputy quartermaster, Isaac Craig, in charge of his shipyards, and set up another soldier friend, Devereux Smith, in grocery distribution. In 1811, they launched the steamboat "New Orleans" for Mississippi River travel.

O'Hara not only was in shipbuilding but shipping. Monongahela rye whiskey was shipped to Europe via O'Hara's Pittsburgh to New Orleans connection. Boatbuilding required many blacksmiths to support the operations, which helped give the area its manufacturing start of making ship parts. Boatbuilding also required thousands of buckets of nails which needed to be produced in mass. By 1802, iron products accounted for $56,548 of Pittsburgh's total value of products and was the largest industry accounting for 16 percent of the total value. Nail production turned blacksmith shops into nail factories in a few short years. By 1810, iron product production had doubled and accounted for 24 percent of Pittsburgh's product production. O'Hara himself built a glassworks and was the first to use coal in his glass making. O'Hara profited from the trade and manufacturing, building one of Pittsburgh's first mansions. This amazing plantation and mansion was built on the outskirts of old Fort Pitt known as the "King's Artillery Garden" on the Allegheny River side of the point. The estate grew and would later become known as "King's Orchard."

O'Hara's Pittsburgh businesses included a retail store, brewery, sawmill, gristmill, glassworks, brick making plant, and shipyard. O'Hara developed housing and real estate throughout the area as well. No one did more to move to Alexander Hamilton's vision of an America as a manufacturing center. O'Hara was a strong Federalist and follower of Alexander Hamilton who believed in the federal use of currency to build manufacturing and transportation. O'Hara's capitalist empire was a monument to Hamilton's vision of America. As a Federalist, O'Hara was a major supporter of a national banking system to stimulate industry. He would be a director of the First United States Bank, establishing a Pittsburgh branch. O'Hara truly used capital, natural resources, and innovation and not the backs of workers to succeed. He created prosperity that allowed for good wages. American manufacturing wages were much higher than in Europe at the time, and O'Hara was exporting to all of Europe. With innovations such as the use of coal as a fuel, he cut costs below that of Europe while increasing wages.

For his time, James O'Hara was more dominant in Pittsburgh than Andrew Carnegie would be many decades later. He used his many ties and networks to build Pittsburgh into an industrial center. O'Hara's fortune is remembered today for Schenley Park in Pittsburgh. At one point, O'Hara owned most of today's Pittsburgh including the East End. When his heir and granddaughter Mary Croghan married Captain Schenley and left Pittsburgh for England, her real estate holdings remained. On her death in 1903, these real estate holdings were estimated at $50 million.

O'Hara's partnership with his junior officer, Isaac Craig, brought O'Hara into the glass and iron industry. In 1784 deputy quartermaster-general Isaac Craig worked for O'Hara and became an early partner. Isaac Craig had been born in Ireland and immigrated to Philadelphia as a carpenter in 1741. In 1775 he joined the American marines and was severely wounded at the Battle of Brandywine in 1777. After the war, he became the quartermaster at Fort Pitt and married the daughter of the area's most prominent resident — General John Neville. Isaac Craig partnered with James O'Hara to build the first glassworks west of the Alleghenies in 1795, which is considered the beginning of the great industrial empire of Pittsburgh. In 1795 he reported: "Today we made the first bottle at a cost of $30,000!" Pittsburgh's rich coal seams made it a natural for glassworks, and O'Hara was one of the first to exploit it. Coal is a much better fuel than wood, which was used by most eastern glassworks. O'Hara appears to have supplied most of the capital for the glass business and was one of the wealthiest citizens with numerous slaves at his mansion house. Although Craig was given the land for the glassworks by the Penn family, all the capital was from O'Hara and his associates. By 1802 the establishment was producing glass bottles, window glass, and decanters. Craig, however, would move into the background as O'Hara built a larger manufacturing base. O'Hara's enterprises and investments were truly amazing.

Craig also introduced O'Hara to the pig iron business. O'Hara did have one excursion directly into the pig iron business. He partnered with John Hopkins of Vermont (a future bishop of the Episcopal Church) in taking over a failed furnace in Westmoreland County. The operation failed, and O'Hara bought out his partner Hopkins to save him from bankruptcy. O'Hara teamed up with Craig to produce cannon shot. As deputy quartermaster under General O'Hara, Isaac Craig was actively involved in the 1790s in supplying the U.S. Army of General Anthony Wayne. General Wayne mustered and supplied his army outside of Pittsburgh for his march on the Northwest Indians. Isaac Craig was working with the charcoal iron furnaces of Fayette and Westmoreland counties to supply shot and cannon for Wayne's army. Military officers such as William Turnbull and General St. Clair had built a number of these furnaces. Actually, the first and failed charcoal furnace in the area was that of George Anshultz in the East End in 1790. As noted, Pittsburgh lacked iron ore to maintain operation of its early iron furnaces. While Pittsburgh was short on iron ore for smelting, it had other assets. Pittsburgh was rich in coal, which was plentiful and cheap. Coal could be used to reheat and melt pig iron for foundry operations. This type of re-melting of pig iron was a more controllable method for foundry operations versus working directly from a charcoal-smelting furnace. Especially for large castings, re-melt air furnaces could supply more molten metal than a single tap of a charcoal furnace. Re-melting also supplied a cleaner and higher quality iron than that direct from charcoal furnaces. Re-melted pig iron was also a raw material for the rolling mills of Pittsburgh for nails, wire, and sheet. Re-melted iron was the preferred raw material for cannon production because of its quality. Shot, however, could be made more cheaply in direct cast at the charcoal furnace. The navigable Monongahela River offered the transportation network to link southwestern Pennsylvania pig iron to Pittsburgh, and Pittsburgh capitalists invested heavily in charcoal furnaces. O'Hara financed many of these "Pig Iron Aristocrats."

The crown of "Iron City" came to Pittsburgh not because of its iron production, but from its use of iron. Whether it was wire, cast steam engine parts, or nails, pig iron was needed. The real boom in the use of pig iron came with the opening of a puddling furnace in 1819 by Union Rolling Mill. Englishman Henry Cort had invented puddling in 1784, but it took another twenty years for it to evolve into an efficient method. Puddling furnaces heated pig iron to a gooey mass which was worked as a ball to remove carbon and produce wrought iron. A skilled puddler would use a hooked rod to pull a pasty mass out of the furnace. The pasty ball was moved to a forging hammer that squeezed and hammered out slag while burning carbon out. A puddling furnace would melt a 500-pound "heat" of pig iron. A puddler could process four to five heats into wrought iron in a nine-hour day. The amount of wrought iron exceeded the 50- to 300-pound wrought iron output of heat and beat process forges. This puddled wrought iron was the raw material for rolling and nail mills. Puddlers were the top paid craftsmen in the country, making as much as $25.00 a day, when labors made $1.25 a day. Puddling made wrought iron production many times more productive. The puddling process would evolve into the steel mills of the 1860s.

Iron nails were the tonnage product in the 1820s and 1830s of Pittsburgh manufacturers. The switch from log cabins to frame housing had caused a super boom in nail demand. Actually, it was more of a co-dependency, as volume nail production for shipbuilding made frame building more economical. Prior to 1800, nails were made by painstakingly long operations of blacksmiths on anvils. As volume increased, blacksmith shops grew into small factories and then into naileries. Nails made Pittsburgh the "Iron City" because of some natural and man-made strategic advantages. Pittsburgh had three nail factories by 1806, but most of these were extended blacksmith operations of southern Scotch–Irish immigrants. Blacksmith operations also became the main suppliers of horseshoes for the army and western pioneers. These Scotch–Irish ironworkers were also moving into eastern Ohio valleys following new ore deposits. Family ties sent the resultant pig iron to Pittsburgh for processing. O'Hara's banking and capital drew investment and technology to Pittsburgh.

Most important was the invention of mechanical nail making machines by Jacob Perkins of Massachusetts in 1795, but its application took a decade. The Perkins machine could produce up to 500 nails per minute. This Boston technology was brought to Pittsburgh by two Boston iron makers — William Stackpole and Ruggles Whiting. In 1811, they built a nail mill known as Stackpole & Whiting. Pittsburgh offered a good supply of pig iron, steam engines, capital, and the world's largest market for nails. British dumping of iron products in the period after the War of 1812 put Stackpole and Ruggles in bankruptcy. Stackpole and Ruggles was considered the most modern nail mill in the world. Key also was the abundance of coal in Pittsburgh for fuel in puddling furnaces for wrought iron production. Coal also fired the local made steam engines that drove the iron rolling mills. There were an amazing eight steam engine companies in Pittsburgh by 1830, and the city led America in engine manufacture. Lastly, Pittsburgh's river connection to the west tied the market demand to the operations. Pittsburgh stood almost alone in the unique combination of resources and technology, but O'Hara added the important ingredient of capital.

Another prominent Scotch–Irish businessman and partner of O'Hara was John Wilkins. The John Wilkins family had come to Pittsburgh in the 1780s and was an early Pittsburgh investor. Like O'Hara and Craig, Wilkins served as a quartermaster of the United States army, and it was there that he came to know General James O'Hara and the Scotch–Irish trading network of Europe. John Wilkins Jr. had opened a window glass factory in the early 1800s and was a director with O'Hara in the formation of the Bank of Pennsylvania branch in 1802. This branch was the first bank west of the Allegheny Mountains. O'Hara and William Wilkins would bring Philadelphian John Thaw to be Chief Clerk. The Thaw family would become one of the area's railroad dynasties. John Wilkins's younger brother, William, founded the Bank of Pittsburgh in 1810. William Wilkins (1779–1865) would eventually become a judge and an ambassador to Russia. He built the first large mansion in the East End in 1832 known as "Homewood." He was first known in politics for his strong support of Democrat Andrew Jackson.

John Wilkins Sr., along with the O'Haras, Dennys, Craigs, Bayards, and Bracken-ridges, are considered the founding families of Pittsburgh Presbyterianism. Wilkins Jr. would serve as Quartermaster General from 1796 to 1802, strengthening his family ties with the O'Hara trading empire. In addition, the Wilkins, O'Haras, Dennys, and Bracken-ridges were considered the founding families of the Federalist Party in Pittsburgh. William Wilkins, the younger brother of John Jr., would become a key politician in the Pig Iron Aristocracy. This protectionist group of Pittsburghers would start out as Federalists, then merge into Whigs, and finally morph into the Republican Party which was born in Pittsburgh. The Wilkins family, however, would take an unusual political turn. John Jr. and William Wilkins were Jacksonian Democrats but were strong protectionists until the 1840s. William's belief in slavery moved him to the Democratic Party, while most East Enders were abolitionists, Whigs, and/or Republicans. William would serve as a Senator, U.S. Representative, Supreme Court Judge, Ambassador to Russia, and Secretary of War. He was visited at his home by then President James Monroe in 1817 and built a mansion in the Homewood section of the East End in 1835. Present day Wilkinsburg is named after him. William was also a bank director and a president of the Bank of Pittsburgh and owned Pittsburgh Manufacturing Company. While a Democrat in the 1840s, he stood strong for tariffs to protect American industry. William Wilkins's sister, Nancy, married another Pittsburgh founder and Scotch–Irishman, Ebenezer Denny, tying these two families together. Pig iron politicians were often given cabinet positions to pander to the iron districts in Pennsylvania and Ohio. This mixing of Federalists and Jeffersonian Democrats, like Germans and Scotch–Irish, was common, but the pig iron regional politicians never compromised the protectionist beliefs.

Ebenezer Denny was O'Hara's real estate partner in the 1790s. Denny's ties had gone back to supplying the British at Fort Pitt. While English, Denny was a member of the Presbyterian Church. He served with O'Hara and others as a director of the Bank of Penn-sylvania, a founder of the First Presbyterian Church, and a member of Masonic Lodge 45.

He was also a veteran of the Revolutionary War. In 1816, Denny became the first mayor of Pittsburgh. The Denny family would remain a prominent Pittsburgh family for decades and a cornerstone of the Pig Iron Aristocracy. Denny's son, Harmar Denny, would marry Elizabeth, the daughter of James O'Hara. Harmar was invested in many of the O'Hara's companies and had also served as a quartermaster in the army. Harmar Denny would help found the Pittsburgh and Steubenville Railroad and the Pennsylvania Canal as well as the Western University of Pennsylvania (a forerunner of the University of Pittsburgh). He founded the socially elite Chemical Society, which fostered chemistry, mineralogy, and the physical sciences. The Denny and Wilkins families were typical of the split in western Pennsylvania politics that took some industrialists out of the Federalist column. Denny even helped in the formation of a church for the poor Catholics, who numbered fewer than 300 in 1825. It took the Whig Party in the 1840s to unite the industrialists under a protectionist banner.

O'Hara, on the other hand, expanded his interests into sawmills, tanneries, salt works, shipbuilding, and gristmills during the same period. In 1803 O'Hara built Pittsburgh Point Brewery, which made a type of porter beer popular with the Scotch-Irish. He teamed up with Ebenezer Denny to build row houses for the city; and by his death, O'Hara was the largest real estate owner in the area. O'Hara also moved into finance and banking. In 1810, pig iron shortages rose as President Jefferson placed an embargo on British products. The decimated iron furnaces struggled to re-open to meet domestic demand. O'Hara bought Hermitage Furnace from General Arthur St. Clair, who had defaulted on a bond from O'Hara. The upcoming War of 1812 created a pig surge, bringing on furnaces in Pennsylvania and Ohio. Many Scotch-Irish iron families moved up from Maryland and Virginia to start furnaces in western Pennsylvania and eastern Ohio. One of these families was the descendant of future President William McKinley. In 1805 another pig iron lord, Joseph McClurg, opened Pittsburgh's first foundry. The foundry was located at Smithfield Street and Fifth Avenue. McClurg would be one of the premier suppliers for the American Army and Navy of 1812, and James O'Hara bankrolled it. In 1810 McClurg purchased a number of bankrupt Westmoreland furnaces to supply pig iron to his Pittsburgh foundry. This combining of Pittsburgh banks, foundries, and rolling mills with the southwestern Pennsylvania Mountain furnaces became the infrastructure of the area's Pig Iron Aristocracy.

Joseph McClurg had come to Pittsburgh with his Scotch-Irish family in the late 1790s. The family had settled on Pittsburgh's south side and later moved to the East End. He had some theological training in Reformed Presbyterianism. The McClurg foundry had two air furnaces to re-melt southwestern Pennsylvania pig iron. The McClurg Foundry appeared to have been financed by the new branch of the Bank of Pennsylvania, which opened in 1805. The bank branch had been established with James O'Hara as president and Ebenezer Denny, Joseph Barker, Anthony Beelen, Thomas Baird, Boyce Irwin, David Evans, and George Wallace. O'Hara was clearly a visionary who saw that many of the products brought in from the east could be manufactured in Pittsburgh such as shovels, axes, hatchets, stoves, andirons, spades, and particularly, nails. O'Hara's bank not only financed McClurg's foundry, but two nail and slitting mills. By 1810 there were six naileries, having a product value of $49,890 or 33 percent of Pittsburgh's metal industries. Nail tonnage was about 200 tons per year. In 1811, O'Hara's many industries would combine efforts to build America's first steamboat, *New Orleans*, for Robert Fulton.

Another product fostered by O'Hara on America's growing frontier was wire. German-born Peter William Eichbaum (1787–1866) had been brought to Pittsburgh in 1797 to manage the bottle glass factory of James O'Hara. It was considered an affront to many, since Eichbaum was a German Catholic; but O'Hara judged only by the ability to make money. Eichbaum turned out to be an extremely talented engineer who mastered bottle making but moved into other industries. Eichbaum applied steam engine power to the cutting of glass, which was adopted by the company of Bakewell and Page. Eichbaum built a wire mill in 1810 with the help of O'Hara money. Lacking full financing from O'Hara, he petitioned the state legislature which was interested in developing manufacturing. The legislative action was stated:

> Whereas it is true policy of this State to give encouragement to works of public utility, to foster our own manufacture and to render ourselves independent of foreign nations for articles of absolute necessity; therefore, be it enacted. That a loan be granted from the State to William Eichbaum of three thousand dollars.

Like O'Hara, Eichbaum moved into navigation and shipping. He even branched into printing and textbook manufacture and patented several innovations. This type of Scotch–Irish finance of O'Hara combining with the German ingenuity of Eichbaum would be typical of East End capitalism. Eichbaum became a very wealthy industrialist and was the first to build a mansion in the East End, naming it "Oakland." Eichbaum means oak tree in German. Eichbaum's mansion was called a "villa." It was a true country estate in the East End (Oakland). The area was popular with German farmers and plantation owners such as Alexander Negley. Many wealthy Germans would follow Eichbaum to the Oakland area prior to the Civil War.

The use of a state loan was typical of the time, and James O'Hara used this route as well to expand the iron industry of the area. Eichbaum's wire mill was on the Monongahela River beside O'Hara's brewery. It was a state of the art mill, using steam power to drive the rolls. Steam engines were being built en mass in Pittsburgh in 1807 at the plant of Oliver Evans, Mark Stackhouse, and Mahlon Rogers. The company was known as the Pittsburgh Steam Engine Company and was financed by O'Hara's bank. A few years later Eichbaum invented a sheet rolling mill that produced world-class quality sheet metal. Besides Eichbaum, waterpower and later steam engines inspired more Pittsburgh rolling mills prior to 1812. Steam power allowed for concentration of manufacturing in a centralized area. Prior to steam, the river power of streams and rivers were needed. Countryside iron processing operations could be brought to the central city of Pittsburgh with steam power. Steam power assured the manufacturing ascendancy of Pittsburgh and its East End capitalists.

Scotch–Irish Christopher Cowan started a sheet mill near Pittsburgh in Shadyside in 1806, and Jeffery Scaife opened a tin plate on Pittsburgh's Market Street around 1802, again with the help of O'Hara money. Tinplate was popular in tableware on the frontier. Jeffery Scaife would become the city's first iron king, and his son, William, would continue the business and expand into real estate in the East End. Jeffery and William Scaife opened one of the first Pittsburgh blacksmith shops to morph into a true factory. Their employees knew the Scaifes for their "patriarchal" approach, which was similar to the management style of O'Hara.[1] The Scaife paternal factory management would augur the approach of future East Enders, George Westinghouse and H. J. Heinz. The Scaifes would become the East End's first land developers as well. In the 1850s, William Scaife became an investor with political boss, William Shinn, to develop the first community housing project in the Pittsburgh area. William Scaife was the inventor of the corrugated iron roof and the kitchen range broiler. The Scaife family would become one of Pittsburgh's oldest and richest. In 1927 the Scaife family and Mellon family (as well as the King family) would combine in marriage and create one of America's greatest fortunes in the East End of Pittsburgh and the nation.

O'Hara's industrial and financial network was anchored by his family ties to the wealth and power of the area. O'Hara was the leader of the Pittsburgh Aristocracy that would later be known as the "Pig Iron Aristocracy," an industrial and political juggernaut of power. James O'Hara's family ties are a story of the Pittsburgh Aristocracy and East End. O'Hara's daughters, Mary Carson and Elizabeth O'Hara, created two lines of aristocracy. Elizabeth married one of his business partner's sons, Harmer Denny. Harmer's father, Ebenezer Denny, was a Revolutionary War veteran and merchant who was a director with the Bank of Pennsylvania; in 1816 he was elected Pittsburgh's first mayor. The marriage of Ebenezer's son and O'Hara's daughter formed a political–industrial–financial merger in the aristocracy. Harmer Denny became a wealthy gentleman through the marriage. He founded Pittsburgh's Chemical and Physiological Society, and by the time of his death in 1851 Harmer Denny had parlayed his O'Hara inheritance into $20 million (about $600 million today). Their daughter, Elizabeth O'Hara Denney, married into the well-known McKnight family.

The other daughter, Mary Carson O'Hara, wed the wealthy merchant William Croghan Jr., thus creating a merger of two of Pittsburgh's oldest land owning families; between them, they owned most of the East End of Pittsburgh. William Croghan Sr. had been the commander of Fort Pitt in the 1780s and had many business dealings and supply arrangements with General James O'Hara. William Jr.'s grandfather George Croghan was one of the first white settlers of the area and had negotiated with the Indians for George Washington; he had been a trader and Indian scout to George Washington and the Ohio Company with O'Hara. Croghan had a mansion four miles up the Allegheny River known as "Croghan's Castle." The couple settled in Pittsburgh's East End, building a huge brick mansion and plantation known as "Picnic." William Croghan died, leaving his widow Mary the wealthiest person in Pittsburgh. His and the O'Hara fortunes came to over $40

---

1 Burton Hersh, *The Mellon Family,* (New York: William Morrow and Company, 1978), p. 174

million (a billionaire in today's terms). This fortune passed to Mary Croghan, who sub-sequently married Captain Schenley, a veteran who had served on the "wrong" side of the War of 1812; Mary and the captain lived their lives out in England. The Croghan family was so upset they had the Pennsylvania Legislature pass a law holding all of the fortune in trust.

Mary Schenley won the fortune in court. Most of her $50 million inheritance was in real estate in Pittsburgh's Point and East End. She had to sell it slowly as to not dis-turb the market. She donated the land covered by old Fort Pitt to the city and a 300-acre park (today's Schenley Park, in the East End, the land where the Carnegie Library stands). Much of Mary Schenley's land would eventually pass to Pittsburgh's greatest capitalist, Henry Clay Frick; and today it is the location of the University of Pittsburgh's Cathedral of Learning and the Heinz Chapel. The eastern district of Pittsburgh known as Oakland today was Schenley Farms then. The East End would, in turn, become the world's wealthi-est neighborhood when O'Hara's capitalist legacy was re-united with his land legacy. Men like Henry Clay Frick would follow in the footsteps of James O'Hara many decades later.

By status, O'Hara was an aristocrat but behaved more like a populist. He had fought and believed in the Revolution. He believed in paternal capitalism and gave liberally to help the poor. He refused to join elitist groups such as the Literary Society and Pitts-burgh's famous Masonic Lodge 45. He often donated to the poor Catholics of the area who were considered below the black slaves of the Scotch-Irish. Still, O'Hara and Wilkins were the last of the area's major slaveholders. For O'Hara, the region was merely an ex-tension of his personal plantation. This was much different than the arrogance that had come to be expected from the wealthy and the hatred between nationalities in the more aristocratic colonies of the east. O'Hara was the fusion of Scotch-Irish beliefs in freedom and moneymaking with his Christian belief in giving. O'Hara was a powerful example of the Scotch-Irish belief that the wealthy must give back to the community. He would be a model for men like Andrew Carnegie in later generations. It must also be remembered that O'Hara, Craig, Croghan, and Eichbaum, while brilliant and hard working, were as much the result of the Scotch-Irish frontier thinking as their own abilities. The Scotch-Irish demanded upward mobility in a society based on their European background where British aristocrats had held them back in their endeavors in Ireland. More importantly, the Scotch-Irish extended their belief in upward mobility, bringing in Germans and even Catholics to build their enterprises. For the Scotch-Irish, the Revolution was about up-ward mobility. They hated the very aristocracy that inherited money often propelled them to, and many were sad to see later generations of their financial legacy corrupted by that money.

CHAPTER 4. THE BIRTH AND GROWTH OF THE NATION'S RICHEST SUBURB

The "East End" of the 1800s included parts of today's Oakland, Wilkinsburg, and Lawrenceville as well as the smaller communities of East Liberty, Squirrel Hill, Shadyside, Homewood, Point Breeze, Highland Park, and Schenley Park. James O'Hara and the Wilkins family owned large sections of farmland in the East End prior to 1800. In the early 1790s, Germans Alexander Negley and George Anshultz, and Englishman Benjamin Bakewell came to the area, building industries and personal fortunes. Anshultz came to the area wealthy and had strong connections to the banking empire of James O'Hara. George Anshultz would build Pittsburgh's iron furnace in the East End's Shadyside in 1790. Anshultz's iron furnace would fail shortly, however, lacking iron ore and fuel. Interestingly, the furnace was within a mile of the future homes of America's greatest iron, steel, and coke masters of the next century.

Alexander Negley came from Germany as a farmer and blacksmith. He actually came to the East End because of its rural setting, which accepted him readily while other Pittsburgh social circles did not. Negley was affected by the spirit and model of the successful capitalist, James O'Hara. O'Hara was a combination of capitalist, political boss, real estate developer, and philanthropist. O'Hara encouraged immigrants, bringing many German craftsmen to his manufacturing enterprises. Unlike most Scotch–Irish, O'Hara had no bigotry towards other nationalities or religions. He encouraged German immigrant farmers and even built churches for society's lowest — the Irish Catholics. He believed Western Pennsylvania was a bastion of liberty and freedom. Negley and his sons became prosperous by running a needed gristmill for the farming community near O'Hara's farm. The Negley gristmill was located in the East End's Point Breeze area on the Greensburg Pike (Penn Avenue). Negley re-invested in land, and by 1830 owned most of what is called East Liberty today. Negley's wealth grew as did his philanthropy to projects such as the

East Liberty Presbyterian Church. He was really a new generation, not of the O'Hara early capitalist empire.

O'Hara the Federalist supported three key political figures in Pittsburgh and the East End. One of these was the young U.S. Senator James Ross. Ross was a fierce protectionist and national bank supporter. His mansion was near Aspinwall. Ross did own land in downtown Pittsburgh and the East End. Others were President Judge of the western branch, Alexander Addison, and Judge William Wilkins. These men were East Enders. These East End Federalists were fighters for the protectionist policies. They supported the Bank of the United States because it injected money into Pittsburgh's industrial growth. Even Judge Wilkins, who left the Federalist Party to join the Democratic Party, remained aligned with the protectionist policies of the Whigs and Republicans. Wilkins joined the Democratic Party because of his strong support of slavery, which had only minor support in the area.

Another friend of the O'Hara Empire was General John Neville. Neville had been a general in the Revolutionary War and moved to Pittsburgh to become Federal Revenue Chief for the district. He had been assigned to Fort Pitt during the war. Neville's son, Colonel Presley Neville, was also a Revolutionary War veteran and came with his father to Pittsburgh. John Neville was at the center of the Whiskey Rebellion as the chief tax collector for the federal government. As the rebellion progressed, Neville was called out to march with President Washington against the rebels. After the rebellion was put down, Neville became a prominent leader of the Federalist Party and supported the election of James Ross to the United States Senate. Ross would be one of the early protectionists in congress. Pittsburgh became the core of protectionist support. Protectionism united politicians in Western Pennsylvania regardless of party. After his senate career, Ross would be a builder of the Fort Wayne Railroad that connected Pittsburgh to the west. Neville and Ross became major landowners throughout Western Pennsylvania and Pittsburgh East Side.

The cradle of East End capitalism and philanthropy may well have been the Presbyterian Church with its deep Scotch–Irish roots. The log pews of the first Presbyterian Church had the names of James O'Hara, Ebenezer Denny, James Ross, Isaac Craig, Judge Addison, John Wilkins, and John Irwin carved in them. These men owned over a third of the state of Pennsylvania. Their pastor, Francis Herron, preached a gospel of philanthropy. Herron pulled industrialists together to create a social safety net in a time when government had no role in helping the poor and homeless. Herron and O'Hara forged the idea of industrial philanthropy based on Scotch–Irish communal beliefs.

In 1819, Jacob Negley donated the land for the East Liberty Presbyterian Church which would become known as the "Cathedral of Capitalism." Other East End churches such as Point Breeze Presbyterian, Sixth Presbyterian, and Shadyside Presbyterians grew during the next few decades. In these churches, capitalism and philanthropy grew and was passed on to new generations. Marriages between Germans and Scotch–Irish furthered the growth of the Presbyterian Church. The Neville family and the Craig family were neighbors and would be united in the marriage of Major Isaac Craig to daughter of

John Neville, Amelia Neville. Their son, Neville B. Craig (1783–1840), would be a promi-nent East Ender. Neville Craig could be considered a true Pittsburgher, having been born in Fort Pitt. Neville Craig became the editor of the *Pittsburgh Gazette* and would become the area's biggest visionary and promoter. Neville Craig was the first to promote Pittsburgh as a transportation center and the "Gateway to the West." His vision of canals and railways was known as "Craig's Spider," and slowly it was a vision that would be realized. His plantation was known as "Bellefield" and remains an East End section today. Craig farmed the area with fields of corn and wheat. Neville Craig became caught in the old schism of the Federalist Party during the Whiskey Rebellion. He moved to the Democrat Party and became ostracized by the new Whig Party in the East End. Craig, however, never wavered from his protectionist core. Neville and Craig streets still commemorate the existence of the Neville Craig plantation.

In the 1820s, a new heir to Pittsburgh's manufacturing base rose as protectionist tar-iffs were enacted. In 1824 Peter Shoenberger built Pittsburgh's successful volume nail mill known as Juniata Works. East Ender Peter Shoenberger came from one of Pennsylvania's German iron working families. Originally the family worked as blacksmiths and ironmon-gers in Lancaster. Coming over the mountains, Shoenberger's father started one of the most successful iron plantations in Western Pennsylvania. Shoenberger was the son of a Pennsylvania iron plantation owner in the Juniata region which expanded into West-ern Pennsylvania. Peter Shoenberger's father had built a large forge and bloomer with his charcoal furnaces east of Pittsburgh. Shoenbergers would own pig iron furnaces through the tri-state iron-making region of Ohio, Pennsylvania, and West Virginia. Nails could now be mass produced, and a booming America needed nails for housing, shipbuilding, and growth. Juniata Iron was on the Allegheny River at Fifteenth Street near the terminus of the Pennsylvania Canal in which Shoenberger had a financial interest. The Pennsylva-nia Canal connected Shoenberger's pig iron furnaces in the Juniata district of southwest-ern Pennsylvania to his rolling mill. True to his iron plantation heritage, Shoenberger built a large East End mansion near the plant. By 1832, Pittsburgher Peter Shoenberger built a nail operation about 50 miles downriver at Wheeling, West Virginia, one of the other strategic locations. Mahoning Valley in Ohio also had the right combinations for nail pro-duction for Shoenberger to expand. His Juniata Works on the east side of the Allegheny River (near the Pennsylvania Canal) used a high-tech nail machine built by iron engineer, John McElroy. The works had six nail machines and a newly invented spike machine of McElroy. The works employed 80 and produced six tons of nails a week. The smoke in the Pittsburgh's skies was becoming thick, and Charles Dickens noted this on his visit in 1842.

In the 1830s, the new tariffs strengthened the iron foundry business. Alexander Brad-ley made a fortune casting iron stoves and built his wooden mansion in East End's Shady-side (Centre and Millvale Avenues). Pittsburgh was fast becoming the center of industry and capitalism with deep roots going back to its Scotch–Irish belief in property rights. When the famous French observer of American greatness, Alexis de Tocqueville, came to Western Pennsylvania in 1838, he noted: "In democratic countries, the majority of the people do not clearly see what they have to gain by revolution, but they continually and in a thousand ways feel what they might lose by one. . . In no country is the love of property more active and more anxious than in the United States."[1] This strong Scotch–Irish belief dominated the Western Pennsylvania area and spread west to Ohio. The German immigrants, who followed and mixed with the Scotch–Irish, adopted it. Inventors, manufacturers, and investors flooded the hills around Pittsburgh with their factories.

Peter Shoenberger would be the German "O'Hara" of the 1830s in Pittsburgh; his manufacturing empire even surpassed that of O'Hara. Shoenberger built his mansion near today's Highland Park in the East End (Penn Avenue). In 1831 Shoenberger formed Shoenberger & Company with his son, John Shoenberger, to produce iron and steel products. In the 1830s, both Peter and John invested in stagecoaches and canals. By 1833 the firm was pioneering the making of blister and crucible steel. The Shoenbergers also were the first in the area to move into wire production, which would lead to the formation of American Steel & Wire. Peter and John would foreshadow Andrew Carnegie in the use of vertical integration, which means owning the whole supply chain such as coalmines, coke ovens, iron furnaces, rolling mills, and the transportation system. John Shoenberger became a director of the newly established Merchants' and Manufacturers' Bank. The Shoenberger family would also be part of the iron industry expansion into Wheeling, West Virginia, and Youngtown, Ohio. Peter Shoenberger's daughter would become the wife of East End songwriter, Stephen Foster. Peter Shoenberger was a founder of both Lutheran and Episcopal churches as well as the social Pittsburgh Club. The Pittsburgh Club was the first of several clubs for industrialists and capitalists. Peter had a pew in the First English Lutheran Church. John Shoenberger was involved with a number of banks, factories, steel mills, hospitals, and churches. Like O'Hara, he continued the tradition of Pittsburgh capitalists for philanthropy. He would be the first of Pittsburgh's great art collectors and an amateur astronomer (like James O'Hara). Shoenberger was a founder of the Allegheny Observatory, one of the first examples of cultural philanthropy. The Shoenbergers would operate iron and steel operations into the 1900s.

Pittsburgh's paper of 1829, the *Gazette*, was edited by Neville B. Craig who was the son of Isaac Craig and Amelia Neville. The paper was a complex mixture of Pittsburgh political currents. It reflected the unusual politics of the Pig Iron Aristocracy and the regional industrialists. The *Gazette* was called "conservative Democratic, Anti-Masonic, and Whig" all in one. The Anti-Masonic movement in Western Pennsylvania was more an anti-Jackson movement, since it was being used nationally to protest Jackson on the basis of his membership in the Masons. Both Neville Craig and Harmar Denny, who led the anti-Masonic movement, were sons of founders of Masonic Lodge 45 in Pittsburgh.

This type of confusion also is an excellent description of the politics of the Pig Iron Aristocracy and the struggle to define their protectionist plank inside a national party. Eventually the Pig Iron Aristocrats would unite as Republicans in the Whig Party, which fully embraced the protectionist plank. Initially the *Gazette* was considered Jacksonian in the 1830s, but its strong stand on protectionism brought it into the Whig Party of the 1840s

---

1 Daniel Long, *Pittsburgh Memoranda*, (Pittsburgh: Benton Books), p. 35

and Republican Party of the 1850s. The common denominator of Western Pennsylvanian and Ohio politics after 1820 was protectionism and industrial growth. It was, as noted, a struggle against the Scotch–Irish whiskey rebels in the population who personally voted Democrat because of the popularity and Scotch–Irish heritage of Andrew Jackson.

Pittsburgh's cotton mills were struggling in the 1838 due to imports, which added to the strong Whig base. The political and financial center of American protectionism was in Pittsburgh's East End. The Whig Party was the political face of protectionism. East Ender and then-congressman Harmar Denny was critical in the nomination of Whig William Henry Harrison in 1838.[1] It would be the first of many elections decided in the East End of Pittsburgh. The protectionist movement in Pittsburgh was an alliance of labor and capital with the campaign slogan of "Two dollars a day and Roast Beef." Harrison won by the largest electoral vote prior to 1840. Harrison made a visit to the East End on his way to the inauguration in Washington, D.C. It was Pittsburgh's greatest celebration with huge parades. Harrison died after only a month as president, but the Whig base was established. Not surprisingly, East End's Shadyside would be home to one of the most powerful Whig U.S. senators, Thomas Howe. Howe was also president of Exchange National Bank. His mansion, "Graystone," was the first in Shadyside.

Neville Craig, editor of the *Pittsburgh Gazette*, became an active member of the Antimasonic Party in the 1830s. Craig's hatred of the Masons put him at odds with Henry Clay as a presidential candidate. In 1842, the paper opposed Clay's presidential run because Clay was a Mason and a slaveholder. While a strong protectionist with his anti-Clay position, Neville Craig became at odds with the Pittsburgh industrialists who were Clay supporters. In 1844, a group of Pittsburgh industrialists including Edward W. Stephens, William Eichbaum, and Thomas Bakewell helped implement a change in the *Gazette*'s editorial approach. From 1844 on, the paper became an advocate of Henry Clay and his "American System" of protectionism. Henry Clay's Whig Party stood for American industrialization and American greatness. This demonstrated the extensive political power of the Pig Iron Aristocracy in western Pennsylvania. In the Clay-Polk presidential election, Polk won handily nationally, but Whig Henry Clay carried Allegheny County. The local Democrats claimed the Pig Iron Aristocrats assured the Democrat Irish were working on Election Day. Still, the Whig victory would augur the great political alliance of management and labor in the future Republican Party. During the formation of the Republican Party, Pittsburgh was a Whig stronghold and its leaders were known as "Iron Whigs." Almost every president and presidential candidate had to call on the Pig Iron Aristocracy with a visit to Pittsburgh. Every president from Lincoln to Teddy Roosevelt visited Pittsburgh and all went to the East End.

In the 1830s, men like William Eichbaum (Oakland) and William Wilkins (Homewood) built mansions in the East End. The area continued to be popular with German and Scotch–Irish farmer immigrants. Both men had ties with O'Hara and probably bought

---

1 "Letters from William Henry Harrison," *The Western Pennsylvania Historical Magazine*, Vol. 45, 1918

their property from him. Another Oakland capitalist and steamboat magnate, Thomas S. Clarke, had bought his land from O'Hara. Other new residents to the East End in the late 1830s were the successful iron and foundry manufacturers. Eichbaum's East End mansion became a draw for the up and coming German middle class to the Oakland section. These professional German craftsmen were young and had money. These middle class Germans brought openness to public drinking that the area's Scotch–Irish had avoided. The area's first and maybe the nation's first "night-clubs" evolved in the German east end. Lawrenceville's Yellow Tavern had a dance floor in the 1840s. The Shakespeare Gardens at Shady and Penn Avenue even had a type of comedic floorshow.

In the 1840s and 1850s, Allegheny City (Pittsburgh's North side) had millionaire's row, but Pittsburgh's East End was developing faster with its horse-drawn streetcars connecting it to downtown Pittsburgh in 1851. The Pittsburgh–Lawrenceville line was the first, and East End businessmen could readily get to their offices and banks in downtown Pittsburgh. The East End was rapidly becoming one of America's first true suburbs. The real boom would come with the Pennsylvania Railroad running down Penn Avenue in the 1850s. In the 1840s, two railroads (Baltimore & Ohio and the Pennsylvania Railroad) were racing to make Neville Craig's vision a reality. In 1851, the Pennsylvania Railroad reached Turtle Creek where passengers could go from stagecoach, a twenty-mile trip to Pittsburgh. At Turtle Creek, a tunnel would be needed to reach Braddock station and then Pittsburgh. On December 10, 1852, the first steam locomotive made the trip from Philadelphia in 15 hours. The East End would have one of the first stations, and the first officials of the Pennsylvania Railroad settled in the East End.

The 1840s would bring one of the East End's greatest residents in Thomas Mellon. Mellon was the son of a Scotch–Irish farmer who went to Pittsburgh's Western Pennsylvania University (now the University of Pittsburgh). Thomas would open a law practice in Pittsburgh. In 1843 after a brief courtship, he married Sarah Jane Negley of the East End. This would bring Mellon into the old East End aristocracy. The Negley family connection would bring the friendship of Senator James Ross, Pittsburgh's wealthiest lawyer. Ross would be a key player to Thomas Mellon and his legal career. Thomas Mellon would come to say his models were Benjamin Franklin and James Ross. Following the lead of the Negley family and James Ross, Mellon started to invest in real estate. By 1849 he was investing in coal lands. Mellon quickly took advantage of linking Pittsburgh's booming industry to the need for banking. Mellon proved skillful in both and quickly amassed a small fortune. In 1851 he built a country estate in the East End (401 Negley Avenue). Mellon continued to profit from the coal business; but in the 1870s, he would enter the banking field for which he is best known. The Mellon, Negley, Alexander, and Ross Scotch–Irish families became one family under old Judge Mellon.

Bankers had been moving to the East End since the 1840s, and the king of the bankers, old Judge Thomas Mellon, would settle there. During the Civil War, Western Pennsylvania became the forge and armorer of the nation. Thomas Mellon moved from law and farming to the booming coal business where fortunes were being made. Coal requirements for Pittsburgh five years prior to the Civil War were 423,000 tons versus 5,500,000 tons during the war. The Connellsville District of Westmoreland County boomed and coke ovens opened. The biggest coal dealer in the area was B. Corey and Company with Judge Andrew Mellon as the majority stockholder. Judge Mellon, with his father, had originally immigrated to coal-rich Westmoreland County to the east of Pittsburgh. B. Corey and Company had a fleet of barges to move coal down the Ohio River to other industrial cities such as Cincinnati and St. Louis, but the Civil War made Pittsburgh the world's greatest consumer of coal. Pittsburgh produced as much as 25 percent of the Union's artillery, 15 percent at Fort Pitt Foundry alone. At least 80 percent of the Union's naval iron plate for ships and most of the Union's armor plate was rolled in Pittsburgh. All of the artillery carriage axles and most railroad axles were forged in Pittsburgh. But most of the raw pig iron, however, came from Ohio, Westmoreland County, and Fayette County, as Pittsburgh had only three blast furnaces but added two more large ones at the end of the war. All of these blast furnaces were using Connellsville coke, creating many Western Pennsylvanian millionaires. The coke boom created the Pittsburgh and Connellsville Railroad following the Monongahela River to Pittsburgh, which was about forty miles long. Coke fueled the Union's great cannon foundries of the Civil War. Mellon prospered from the war production of Pittsburgh.

Thomas Mellon became interested in making money beyond all else. Mellon, a 35-year-old Pittsburgh (formerly of Westmoreland) lawyer, had made his first investment in a coalfield north of Pittsburgh on the Pennsylvania Canal. Thomas was living at the new family estate in the East End when he followed his neighbors, William Thaw and Samuel Kier, into canal-related businesses. The canal would bring much wealth to the family. It would prove highly profitable by supplying fuel to the city of Pittsburgh for home and industrial heating. The Pittsburgh of 1849 produced no pig iron or steel, but its forges and nail mills were the major consumers of pig iron from Westmoreland County. It had already earned the name of the "Smoky City" due to its use of coal to power industry and heat homes. Pittsburgh burned more coal than any other American city at the time. The city was starting to come out of a nation-wide recession by 1849.

The Pig Iron Aristocrats, capitalists, protectionist politicians, and Whig industrialists started to migrate to the East End. While these industrialist giants were the best remembered, in their shadow was one of the area's most unusual residents — Jane Grey Swisshelm. She was one of America's first feminists and anti-war protestors, but she was probably best known as an abolitionist. She was born in a log cabin near today's USS Building (Trinity Cemetery) and moved east to Wilkinsburg. From her small East End home near that of Judge Wilkins, she got her education by traveling each day to a school in Braddock. She became known in the 1840s for her anti-Mexican War protests and the support of the Pennsylvania Married Women's Property Law of 1848. The law allowed married women to inherit money from their parents. In the 1850s, Jane turned to the anti-slavery movement, finding unusual allies in the Whig (and Republican) capitalists of the East End. At the same time, however, Swisshelm's anti-Catholic views made enemies with the area workers. Her anti-Catholic views helped pull some workers out of the area's fast-growing Republican Party. After the Civil War, Swisshelm turned her energies to Women's Suffrage.

By the 1850s, the industrial, banking, and legal aristocracy resided in the East End. The area had strong interconnecting ties consisting of Scotch–Irish heritage, German heritage, the Presbyterian Church, the Masonic Lodge, and social organizations. Marriage had brought together the aristocratic Scotch–Irish and Germans. Success was becoming a matter of family ties and connections in the East End. In the near future it would bring the young Scotch–Irish Andrew Carnegie and the young German Frick to the neighborhood. Unlike the old aristocratic families of the east, the Pittsburgh aristocracy was open to new members. Capitalism and money had and would prove the stronger bond than family heritage and inherited wealth. The East End would become the nucleus and seed of American industrial might. It would also become the financial cradle of American presidents.

CHAPTER 5. THE GLASS CITY AND THE EAST END GLASS MEN

Few people are aware that Pittsburgh was known as the Glass City for many years. It was, of course, O'Hara who brought the glass industry to Pittsburgh. James O'Hara and Isaac Craig had set up a glass factory on Pittsburgh's Southside in 1798. O'Hara's glass works had been a green glass factory, with green being a natural color of glass with impurities. From that simple beginning, glass factories grew. The mountains between the west and east coast made shipping of glass difficult. Monongahela and Pittsburgh sand was low in impurities, which allowed for some of the best leaded and cut glass to be produced in the area. O'Hara was also the first to use coal versus wood as the fuel. O'Hara's glassworks was amazingly profitable. O'Hara was responsible for bring America's greatest glassmaker, William Peter Eichbaum, to Pittsburgh in the 1790s. In the early 1800s, Eichbaum switched to the firm of Bakewell & Page. Bakewell & Page would be the incubator of the American glass industry.

The growth and dominance of the glass industry of Pittsburgh was amazing. In 1797, there were two glasshouses in Pittsburgh; but by 1824, there were five in Pittsburgh and four more in the surrounding area. By the Civil War there were 25 glasshouses; and by 1885, Pittsburgh had over 50 glasshouses. In 1885, Allegheny County had 51 of America's 211 glasshouses. The only county close to Allegheny was Kings County of New York (Brooklyn) with 12 glasshouses. O'Hara had started what would become the backbone industry of Pittsburgh.

O'Hara had produced all types of glass in his Southside factory in the late 1790s. He mined the coal from "Coal Hill," today's Mount Washington. O'Hara pioneered the model for paternal capitalism at his factory. He had to import skilled glassmakers. To entice them, he built houses with gardens near the factory. He paid the costs of crossing from Europe with their families. He supplied free coal to heat their homes. O'Hara expanded from glass bottles and containers into window glass, which was becoming popular in the west. O'Hara's success was his ability to bring in raw materials from all over the world to make his diverse products.

Another East Ender, by the name of Benjamin Bakewell (1767–1844), changed the face of America and of Pittsburgh glass making. Bakewell entered the cut glass (lead, flint glass) market in 1808. In the early nineteenth century, imported glass controlled the market. Benjamin Bakewell and Benjamin Page formed Pittsburgh Flint Glass with the help of East Ender William Eichbaum, who was also a cut flint glass artisan. Benjamin Page had been an importer of glass; but with protectionist policies, Page decided to invest in his neighbor Bakewell's glass plant. The firm became one of America's biggest importers using the Monongahela River to ship to places like Mexico, Peru, and Brazil. Benjamin Bakewell's son, Thomas, would head America's premier glass company a few years later. The Bakewell family is now considered a founding family of Pittsburgh's East End. Lucy Bakewell, daughter of Benjamin Bakewell, married the famous bird artist and ornithologist John James Audubon (1780–1851). In fact, Audubon painted his passenger pigeon print near the East End where these pigeons once darkened the skies and filled the markets. While living on the Allegheny River, "He once witnessed a huge flock of birds [Passenger Pigeons] in 1813 that he estimated at over a billion birds in such numbers that they darkened the sky for many hours."[1] For a short time Audubon operated a gristmill in the East End with his brother-in-law, Thomas W. Bakewell (1778–1874); but it failed, and Audubon moved to Kentucky. Bakewell's glass works would survive for many decades.

Bakewell had studied the cut-leaded glass manufacturers of England and Ireland. He was a great student and learner who took copious notes. Bakewell realized he needed to import skilled glasscutters as well as glass blowers. Most European nations had made it illegal for glassmakers to immigrate to the United States. The Venetians went so far as to center their glass houses on an island so glassmakers could not leave. Bakewell and other glass manufacturers had to smuggle glass artisans into the United States. America had other resource problems when it came to the production of leaded cut glass. The needed Venetian expertise, lead ore, master glasscutters, and pure sand came to America in the 1790s. Sand, for example, was brought from England as ballast on ships, but it was expensive and almost economically impossible to get it to Pittsburgh.

Lead was the critical resource, however, if Bakewell were to be successful. The Embargo Act of 1807 and the beginning of the War of 1812 cut off the supply of lead ore which crippled American glass manufacture. England controlled the world's only source of quality lead ore for glass making. It was known as red lead, and was a secondary concentrated processed ore of roasted lead ore. After the War of 1812, England continued economic warfare, dumping cheap glass products on the market and keeping the price of red lead high to prevent American companies from competing in the flint glass markets. The company would produce leaded glass for art and tableware pieces, but lead ore shortages and skilled labor shortages again doomed the company. In addition, the high price for

---

1 Charles McCollester, *The Point of Pittsburgh*, (Pittsburgh: Battle of Homestead Foundation, 2008), p. 63

imported red lead made finished American glass more expensive. Bakewell, O'Hara, and the Pittsburgh Federalists would petition Congress for help. Pittsburgh had developed a powerful political machine, and tariff protection united the Federalists and Jeffersonians. Tariff protection would save the Pittsburgh glass industry until process innovation could be developed. A New Englander trained by Bakewell would find a way to produce red lead in America. Once Bakewell and Page found red lead and good Monongahela River sand, the tariffs of the 1820s favored domestic production of high quality glass.

New England glassmaker Deming Jarves found the secret to producing red lead in America. He traded that knowledge with William Bakewell for knowledge of flint glass making. In the 1820s, Jarves came to Pittsburgh to learn cut flint glass manufacture. Jarves would go on to found New England Glass and ultimately Libbey Glass. Jarves was not alone, as many of America's great glassmakers apprenticed at Pittsburgh Flint Glass. William Bakewell would become known as the "father of American glass," and his glass was world renowned. Bakewell was a leader in the early roots of the protectionist Federalists who would morph into the Whig and eventually the Republican Party. More importantly, Bakewell and Pittsburgh's East Enders would lead a political revolution, changing the American vision from an agrarian one to a manufacturing one. Initially, Federalists like O'Hara, Ross, and Wilkins controlled Pittsburgh industry. The political roots of Pittsburgh's East End ran deep, first as part of Clay's Whig Party, then as birthplace of the Republican Party. Eventually a huge majority of 10,000 votes in the area carried Abe Lincoln to the first Republican presidency. The Speaker of the House in 1820s, Henry Clay, became the founder of the Whig Party and would visit East End industrialists a number of times. Interestingly, the commitment to Henry Clay in Western Pennsylvania would result in the name of the East End's future wealthiest resident — Henry Clay Frick.

The Pittsburgh industrialists and arms suppliers were directly related to the political foundation of Henry Clay's "American System." Henry Clay of Kentucky became head of the Hamiltonian Federalists. Clay's American System was a protectionist approach to protect American industries via tariffs and an aggressive approach to national improvements. To fully grasp the roots of Clay's economic philosophy, one must first understand Thomas Jefferson's vision of the nation. Jefferson envisioned an agrarian society of farmers and merchants. In 1790, an estimated 90 percent of the American population was employed in agriculture. His vision demanded free trade to assure that American crops could move into foreign markets readily. Jefferson had grown up in a tobacco and cotton culture that depended on European purchases and their crops. While he believed in farm self-sufficiency, he feared the industrialization that he had seen in Europe. Hamilton, on the other hand, saw America's freedom rooted in its ability to achieve economic freedom through manufacturing and banking. Hamilton, the soldier, was well aware of the role of technology and manufacturing in the ability of a nation to win wars and believed that manufacturing was fundamental to America's freedom. As a young officer, Hamilton found the colonial army constrained by a shortage of iron cannon and rifles because of the lack of American manufacture. Hamilton, however, remained a free trader like many of his Federalist friends, believing that financial systems were the basis for industrialization. Actually, the Federalists were split on tariffs, some seeing no need for them because America lacked manufacturing, and others seeing tariffs as a source of federal revenue. A strong protectionist branch of the Federalist Party evolved out of Pittsburgh's East End and manufacturers.

Initially, Western Pennsylvania was agricultural based and Jeffersonian. Both Jefferson and Hamilton were constrained by the agricultural nature and lack of manufacturing in America at the time, as well as by earlier colonial British constraints on industries such as iron making. These British prohibitions such as the British Iron Act of 1750 had infuriated Scotch–Irish iron makers in western Pennsylvania. In particular, the Scotch–Irish moved to the Ohio frontier to avoid tax laws. The Iron Act of 1750 allowed for all raw bars of smelted iron known as pig iron to be shipped to England duty-free, but outlawed the production of iron products such as kettles, skillets, stoves, forged iron for guns, and steel for the blacksmith shop. One of the families fleeing Western Pennsylvania and the Iron Act was that of William McKinley, who would become Western Pennsylvania's most popular president (carrying Allegheny County by an amazing 70 percent in 1900) and a close friend to Pittsburgh East Enders. The fleeing frontiersmen remembered and vowed never to be economically restrained again by any government, and they would be the core of the future Whig party. More of these same Scotch–Irish would flee western Pennsylvania to Ohio, Kentucky, and Tennessee to avoid the federal tax on whiskey manufacture in 1794 and would become part of the political base of frontier politician, Henry Clay. It would be a base that often disagreed with Clay wanting cheap imported goods.

More than anything, the Whiskey Rebellion caused a political divide in the Scotch–Irish along economic lines in Pittsburgh. The wealthy Scotch–Irish industrialists and the Presbyterian Church leaders had supported the Federalist application of the law in Pittsburgh. Their poorer cousins in the Pennsylvanian hills opposed a strong central government and taxes. The whiskey tax forced the frontier Scotch–Irish into Jefferson's "Republican" Party. In the 1810s, "the clapboard junto" of Pittsburgh (those who lived in clapboard houses) put together a strong opposition to the Federalist manufacturers. The Jacksonian Democratic Party (known as the clapboard democracy) controlled the area, but Pittsburgh's congressmen were protectionists who sided with Henry Clay in Congress. Henry Clay would make many trips to Pittsburgh where he was often greeted as a hero. Even on his trips through Pittsburgh on his way from Kentucky to Washington, he drew large crowds of supporters.

East Enders James O'Hara and John Wilkins represented the political split in Western Pennsylvania. John Wilkins became a good friend of James O'Hara and would become a partner of O'Hara in Pittsburgh's first bank in 1804. Like O'Hara, John Wilkins was an early industrialist who built a Southside glass window factory in 1800. John Wilkins's son, John Jr., became a brigadier general of the local militia and an associate judge. Wilkins Jr. led the Pittsburgh militia in the Whiskey Rebellion. His brother, William Wilkins, would build a major mansion in the Homewood section of the East End. William was an important judge, banker, and industrialist. He was also a good friend of Henry Clay. Politically, the Wilkins families were strong Federalists, but William would join the Jacksonian Democrats and become a congressman. William Wilkins was always a strong protectionist and voted with Henry Clay on trade issues. The Wilkins family had supported slavery, which prevented them from supporting the Republicans; but Wilkins would often stand with the Whigs and Republicans on protectionist issues. Wilkins represented the alliance of industry and politics in Pittsburgh. Pittsburgh needed the protection of its iron and glass industries to grow. Its glass industry was dominant locally and nationally. In 1803 Pittsburgh's two glasshouses produced $13,000 in glass (over a half million in today's money); in 1810, three glasshouses produced $63,000 in glass; and 1815, six glasshouses produced over $235,000 ($10 million today).[1]

President James Monroe had made the first visit to Pittsburgh's East End in 1812 to meet with Judge William Wilkins and Thomas Bakewell to discuss protection of the glass industry. He would be one of many presidents who would visit the East End capitalists. Bakewell had given President Monroe a beautiful 328-piece set of engraved flint glass tableware. A few years later Andrew Jackson ordered a complete table set of Bakewell glass at a price of $1,500. Bakewell's glass factory had commanded visits from President Monroe, Speaker of the House Henry Clay, and famous ornithologists — Alexander Wilson and John Audubon — and the original founder of Libbey Glass — Deming Jarves. Even the infamous Vice-President Aaron Burr came to Bakewell and Wilkins to solicit help in his rebellion. When General Lafayette visited Bakewell's home and factory in 1825, he was impressed with the high quality and would purchase pieces for friends. Lafayette received a beautiful set of cut glass vases which were exhibited at the 1893 Chicago World Fair years later. Benjamin Page also became wealthy from the popularity of Pittsburgh cut glass. Page founded Pittsburgh's first library system, although members had to pay to belong.

Pennsylvania Representative Henry Baldwin supported Henry Clay's American System with an iron fist and would help pass the "cut glass bill," which offered protection for American cut flint glass in 1824. For years Henry Baldwin chaired the U.S. House Committee on Manufacturers. The British, French, and Irish imports controlled the market with Pittsburgh's Bakewell & Company, having a small domestic share until they won protectionist policies from Washington. Bakewell often sent special glass pieces to politicians and presidents to promote Clay's "American System." East End Senator Judge Wilkins became known as the "iron knight" in his support of iron and glass tariffs. Clay's great tariff of 1824 assured the growth of Bakewell's glass company and many American manufacturers. The manufacturers ultimately wrestled the vote away from the Democrats as Andrew Jackson's policies turned anti-manufacturing. These manufacturers often held dinners for national protectionists such as Mathew Carey and Henry Clay. Clay and Carey often visited Pittsburgh for protectionist dinners given by Bakewell, Wilkins, Henry Baldwin, and other East Enders. Nearby manufacturing cities such as Steubenville, Ohio, and Wheeling, West Virginia, developed a manufacturing network through Clay and Carey; and ultimately, even the Jacksonians paid tribute to the East Enders of Pittsburgh.

The political link between the Pittsburgh industrialists and national politicians increased as the Civil War approached. Pittsburgh's iron and glass men stood united, sup-

---

1 Richard Wade, *The Urban Frontier*, (Urbana: University of Chicago Press, 1959), p. 48

porting the new Whig Party and Republican Party. The area had been strongly abolitionist and had given Lincoln his presidential victory. Pittsburgh historian Stefan Lorant noted: "Abraham Lincoln had polled a record-breaking majority of 10,000 in Allegheny County, and Republicans jokingly referred to the county as 'the State of Allegheny'."[1] President-elect Abraham Lincoln spent the night at Pittsburgh's Monongahela House on his way to Washington. Thousands surrounded the hotel as Lincoln went to the balcony to give a short speech to the crowd. The young middle class and future residents of the East End such as Andrew Carnegie and Henry Clay Frick were staunch Republicans coming from abolitionist and Whig families. The Wilkins family of the East End was the exception with Southern and slavery ties of old. However, once war was declared, Wilkins lined up with the Union and actually headed up the Committee of Public Safety.

Pittsburgh banks had reaped the rewards of federal grants over the years, and many Pittsburgh industrialists were also bankers. The Bank of the United States in 1823 had directors such as Thomas Bakewell, George Boggs, and James Park. William Wilkins was also involved in the branch of the Second Bank of the United States which brought another future industrialist, John Thaw, to the city. John Thaw's son, William, would be part of the Pittsburgh iron empire and Pig Iron Aristocracy. Men like William Thaw, Harry Thaw (son of William), Benjamin Jones, James Laughlin, John Shoenberger, E. Stevens, Henry Phipps, Henry Oliver, James Park, and Henry Buhl were the Pig Iron Aristocrats of Pittsburgh. They actually lived on Pittsburgh's north side, then known as Allegheny City. In the 1850s, the original "Millionaire's Row" prior to the East End was Allegheny City's Ridge Avenue. Allegheny City became the classy suburb of Pittsburgh industrialists for a short period. Lincoln would even make a brief stop there prior to going to his hotel in Pittsburgh on his way to the White House. President Grant and Rutherford Hayes would also visit this aristocratic city of Allegheny of pig iron manufacturers.

The East End started to become the preferred residency of millionaires because of its ease of access to the Pittsburgh financial center. Also, the location of the East End spared it from the heavy smoke of Pittsburgh's industrial plants. The main drawback to Allegheny City was its then awkward location on the other side of the Allegheny River, decline of the cotton mills, and the rise of the city's first ghettos. Interestingly, some future millionaire residents of the East End such as Carnegie grew up in Allegheny City ghettos. The 1840s Allegheny gang of the "bottom hooshiers" had some of the future East End and Pittsburgh industrialists in Henry Phipps, Henry Oliver, Robert Pitcairn, and Thomas Miller. Furthermore, the East End had been the first suburb of Pittsburgh to have an extensive horse drawn streetcar system, which allowed quick access to the Pittsburgh banks for the iron and glass manufacturers. Many iron and glass aristocrats moved to the East End and helped its development as Pittsburgh's best suburb. Protectionism was at the heart of the rise of a millionaire class of iron and glass manufacturers.

Bakewell was not alone as a Glass King in the East End. One of the richest men was Alexander King (1816–1890). King had come from Ireland to Pittsburgh in his early twen-

---

1 Lorant, p. 133

ties to enter the grocery business. King quickly tapped into the old Scotch–Irish trading ties of Pittsburgh and started importing. He became the leading importer of English soda ash needed by glassmakers throughout the area. Eventually he entered into glass production himself. Making a small fortune in glass, Alexander King moved into banking. In 1880, King built his East End mansion "Baywood" on land originally owned by James Negley, having outgrown his Shadyside townhouse. Today the King mansion is part of Highland Park. King was known for philanthropy with the poor of Pittsburgh. Like O'Hara and Scaife, King set a standard in Scotch–Irish philanthropy to be followed. His daughter, Jennie, would marry Richard Beatty Mellon, creating another East End aristocratic line. Both the King and Mellon families were prominent members of East Liberty Presbyterian Church. Another prominent East End glassmaker was Edward Dithridge (1804–1889) who invented an oil lamp chimney in 1860. He would be one of the first of many creative inventors who settled in the East End. He built his mansion on the south part of the old Neville Craig farm in Bellefield. Dithridge had been inspired by the success of East Enders in the first distillation of newly found Pennsylvania oil to kerosene. He would make a fortune with his oil chimney lamps.

Maybe more important was the contribution of East End glass men to social institutions such as the Pittsburgh Permanent Library Association and the Bible Association. Benjamin Page, Thomas Bakewell, and Peter William Eichbaum founded the Pittsburgh Permanent Library Association in 1813. The Library was established in a Pittsburgh Courthouse and was open on Saturday evenings. This high value on education would become the distinguishing characteristic of East End philanthropy. Thomas Bakewell also organized the Pittsburgh Humane Society to take care of Pittsburgh's poor and hungry. Two other institutions of the early East Enders were the Presbyterian Church and the famous Masonic Lodge 45. The East End Germans often entered the Presbyterian Church through marriage or a desire to enter the mainstream of East End society. Even British Americans such as Benjamin Bakewell were loosely associated with the Presbyterian Church. Ultimately, East End Presbyterian Churches would become the "cathedral of capitalism."

The glass boom of the 1850s earned Pittsburgh the title of "Glass City," as the area had over 15 glassworks. Coal had fueled the glass boom, bringing many New England and East Coast glass companies to Pittsburgh. By the 1870s, the city had 32 glassworks and manufacturing products worth $5,832,492. Pittsburgh's annual glass exhibition at the famous Monongahela House was world renowned. The glass heritage of O'Hara, Eichbaum, Bakewell, Page, Denny, King, and Wilkins had created the nation's glass industry. Bakewell and Page was one of the world's best cut flint glass manufacturers; Bryce Higbee on Pittsburgh's Southside was known for its pressed glass; and Pittsburgh's window glass production led the country in volume. For the 1830s, 1840s and 1850s, Pittsburgh held the title of "Glass City." In the 1850s, its old iron industry would rise again and take the title back, but glass remained a major industry into the 1950s.

Later glass companies became important in the 1880s. East Enders George Macbeth and Thomas Evans had control of the chimney glass market. Both of these producers controlled a market of over 25 million lamps per year. Both companies were Pittsburgh based with plants in Pennsylvania and Indiana. They were hand-blown operations, which would doom them in a head-on competition with the new Michael Owens automated glass process. Evans and Macbeth went directly to glass magnate Edward Libbey in Toledo to discuss a solution. The deal was made to sell Libbey's Toledo Glass automated chimney operation for cash and stock in a new company, Macbeth-Evans. Shareholders in Toledo Glass received a 100 percent dividend with shares in Macbeth-Evans. Toledo Glass would control about 15 percent of Macbeth-Evans. Macbeth and Evans would dominate the glass chimney market. Libbey served as a vice-president and a director of the new company. Michael Owens was superintendent of the Macbeth-Evans Toledo plant.

One of the greatest glass industrialists would be East Ender John Pitcairn Jr. (1841–1916), the brother of Carnegie associate and Pennsylvania Railroad executive Robert Pitcairn. The Pitcairn family had emigrated from Scotland to Pittsburgh's north side, the same year as the Carnegie family. John would rise through the Pennsylvania Railroad. He invested with J. J. Vandergrift (future partner in Standard Oil) of the East End in the emerging oil industry. Making his fortune in oil, John Pitcairn partnered with Captain John Ford to form Pittsburgh Plate Glass in 1883. The plant was built 20 miles north of Pittsburgh at Creighton, Pennsylvania. In 1900, Pittsburgh Plate Glass controlled 65 percent of the plate glass market. His partner John Ford would later break off and form Libbey–Owens–Ford in Toledo, Ohio.

CHAPTER 6. THE "IRON CITY"

The label "Iron City" of the 1820s and 1830s applied to the iron-working factories of early Pittsburgh, not its production of iron. Pittsburgh's factories were the world's biggest consumers of pig iron. The rolling mills, nail factories, and cast foundries had an endless appetite for pig iron. No pig iron had been made in Pittsburgh until the 1850s after the initial failure of Pittsburgh's East End furnace of George Anshultz in the 1790s. Most of the pig iron was coming from the relatively close hills of Western Pennsylvania and Eastern Ohio. With Pittsburgh as the biggest user of pig iron, the capitalists found the technology and capital to allow pig iron to be made in Pittsburgh. The early Pittsburgh blast furnaces of the 1850s were built to produce pig iron for connected iron operations and distant pig iron users. The blast furnace could stand on its own, shipping and supplying pigs to many different foundries and rolling mills at points distant from the operation, using the emerging railroad system. The pig iron producers started to look at more integrated operations during and after the Civil War — blast furnaces and finishing operations in the same manufacturing complex — which would make the Pittsburgh the world's biggest producer and consumer.

In the 1840s, Pittsburgh was an amalgamation of blacksmith factories, foundries, nail factories, and metalworking shops. The city was well known as the smoky city as coal was the fuel. When Charles Dickens visited in 1842, he noted "Pittsburgh is like Birmingham in England; at least, at least its townspeople say so; setting aside the streets, the shops, the houses, wagons, factories, public buildings, and population, perhaps it maybe. It certainly has a great quantity of smoke hanging about it, and is famous for its ironworks."[1] Pittsburgh was the major supplier to the nation of cannonball, cannon, nails, stoves, steam engines, and horseshoes. In 1845, Pittsburgh supplied 100,000 horseshoes to the military

1 Charles Dickens, *American Notes: A Journey*, (New York: International Publishing, 1985), pp. 152-154

during the Mexican War. Still, Pittsburgh was an ironmonger and not an iron maker in the 1840s. Pittsburgh used more iron than any city in the world, and capitalists started to look to putting their blast furnaces in the city. Soon the demand for pig iron led to the need for local blast furnaces.

The story of the blast furnace in Pittsburgh is the story of Jones and Laughlin Steel. That story begins with the world's first oil baron, Samuel Kier, and Kier's young bank manager, Benjamin Franklin Jones. Both men had invested earlier in canals. In 1850, Kier focused his energy on oil while Jones invested in puddling furnaces and rolling mills on Pittsburgh's Southside (known as Brownstown). Another Pittsburgh East End investor, William Thaw, teamed up with Kier to extend canals to connect Pittsburgh and Youngstown. Then he moved into iron. Benjamin Jones was Scotch–Irish from a modest background, but as a young boy showed an attitude for business. Jones had been manager of the Pennsylvania Canal prior to this move in 1850, but in the 1840s he was a partner of a charcoal furnace and forge in Pennsylvania's Indiana County. The furnace failed with a reduction in national tariffs of the 1840s under the Democrats, allowing more imports. Jones had gotten the bug for the pig iron industry and its potential. The depression of the pig iron industry caused by lower tariffs left a lasting impression on Jones. He switched from the Democrat Party of his upbringing to the new protectionist Republican Party of the 1850s. B. F. Jones would become the nation's leader in support of a protectionist tariff policy and the political leader of the East End. He would become an important member of the old First Presbyterian Church of earlier Pig Iron Aristocrats and would lead the exodus of the Pig Iron Aristocrats from Allegheny City to Pittsburgh's east end. Jones would start a blast furnace/rolling mill operation on Pittsburgh's Southside.

Pig Iron Aristocrat Jones never got his Southside works fully running, but in 1853 teamed up with two German ironmasters — Bernard and John Lauth. Samuel Kier was also an investor in the company known as Jones, Lauth, and Company. The 1853 partnership agreement of B. F. Jones would augur that of the future steel king — Andrew Carnegie. The agreement called for all profits to be re-invested in the operation. Furthermore, the partnership was the first to apply the idea of vertical integration in the pig iron industry. Vertical integration meant owning the full manufacturing chain from raw materials to distribution. The new business model of vertical integration would become that of other East Enders such as Andrew Carnegie, H. J. Heinz, and Henry Clay Frick. This was the idea of Jones who opened warehouses in Chicago and Philadelphia to market iron products. Jones focused in particular on the needs of the railroad industry. The Southside operation in 1855 was known as the American Iron Works and got most of its pig iron from the Falcon Furnaces of Youngstown, Ohio. The plant rolled bar and rails. The Lauth brothers were brilliant engineers, and the American Iron Works became the most productive rolling mills in the country as well as a major consumer of pig iron. Jones's partners, the Lauths, were inventive and energetic partners who made Jones a wealthy industrialist. The Lauths also invented the cold rolling process to produce polished bar surfaces. They were German-Catholic, however, and could never gain acceptance in the elite Pig Iron Aristocracy of Pittsburgh.

In 1859, another partner who was a Pittsburgh banker and an East Ender, Scotch-Irish James Laughlin, brought with him a major infusion of cash and pig iron from his Ohio furnaces. Earlier, James Laughlin's Youngtown furnaces were supplying the American Iron Works of the Lauth brothers. The pig iron requirements for the Pittsburgh rolling mills were soon outstripping the ability of Pennsylvania and Ohio furnaces to supply them. As part of Laughlin's vertical integration, he set up two Pittsburgh blast furnaces (Eliza Furnaces) on the north side of the Monongahela River. Additional integration included the building of coke beehive furnaces. Coal was brought down the river from Connellsville while iron ore was brought in from Missouri and the Great Lakes. Vertical integration allowed Jones and Laughlin to become the low cost producer, a lesson that a young Andrew Carnegie would note. The basic layout of the operations would remain intact until 1980! Thus in 1861, the Jones and Laughlin Company became the first integrated iron works. Both Jones and Laughlin worked behind the scenes with the Pig Iron lobby to assure Lincoln's protectionist policies. Their support was a key reason behind Lincoln carrying Allegheny County by an overwhelming majority, and Jones would lead the Allegheny Republican Party for decades.

One difference between banker/investors of the east and the Pig Iron Aristocrats was who controlled the operations. The Pig Iron Aristocrats were operators first. They used their banking connections and political connections to finance and invest in their operations. They loved the size and mastery of their furnaces and mills. They rarely became politicians, looking at politicians as lower class. The success of the Pig Iron Aristocrats assured the success of the bankers, but unlike New York capitalism, the Pittsburgh bankers were the tail of the dog. When the corporate steel kings took over in the 1890s, the bankers took control of the operations and the politicians' limited operations. The Pig Iron Aristocrats expanded with the political success of the protectionist Republicans into other iron districts in Ohio, Michigan, West Virginia, and Illinois. They would deliver the presidential election for Abe Lincoln and Republican presidents into the 1930s.

The Pig Iron Aristocrats of Pennsylvania had brought war, not by their abolitionism but from their protectionism. The iron districts of Ohio, Maryland, Connecticut, and Pennsylvania had given Lincoln a resounding victory in 1860. He had been the first national candidate since Henry Clay to have the united support of the Pig Iron Aristocrats. Lincoln's majority would control Allegheny County around Pittsburgh and the Mahoning Valley of Ohio for the next 70 years. Ohio would become the birthplace of presidents, and Pennsylvania would be the financier of presidents. Pittsburgh had finally overcome the divides of the 1794 Whiskey Rebellion and united under the protectionist plank of the emerging Republicans. The margins were similar in the iron districts of Ohio. The Iron Whigs and protectionist Democrats had found a new home in the Republican Party. In western Virginia, the Pig Iron Aristocrats' support of the protectionist Lincoln split the state and created West Virginia. These Pig Iron Aristocrats had forged an alliance with iron labor as well. A strong pig iron industry was necessary for both management and labor.

The German and Irish immigrants of the 1840s came for economic opportunity, and they united with wealthy Scotch-Irish to form a new culture and a Republican machine in the iron districts. The Pig Iron Aristocrats of the North side started to build their mansions in the East End of Pittsburgh in the 1850s. Jones's annual earnings had reached $325,000 (near $8 million today) and allowed for the type of opulent living never seen in this industrial burgh. Jones would be the inspiration of a young telegram boy, Andrew Carnegie, who always remembered his large and generous tips. This would be the root of the Pittsburgh's industrial Republican machine of the East End. Industry growth took priority over unionism and profits. The owners and workers knew the economic recessions that had gone hand in hand with earlier free trade policies. As a result of war and protectionism, the pig iron industry would see great advances in technology. The Pig Iron Aristocrats were rewarded for their votes with the 1862 tariff act, which was the highest ever on pig iron at 32 percent. As the Pig Iron Aristocrats responded with massive investments in industry, Congress moved the rate to 47 percent in 1864. The pig iron industry grew an amazing 65 percent during the Civil War. By the end of the war, the Pig Iron Aristocrats were a real national political force with wealth and the ability to employ tens of thousands.

Besides technology, demand would drive Pittsburgh pig iron production, and there is no demand such as that of war. As much as 25 percent of the Union's artillery (15 percent at Fort Pitt Foundry alone) was made in Pittsburgh, and at least 80 percent of the Union's naval iron plate for ships. Most of the Union's armor plate was rolled in Pittsburgh. All of the artillery carriage axles and most railroad axles were forged in Pittsburgh. But most of the raw pig iron, however, came from Ohio. The Pig Iron Aristocrats were not only the ones who won the war but also the ones who profited the most. It would set the stage for the wealthy industrialists of Pittsburgh's East Side. The Republican tariffs assured a boom in national production. The great iron triangle of Ohio, West Virginia, and Pennsylvania saw growth as never before. The war would also stimulate huge leaps in pig iron technology. The huge profit margins in the pig iron related businesses assured that those profits were poured back into the businesses and expanded employment. Just as important, the pig iron end users such as the railroads experienced similar growth. The expansion of American industry during the war would be the infrastructure in place to make America the premier industrial nation.

The Jones and Laughlin furnaces at Pittsburgh expanded but could only supply their south side rolling mills. The war brought not only expansion of the Jones and Laughlin Eliza Furnaces, but also the twin monster blast furnaces in Pittsburgh of Shoenberger, Blair, and Company known as Superior furnaces. These furnaces built in 1865 stood 65 feet high (the largest in Pittsburgh) and had a dual capacity of 48,000 tons annually. The eyes of the nation were not focused on blast furnaces, but the great foundries and the world's largest cannon. The greatest producer of mammoth cannon was the Fort Pitt Foundry in Pittsburgh. Fort Pitt Foundry was the direct descendent of the Joseph McClurg works of 1804. This foundry would produce 60 percent of the Union's heavy artillery and 15 percent of all Union artillery. The Fort Pitt Foundry became famous throughout the war across Europe as reporters marveled at the huge guns cast there.

Fort Pitt Foundry had led the country in the development of heavy cast iron in the 1850s. It was located on the north side of Pittsburgh (Allegheny City) on 28th Street. Charles Knapp then owned the foundry, purchasing it from the sons of Joseph McClurg in 1841. The real advance in heavy artillery came from the work of army Major Thomas Jefferson Rodman. Major Rodman was the superintendent of the Watertown Arsenal in Massachusetts. Large cast cannon had become problematic since these hot cast cannon cooled, creating internal strains. The strains would cause the cast cannon to break on cooling, split during transport, or burst in firing. Rodman had worked out a revolutionary process of cooling the cannon from the inside core. This allowed for a hollow tube to be cast. Prior to this, large cannon in America and at Germany's Krupp Works were cast solid and bored out. Rodman had received a patent in 1847, but the army was less impressed. In 1849, Rodman signed a contract to develop large cannon at Knapp's Fort Pitt Foundry.

Rodman moved to Pittsburgh's East End and started a series of production experiments that made news around the world. It's hard for us to understand the Victorian mind that loved to read of the great accomplishments of industry; but remember, they lacked movie stars and sports rivalries. Over the next ten years Rodman perfected his process of hollow cast cannon. The larger size of the Rodman cannon posed additional technical problems beyond casting. Pig iron purity was critical to prevent bursting, and Rodman settled on Hocking Hills pig iron because of it purity. Pig iron was then re-melted in improved air furnaces. The breech was another area of concern for larger cannon. Solid cast cannon had moved to the use of a wrought iron hoop around the breech. Robert Parrott of West Point Foundry in New York had developed this technique. John Dahlgren had cast bottle-shaped breeches to better withstand the greater gunpowder charge. Krupp Works in Germany was experimenting with tougher steel castings. Rodman did increase the width of the breech like Dahlgren, but less was needed because of his strain free casting system and pure pig iron. In 1860 the Fort Pitt Foundry cast a pair of 15-inch Rodman "Columbiads" — the largest in the world. The Pig Iron Aristocrats were now the pride of the country and heroes worldwide. The foundry had stockpiled a smaller 10-inch version to supply the army.

As the war progressed, Rodman began work on a 20-inch cannon which would weigh over 50 tons and fire a half-ton shot four miles. The estimated cost of the finished gun was over $32,000. It was the birth of the industrial-military complex that only added to the political power of the Pig Iron Aristocrats. Rodman stated: "It is not deemed probable that any naval structure, proof against that caliber, will soon if ever be built." The casting of the proposed gun was planned for early 1864, and it gained the attention of the world. Reporters and military observers from all over descended on Pittsburgh and the supply furnaces in Ohio. There were military officers from Prussia, England, France, Austria, Russia, Spain, Sweden, and Denmark. The core would be water-cooled using the Rodman process. Rodman's process was used to produce guns for the Union's fleet of monitors. Rodman also proposed the casting of the world's largest gun.

On February 11, 1864, the world press gathered in Pittsburgh for the great event. The cast cannon took ten days to completely cool. The gun required twenty-four horses to move it to the Pennsylvania Railroad special car. The weight restricted the train to 30 miles an hour on its trip to Fort Hamilton, New York. The firing of the gun showed a range of five miles. It was never used in the Civil War but remained on seacoast duty through World War I. The story resulted in the novel *From the Earth to the Moon* by Jules Verne. A few months later, the Fort Pitt Foundry cast another great 20-inch gun, the XX-Dahlgren known as "Beelzebub." This would be the first of a series of XX-Dahlgrens: Satan, Lucifer, and Moloch. These guns were made too late for service in the Civil War, however. The mass demand on pig iron caused a 100 percent increase in price and a world-class metal industry. The reports of the manufacture of these great guns in *Scientific American* and *Harpers* put metalworking in the public's attention. There evolved a type of national pride in what industry could accomplish. This pride was an important element in forging an alliance between labor and the Pig Iron Aristocrats and would be an important element in Pittsburgh's general acceptance of East End millionaires.

Pittsburgh was the most important strategic target of the South with its iron and steel manufacturing. Fort Pitt Foundry and Knapp Rudd Company made most of the Union's large cast iron cannon and artillery pieces. Not surprisingly, East Ender Thomas Scott of the Pennsylvania Railroad was Lincoln's Assistant Secretary of War. During the war several East Enders — Judge Wilkins, Thomas Moore, and William Johnstown — headed the hometown defense. Military camps were located in Shadyside, Oakland, East Liberty, and Wilkinsburg. Some of this was because of the rolling mills and foundries in the Lawrenceville area. There were several panics in the East End over possible raids of Pittsburgh's foundries, mills, and factories. In 1863, General Morgan's Cavalry was raiding West Virginia and that caused East Enders to bury valuables in the woods for fear of attack. J.E.B. Stuart's cavalry caused a similar panic about the same time at the Battle of Gettysburg. There is some evidence that J.E.B. Stewart planned a raid on Pittsburgh's iron industry, including the East End homes of the Pig Iron Aristocrats such as Tom Miller, Henry Oliver, William Thaw, B. F. Jones, and the Carnegie brothers, as well as the home of the Assistant Secretary of War and, essentially, the heart of the Republican Party.

Pittsburgh was truly the forge of the Union. The city had over 400 puddling furnaces in operation during the war. Puddling was a craftsman process of steelmaking. Most of the pig iron was coming in from Ohio to run Pittsburgh's furnaces and rolling mills. The war united the Pig Iron Aristocrats and pig iron-related states of Ohio, West Virginia, Pennsylvania, Michigan, Kentucky, Missouri, Illinois, New York, and Connecticut. All of these states would be the iron heart of the new Republican Party's protectionist policies. The protectionist policies of Lincoln would become the most important core policy of the Republicans. Protectionism not only spurred the iron industry but fueled research into the new iron product of steel. Pittsburgh was experimenting with a new iron product known as cast steel.

Steel was being made by the "German method," a "high" volume variation of crucible steel. This required pig iron to be heated in crucibles in coal fired furnaces for days. Then carbon was re-added to produce steel. One crucible might only hold 200 to 1,000 pounds of steel. Larger castings required a simultaneous pouring and mixing of the liquid steel. Several Pittsburgh foundries such as Singer, Nimick, & Company were casting small rifle (3-inch) steel cannons to compete with German and British guns. By 1864, Pittsburgh's Hussey, Wells and Company, using the crucible and German method, could produce 20 tons of cast steel a day (when most steel companies were lucky to cast a ton a day). Steel would never be a factor during the Civil War but would bring the Pig Iron Aristocrats much wealth; and ultimately, mass-produced Bessemer steel would spell the end of the Pig Iron Aristocracy and usher in the steel barons. Pittsburgh stood alone in the casting of steel, which would draw a young George Westinghouse to come to Pittsburgh to cast his new railroad products.

While many Pig Iron Aristocrats morphed into steel barons, there were exceptions such as Curtis Hussey (1802–1893). East Ender Hussey had primarily been in the copper business and rolling mill prior to moving into crucible steel making in 1858. It would be the success of Hussey's crucible steel casting that would attract a young George Westinghouse to Pittsburgh a few years later. Hussey would initially give George Westinghouse a large loan to help him start his business. In actual dollars, C. C. Hussey was Pittsburgh's first millionaire. He would also be the area's first commercial manufacturer of tin plated steel. He was a medical doctor who had built a grocery business in Pittsburgh. Hussey was a friend of Henry Clay Frick and a member of the South Fork Hunting Club of East Enders. Hussey was also a great philanthropist, creating schools and colleges for women. He was an early supporter of abolition, the Underground Railroad, women's suffrage, and the temperance movement. Hussey was never a pig iron producer, but he had close personal and investment ties with the Pig Iron Aristocrats such as Jones, Thaw, Laughlin, the Park brothers, and Shoenberger. Hussey was often part of the Pig Iron daily lunch at "Room #6" of the Duquesne Club in Pittsburgh. He would also invest in the Pig Iron Aristocrats' last-ditch effort of Pittsburgh Bessemer to stop a Carnegie monopoly.

As a telegraph boy in the 1850s, Carnegie got to know and admire the Pig Iron Aristocrats. The Pig Iron Aristocrats foreshadowed the robber barons in their philanthropy. They followed the tradition set in the 1790s by James O'Hara. They built parks, donated churches, and contributed to cultural endeavors. William Thaw, Henry Buhl, and Henry Phipps contributed to the building of Allegheny Observatory in the 1860s. Even before his son, William Thaw had supplied the first funds in the 1860s. Henry Buhl donated a planetarium, and Henry Phipps built a conservatory. Christopher Magee built the Pittsburgh Zoo. This philanthropy is fascinating since it did not have European roots but was a type of Scotch–Irish frontier tradition. While Europe promoted a type of paternalistic capitalism, the Pittsburgh industrialists favored their own style of philanthropic capitalism. Both approaches seemed to be influenced by the revolutionary unrest in Europe during the 1840s and 1850s.

CHAPTER 7. KIER'S ROCK OIL: "THE MOST WONDERFUL REMEDY EVER"

Few realize that at one point the world oil market and the world's refineries were located in Pittsburgh and managed by a number of East Enders. A type of "rock oil" (petroleum) was found in salt mining operations north of Pittsburgh in the 1840s. A young Pittsburgh clerk, Samuel Kier, figured out this ground oil could be used in lamps to replace costly sperm whale oil. However, Kier found demand to be greater than supply in the 1850s. Pittsburgh and oil go back to Edwin Drake's first commercial oil well north on the Allegheny River from Pittsburgh. The oil slowly found application in lubricants and illuminating oil for lamps. Initially, the oil was transported down river in barrels on barges. Pittsburgh rapidly became the oil center of the oil. By 1871, there were 60 oil refineries with a capacity of 36,000 barrels per day. The oil market in Pittsburgh set the world price per barrel. The first oil boom turned the East End into Saudi Arabia, and many residents were princes.

Pittsburgh and the East Enders predated Rockefeller and the Cleveland refineries because it was the birthplace of Standard Oil. The actual distillation process had been perfected for decades by the area's Scotch–Irish whiskey stills. It would be Rockefeller who came to Pittsburgh to create his monopoly. The formation of Standard Oil took place in secret meetings at the East End home of Charles Lockhart, but the story begins even earlier with what some call the first refinery in the world. One of the least remembered of the East End capitalists was Samuel M. Kier (1813–1874), yet he was one of the most versatile and diversified capitalists since James O'Hara. Kier represents the beginning of America's oil industry and the "Grandfather of Modern Petroleum Refining." Kier was an iron baron, merchant, salt manufacturer, druggist, canal builder, railroad man, oilman, oil refiner, and brick maker. He made fortunes in all of these endeavors, and like O'Hara, many of his employees would go on to build other industrial empires. Kier's father owned a number of salt mines north of Pittsburgh in Tarentum, Pennsylvania. While Kier maintained a financial interest in these salt mines, he went to Pittsburgh to begin a career as a merchant.

Like most East Enders, Kier was armed with a common school education based on the *McGuffey Readers*. He started with a railway express company and progressed to a partner, only to see the firm fail in the Panic of 1837. In 1838, Samuel Kier got involved in the Pennsylvania Canal by taking advantage of government grants. Kier moved to Lawrenceville on the east side of Pittsburgh where he would live the rest of his life. Kier would team up with East Ender William Thaw (1818–1889) and Thaw's brother-in-law and East Ender, Thomas S. Clarke (1801–1867). Another investor in the canal project was future president, James Buchanan. The vision for the canal and Pittsburgh as a transportation center had been that of East Ender Neville Craig, editor of the Pittsburgh *Gazette* years earlier. The Pennsylvania Canal was America's greatest achievement running the east–west length of Pennsylvania over the mountains via aqueducts and incline railroads for canal boats. The canal was 395 miles long and became world famous when Charles Dickens took a trip on it in 1842. However, it was a financial failure of the United States Bank of Pennsylvania which had been forced by its government charter to invest in public works. While it was an engineering wonder, its cost was an amazing $25 million (close to a billion in today's dollars). Kier, however, became wealthy. He teamed up with Pittsburgher Benjamin Jones (founder of Jones and Laughlin Steel) to buy iron furnaces in the mountains and ship iron via the canal to Pittsburgh. Maybe more importantly, Kier had joined the exclusive club of Pittsburgh capitalists, creating an interconnecting network of industries.

Kier had proved to be a successful engineer with his specially designed boats, but his real inventive genius would be seen in the oil business. The family salt mines continued to be polluted with "rock oil," and Kier began to study it for uses. In 1848, after realizing that the mechanic oil the doctor had prescribed for his wife's tuberculosis was really his rock oil, Kier started to bottle it as a medicine. He sold a half pint bottle as "Seneca Oil" for 50 cents. The Seneca Indians of the area had long used it as a medicine. He also sold "petroleum butter," which today we call petroleum jelly. Kier had it analyzed by a Philadelphia chemist, who suggested that he could distill it into other products. Kier experimented with the distilling process and achieved better oil through double distillation. His double distillation earned him the title of "the father of modern petroleum refining."

The distilling technology of the world could be found in the Scotch–Irish whiskey stills of the last 100 hundred years. Kier developed the product later known as kerosene, which he called illuminating oil. Using an old Scotch–Irish whiskey still, he could produce three gallons a day. He used it to light lamps for home lighting, replacing whale oil, which was very timely as whale fishing could not keep up with the demand for whale oil. The illuminating oil sold at $1.50 a gallon (about $40.00 today) versus $2.50 a gallon for whale oil. Kier never patented any of this; but his new oil would launch the career of two other East Enders — Charles Lockhart, co-founder of Standard Oil, and George Macbeth, a glass oil lamp manufacturer. Kier did set up a Lawrenceville refinery and made his fortune. In 1854, Kier improved his distillation process by opening up a Pittsburgh refinery. The site was at Seventh and Grant Street, the present location of the United States Steel Building.

The refinery was considered the first in the Western Hemisphere and had a capacity of six barrels a day. The smell caused problems, and Kier moved the refinery to the East End (Lawrenceville). The refinery became known as the Radiant Oil Works. Kier lived nearby on 51st Street in Lawrenceville. The problem was Kier couldn't get enough of the stuff to sell. All the oil he was getting was a byproduct of salt mining. Kier had created demand, and incentive for profit, which spurred exploration and technology. The abundance of oil in the woods north of Pittsburgh was a well-known fact, but a method was needed to increase the volume. That method came from the drilling operation of Edwin Drake in Titusville, Pennsylvania. Actually, the drilling had been borrowed from salt miners. Drake's real genius was to transport the oil in "Pennsylvania barrels," which were equal to 42 gallons. The 42-gallon barrel remains the standard to this day. Teamsters then took the barrels several miles to the Allegheny River for barge transportation to Pittsburgh. The other way was to go on the Cuyahoga River then to Cleveland refiners. By 1865 a great oil boom was underway, and a battle between Pittsburgh and Cleveland refineries had begun. Kier built his fortune by investing his oil money in brick making, coal mining, and banking. He became a philanthropist, true to his Scotch–Irish background, and gave most of his fortune away to churches and hospitals.

One of the early business contacts of Samuel Kier was Pittsburgh East Ender Charles Lockhart. In the 1850s, oil was the hot topic at East End parties. Lockhart had emigrated from Scotland with his family in 1836. He was born less than fifty miles from Carnegie in Scotland. He started work as an errand boy for Pittsburgh's McCully Dry Goods. McCully was an East Ender owning some of the old Negley family farmland. He eventually became a partner in the dry goods business. One of the partners had a salt mine north of Pittsburgh and had some crude oil as a by-product of the mines. Lockhart purchased it for 31 cents a gallon and then sold it to Kier's refinery for 61 cents a gallon. Lockhart contracted to buy all the crude that could be produced at the salt mines. He invested more in the oil fields north of Pittsburgh on the Allegheny River. He partnered with William Phillips, William Frew, John Vannausdall, and A. V. Kipp to form Phillips, Frew & Co. He also lined up a barge company to transport crude oil down river. Lockhart teamed up with boat captain, J. J. Vandergrift. Vandergrift made his fortune shipping oil down the Allegheny River to Pittsburgh refiners. The business expanded and vertically integrated to drilling, transportation, and refining. Business boomed for Kier; and in 1861, he built a commercial refinery on the south bank of the Allegheny River at Negley Creek, which was part of the Negley-McCully tract. This was the first real commercial refinery with extensive condensing equipment and chemical treatment. The capacity was an amazing 250 barrels of oil a day. Kier and Lockhart weren't the only East Enders investing in the Pennsylvanian oil boom. Railroad magnate Thomas Scott and his East End friends, J. J. Vandergrift and John Pitcairn, were investing in oil companies as well. Scott was a true visionary seeing a railroad-related boom. In particular, refined oil moved on his newly finished Pittsburgh-Philadelphia line, which would bring oil to ships and the European market. The oil boom was causing Pittsburgh capitalists to move into all facets of the energy business.

Lockhart expanded in the 1860s by traveling to and creating a market in Europe. His new company of Lockhart & Frew built a total of seven refineries and controlled about 60 percent of the world refined oil market. Pittsburgh had a total of 58 refineries by 1867. World oil futures were traded on the Pittsburgh exchange. Lockhart built a refinery in Philadelphia to ship oil to Europe. His network of refining brought the railroads into the business. Another East Ender, Thomas Scott of the Pennsylvania Railroad, started to meet with his neighbor, Charles Lockhart, to cut new transportation deals. Lockhart was searching for an edge on his major competitor, John D. Rockefeller and the Cleveland refineries. Rockefeller realized the problem and teamed up with Scott and Lockhart to form a secret cartel known as South Improvement Company to divide up the oil business. The cartel had grown out of a number of meetings in Pittsburgh's East End, which was off limits for the press and public. This new cartel, like so many in the future, functioned in the parlors of East End homes. The powerful cartel would have both refiners and railroads. The railroads would split the business — 45 percent to the Pennsylvania Railroad, 27.5 percent to the Erie Railroad, and 27.5 percent to the New York Central. Refiners in the cartel would get special rates. This became the "Pittsburgh Plan." Meeting at the homes of Lockhart and Scott in the privacy of East Liberty allowed Rockefeller to avoid the press. The secret deal cut out many small Pennsylvania and Cleveland refiners as well as New York refiners. When South Improvement became known, there was a major uproar. Still, the deal laid the groundwork for Standard Oil's takeover of smaller operations and crushed competitors.

Rockefeller was still fearful of the East End alliance of Pennsylvania oil, refining, and the Pennsylvania Railroad. He needed to take more ownership of the cartel. In the summer of 1874, Rockefeller held a secret summit at the resort of the wealthy at Saratoga Springs. He proposed a merger of Pittsburgh and Philadelphia refiners into Standard Oil. The meeting was followed by more secret meetings in Pittsburgh's East End. Charles Lockhart and his old partner, William Frew, who sold bottled medicinal oil with him, were at these meetings. Lockhart and Frew would bring in twenty-one Pittsburgh refiners, leaving only one independent refiner in Pittsburgh. Lockhart would be named president of this powerful new Standard Oil. He was now the East End's wealthiest resident, although few realized it.

Lockhart became extremely active in a number of investments and expanded his home at 608 North Highland Avenue, East Liberty. He gave freely to the Presbyterian Church, Pittsburgh hospitals, and children charities. He was a strict Presbyterian throughout his life to the point of removing his daughter from the will for eloping with the family dentist. Lockhart approached the grandfather of Pittsburgh capitalists, James O'Hara, in the diversity of his investments. He was a director of the Pittsburgh Bank of Commerce and was a major stockholder in other East End investments such as Pittsburgh Plate Glass. Later in life he was a major investor in Union Trust owned by Andrew Mellon and Henry Clay Frick. Lockhart was a good friend of neighbors, Henry Clay Frick and Andrew Mellon, and a major art collector. The art collected by these men is the core of today's National Gallery in Washington, D.C., and most of America's great art masterpieces were owned by the three men. Lockhart was instrumental in setting up the Carnegie Art Exhibition with Frick and Carnegie in 1895. Lockhart built a three-story community hall known as Liberty Hall on Penn and Centre Avenues for the YMCA and social gatherings in 1895. He amazed the financial community when his estate was estimated at $200 million![1] Consider that Carnegie's estate was $300 million, John Rockefeller had $250 million, Henry Clay Frick was at $70 million, and J. P. Morgan was at $60 million. Lockhart ranks in Pittsburgh's top five richest capitalists and America's top ten.

East End Pennsylvania railroad executives Tom Scott and A. J. Cassatt did not buy in to the new Standard Oil nor did they want to be controlled by this new company. Rockefeller then launched a war on Scott and the Pennsylvania Railroad. He tried to starve out the railroad by closing his newly acquired Pittsburgh refineries. In an effort to generate cash, Scott cut wages of the railroad workers, which led to the bloodiest national strike, and most of that blood ran in Pittsburgh. The high costs of the strike forced Scott to play ball with Rockefeller. We'll discuss the Great Railroad Strike of 1877 in a later chapter.

The real impact of the oil industry on the nation and on the East End came not so much from the founders of Standard Oil, but from the creation of super millionaire Andrew Carnegie. Carnegie had been born in 1835 in Dunfernline, Scotland, the son of a hand weaver. Ironically, the Carnegie family and his father were true victims of the Industrial Revolution in Europe, which destroyed the craft of weaving. Power looms drove John Carnegie out of business, finally forcing the family to migrate to the United States in 1847. They came by boat via canal to Pittsburgh, which at the time had booming cotton mills. The family settled in Allegheny City (today Pittsburgh's north side) where many Scotch immigrants worked in the cotton mills. Young Andrew found a job as a bobbin boy in a local cotton mill at $1.20 a week. Andy worked 12-hour days, six days a day. Sundays were strictly adhered to in this Scotch–Irish Presbyterian area. Interestingly, it would be Carnegie who later forced Sunday work in his steel mills. He also started night school at Pittsburgh's Duff's College. Carnegie took accounting course at Duff's, which would also train many of the young future East Enders of the period.

Andy's real break came at fourteen when he landed a job as a telegraph boy delivering messages to Pittsburgh businesses. The telegraph was a new technology, the line arriving in Pittsburgh a few months before Carnegie had arrived. Andy made friends with two boys there who were also destined to be tycoons. Those boys were Robert Pitcairn (future railroad executive) and Henry Oliver (iron and ore magnate). Andy took to the work and expanded on it by learning Morse code and telegraph operation. Carnegie took messages throughout the city to the area's wealthiest capitalists and become friends with many of them including the "King of the Pig Iron Aristocrats," B. F. Jones. This knowledge and contacts would eventually lead him to a job with the railroads, which were just expanding to Pittsburgh in the early 1850s. Carnegie would invest in railroads and related industries to make his first million.

---

1 *New York Times*, February 4, 1906

While it was his investment in railroads that had pushed Carnegie to his first million dollars, it was a timely oil investment that created five million dollars and helped Carnegie to retire from being an employee. He was then able to invest in the iron and steel business early with tips from Pittsburgh's wealthiest capitalists. Carnegie's profits were amazing, finding success with each investment. He also increased his investment with Tom Scott in the Pennsylvania Railroad, which had completed a branch to connect the oil fields to Pittsburgh. The profits also allowed him to purchase a large piece of land and build a mansion for his mother in the East End's Homewood section. Carnegie's future partner, then Pennsylvania Road's freight agent David Stewart, suggested the beautiful suburb of Homewood where he and his uncle, Tom Scott, president of the Pennsylvania Railroad, lived. The land Carnegie purchased had been that of Judge Wilkins. Tom and Andrew had gone to many parties at this "Homewood" mansion. The area of three blocks on Penn Avenue became known as "Homewood" and "Carnegie County." It would be there the Carnegies would rejoin childhood friends from the North side ghetto — Tom Miller, Robert Pitcairn, David McCandless, and Henry Phipps in Homewood. The oil investment came from his two East Enders — Tom Carnegie and William Coleman. Tom and Coleman were good friends and rode the streetcar to Pittsburgh each day. Eventually, Tom would marry Coleman's daughter, Lucy, and live next door to him in Homewood. Coleman was from the old Pig Iron Aristocracy, and his family had made money in the charcoal iron furnace industry of Western Pennsylvania, which supplied iron to Pittsburgh. The real buzz at the neighborhood parties was oil. Railroad men like Thomas Scott, Robert Pitcairn, and John Pitcairn were investing large sums in oil. At neighborhood social functions, Tom Carnegie was picking up on the buzz and investment tips.

It was in Homewood that a young Tom and Andrew Carnegie would learn their social skills as well. It was here that the Carnegies met the East End aristocrat, Judge Wilkins, in the early 1860s. The Judge died in 1865. If you remember, Judge Wilkins was an industrialist and had been minister to Russia under President Andrew Jackson and Secretary of War for President John Tyler. At the time the Judge's 650-acre homestead was the area's largest. It was said: "Judge Wilkins, now in his eightieth year, ruled over Homestead like a feudal baron, and his home."[1] The judge's wife was the daughter of George Dallas, then the vice-president of the United States. The mansion had hosted presidents and world leaders. Andrew Carnegie became a regular guest at the Wilkins Mansion. He would later note: "Musical parties, charades, and theatricals, in which Miss Wilkins took the leading parts furnished me with another means of self improvement."[2]

Carnegie learned much about the history of Pittsburgh capitalism at the mansion. He also got to know Wilkins's neighbor and Pig Iron Aristocrat, John F. Singer. Singer was a member of B.F. Jones's Duquesne Club capitalist lunches. The Wilkins parties brought together men like Carnegie, Charles Lockhart, John Pitcairn, Robert Pitcairn, and many other East End capitalists. The only difference Carnegie had with the Wilkins was that

---

1 Joseph Frazier Wall, *Andrew Carnegie*, (Pittsburgh: University of Pittsburgh Press, 1989), p. 146
2 Peter Krass, *Carnegie*, (New York: John Wiley & Sons, 2002), p. 58

Carnegie was an abolitionist, supporter of Lincoln, and a Republican. Wilkins was a unionist but a Democrat opposed to abolition, and Carnegie learned from Mrs. Wilkins that such politics should not be discussed at the mansion. Carnegie also participated in the neighborhood's popular sports such as fishing, ice skating, and horseback riding. Here again, the torch of capitalism was passed from earlier generations to the new. The talk of the day in the early 1860s was more oil than war. Homewood would be the real birthplace of the great Carnegie Empire, and most of his rich partners and associates would eventually populate the East End and the Homewood section.

The story of Carnegie's oil investment started with an 1862 visit to Pennsylvania oil country with his brother's friend, William Coleman, who was in the iron and coal business. Prior to the trip, Carnegie had made some small investments in oil based on advice by his East End friends. He then purchased a $40,000 share in an oil venture known as Columbia Oil. Carnegie and Coleman even dug a "lake" (known today as "Carnegie's Pond") to hold oil in hopes of a future shortage. In the end, oil seemed in endless supply, and the stock did return over 400 percent! Not surprisingly, the president of Columbia Oil was Charles Lockhart. Carnegie made a philosophical comment in his autobiography about how cheap and abundant oil had become since Kier and others were selling it for 50 cents a small bottle. Carnegie commented: "The oil gathered by the Indians in early days was bottled in Pittsburgh and sold at high prices as a medicine — a dollar for a small vial. It had a general reputation as a sure cure for rheumatic tendencies. As it became plentiful and cheap, its virtues vanished. What fools we mortal be!"[1] It is also suggested that Carnegie's experience with Columbia Oil was his first taste of philanthropy. Columbia Oil provided housing and had built a library for the town of Columbia Farm.

East Enders Andrew and Richard Mellon were late investors in oil, but they would have a major impact on the industry. Andrew Mellon and Henry Clay Frick had been major investors in coal from its earlier days and had avoided oil investment and speculation, although it was often part of their conversation at the Duquesne Club. Frick probably viewed it as coal competition in some areas. In 1889, oil was discovered in Mellon's backyard in Coraopolis, Pennsylvania, known as McDonald's Field. Mellon was now interested as wildcatters and friends — Sam Galey, John Galey, and James Guffey — pushed Mellon's interest. The Mellon family had a new rising business star in Judge Mellon's eldest grandson, William Larimer Mellon (1868-1949), who was the son of James Ross Mellon (1846-1934), the brother of Andrew. Young William Larimer Mellon had worked for John Galey at McDonald's Field. Frick decided not to invest, fearing the wrath of Rockefeller. The Mellons then moved to develop Crescent Oil Company, which gathered oil in Coraopolis and pipelined it to Philadelphia to ship to Europe. They defeat efforts by Rockefeller and the Pennsylvania Railroad to buy up land and stop the 271-mile pipeline. It was the biggest Mellon investment to date at $2.5 million, and it was headed by William Larimer Mellon. William Larimer Mellon would build an East End mansion known as "Ben Elm" at 5340 Forbes Avenue in the Squirrel Hill area.

---

1 Andrew Carnegie, *The Autobiography of Andrew Carnegie* (New York: Signet Classic)

The pipeline company made profits and competed well against Standard Oil. Mellon's biggest interests in oil came after the Pennsylvania oil boom. In 1900, wildcatters such as James Guffey and John Galey followed the oil boom to Texas. They formed James Guffey Petroleum Company with the aid of the Mellon brothers — Andrew and Richard. East Enders William Flinn and James Reed came into the oil group with the Mellons. Interestingly, Henry Clay Frick again declined to participate in the oil investment. Gulf Oil refining was formed as a subsidiary of Guffey Petroleum. Gulf Oil boomed, as Teddy Roosevelt filed anti-trust suits to prevent Standard Oil from moving into new Oklahoma fields. In 1906, the Mellon family took over Gulf Oil. William L. Mellon became president. Gulf Oil used the Carnegie and Heinz strategy of vertical integration taking crude oil drilling to retail selling. One of the first gasoline stations in America was a Gulf Oil station in the East End. Gulf Oil headquarters would be in Pittsburgh, and the oil legacy would remain in Pittsburgh until the 1950s.

CHAPTER 8. A PENNSYLVANIA RAILROAD

The real boom of Pittsburgh's East Side came on December 10, 1852 when a wood-burning locomotive and four railcars arrived from Philadelphia. The people at the station that day included some of the East End's future residents such as Andrew and Tom Carnegie, Henry Phipps, and Tom Scott. Waiting at the station was East Ender and musician, Stephen Foster, to watch his brother engineer bring in the steam locomotive. The railroad company had built a station in the East End prior to its stop in Pittsburgh, allowing the East End to become a commuter suburb. In the summer the train would take wealthy East Ender families to their mountain top lake resort in the Allegheny Mountains. Years later the Pennsylvania Railroad would put a non-stop express from the East End to the financial district of New York. Decades later the railroad would allow George Westinghouse to commute daily to his plants in the Turtle Creek Valley. His neighbor, H. J. Heinz, would take it monthly to his Sunday School Society meeting in Philadelphia. Henry Clay Frick, Heinz, and Westinghouse would take the direct line trip on the "Pittsburgher" to the financial district of New York. Men like Westinghouse would have a special East End station and his own Pullman railroad car for personal travel. The Pennsylvania Railroad, of course, was where young immigrant boys such as Andrew Carnegie and Henry Phipps started their working careers. The Pennsylvania Railroad was the mother of Pittsburgh capitalism behind the glass, oil, iron, and steel industries. The railroad made Pittsburgh a convention center, and on Washington's Birthday in 1856, the first Republican National Convention would be held in Lafayette Hall at Wood and Fourth Avenues. This convention fused the "Iron Whigs" into the new Republican Party. It was here that the anti-slavery plank went into the Republican Party that Lincoln would bring to the White House. The East End would be the strongest bastion in the country of the Republican Party.

The coming of the railroad to Pittsburgh would create yet another industrial advantage for the city, while Pittsburgh's river system had made it an international port since its founding. Transportation had always been at the heart of Pittsburgh's growth following the hub of old Indian trails that converged on Pittsburgh. The city forged axes, produced oil lamps, made nails, and manufactured guns for western migrants. It was the west's only inland harbor that had access to shipping to Europe. Beaver fur from Western Pennsylvania adorned the heads of many Europeans, and Monongahela rye whiskey was drunk all over Europe. Western Pennsylvania ginseng was popular throughout Europe as a medical herb. Bakewell glass was on many European tables. Tons of animal furs passed through the markets of Scottish capitalists. The iron and eventually the steel industry came to Pittsburgh not because of iron ore (it had little) or even coal, but because it was a transportation hub where all the necessary resources could be brought together. The Pennsylvania Canal was 395 miles long, connecting Pittsburgh and Philadelphia, and it had been functioning since the late 1830s. Wooden plank turnpikes were used for shorter hauls.

Railroads were a natural outgrowth of the booming industry, and Pittsburgh was a national center of production. The metropolitan area had over 200,000 people and was the fastest growing area in the nation in 1855. By 1860, Allegheny County had 1,191 factories with 20,500 laborers producing goods worth over $26 million. Pittsburgh desperately needed pig iron and coal from the east, and a shorter route to the east coast for its glass, iron, oil, and whiskey. The first railroad chartered in Pittsburgh was the Pennsylvania Railroad in 1846, but the Baltimore and Ohio Railroad was not far behind. The track started in Pittsburgh and expanded to Turtle Creek in 1851 with a locomotive brought in by canal boat. A large hill at the Braddock/Turtle Creek boundary prevented the Pennsylvania Railroad any further progress until a tunnel could be built. Passengers were forced to disembark and take a stagecoach 28 miles to Pittsburgh. In 1853, the Pennsylvania Railroad was connected between Pittsburgh and Philadelphia. This was the same year a young Andrew Carnegie was hired by the Pennsylvania Railroad as a secretary to East Ender and Divisional Superintendent Thomas Scott for a monthly salary of $35.00. The Pennsylvania Railroad would pass through Pittsburgh's East End following an old Indian trail. A small stop in the East End now allowed for Pittsburgh commuters. This type of commuter suburb was something new.

Thomas Scott would also become Assistant Secretary of War under Abe Lincoln. It had been Tom Scott who had promoted a young Carnegie to his first management position. Tom Scott would prove brilliant as a logistical commander of the northern troops. Carnegie was soon leading crews of the railroad in setting up telegraph lines. During the war Carnegie worked as Superintendent of the Pittsburgh Division of the Pennsylvania Railroad. He would play a key role in the North's advantage in rail logistics and communications. Shortly after the war, Carnegie left the railroad to become a full-time investor and capitalist. He still had extensive ties with the Pennsylvania Railroad, which would be critical for his future. He would be a life-long friend of Thomas Scott who had given him his start.

In 1855 the Baltimore & Ohio Railroad connected Pittsburgh to Baltimore as well as points west into Ohio. The Fort Wayne Railroad had been operating out of Pittsburgh's North side (then Allegheny City) for years. The Pennsylvania Railroad and the Fort

Wayne Railroad could not connect to downtown Pittsburgh until a bridge was completed in 1858. Being at the confluence of three great rivers (Allegheny, Monongahela, and Ohio), Pittsburgh offered a natural merger point for river transportation with railroads. Pittsburgh represented a true international port with a river connection to New Orleans and the Atlantic Ocean. By 1870 Pittsburgh's major employer was the railroad industry. But the industry also brought a lethal combination of smoke, dust, and oily mist to Pittsburgh. The railroads, however, would connect the forge of the nation to the Union Army during the Civil War and created an economic burst.

As we have seen, Pittsburgh was the Union Army's manufacturing center, but it also was the North's logistics and transportation center. Soldiers going to and coming back from war passed through Pittsburgh. Three East Enders headed up the Subsistence Committee of the Committee of Public Safety (chaired by Judge Wilkins). The Subsistence Committee was led by Thomas Howe (Pig Iron Aristocrat, U. S Senator, and copper baron), B. F. Jones (Pig Iron Aristocrat), and William Thaw (Pig Iron Aristocrat). These men pulled donations to operate a remarkable effort to feed and care for soldiers passing through Pittsburgh to the point that the railroad and the army planned stops in Pittsburgh. Two large dining halls were set up on Penn Avenue and at the Diamond. Leland Baldwin reported: "during a period of more than four years, over four hundred thousand meals were served at a cost of five cents per meal."[1] A Soldiers Home was set up in the East End at 34 Liberty Street. It cared for over 100,000 soldiers over the four years. The Subsistence Committee set up an efficient network of Pittsburgh hospitals to handle the wounded after major battles. This would be the start of a truly amazing record of financial aid to the country's soldiers and sailors by East Enders.

Two Union officers and future United States presidents would play a key role in the defense of Pittsburgh. In October 1862, the 23rd Ohio was ordered to Pennsylvania to protect against possible cavalry raids on the iron valleys of Pittsburgh and Ohio's nearby Mahoning Valley. The Ohio 23rd was headed by future president, Rutherford B. Hayes, and had William McKinley as its supply quartermaster. Through the spring of 1863, there were rumors of confederate cavalry near these manufacturing centers. Most of these never proved out, but Hayes did cut off an attempted raid of Jim Morgan into Ohio to cut rail connections. The southeastern counties of Ohio were the major producers of pig iron during the war, which was being shipped to Pittsburgh gun foundries. This "Hanging Rock Iron District" of Southern Ohio was a 30-mile belt in the counties of Scioto, Lawrence, and Gallia on the Kentucky border and on the Ohio River. Some of the largest Union blast furnaces were in this strategic area. Even the British had found this Ohio ore superior to their own cannons and had used large amounts of it to produce armaments for the Crimean War (1854–1856). The 23rd was one of many regiments used to defend against planned confederate raids. This area would be part of the "Pig Iron Aristocracy" that supported McKinley's presidential runs. McKinley and Pittsburgh's Pig Iron Aristocracy would

---

1 Leland Baldwin, *Pittsburgh: The Story of a City*, (Pittsburgh: University of Pittsburgh Press, 1937), p. 300

always remember the importance of railroads and iron in the Union victory. McKinley would become the "apostle of protectionism" for Pittsburgh's iron and steel industries. Furthermore, McKinley's election to the presidency owed much to the parlors and game rooms of the East End mansions.

One of the battles to cut off Confederate Morgan in the Hanging Rock area was the battle of Buffington's Island. Confederate General Morgan had entered Ohio near Gallipolis about 30 miles from some of the Union's largest blast furnaces in the summer of 1863. Furthermore, McKinley used Gallipolis as a depot for shipments of pig to Pittsburgh. The 23rd Ohio, the 13th West Virginia, Union gunboats, and Union regulars amassed to chase off Morgan's cavalry. At Buffington's Island, this combined force killed over 800 and captured 2,300 confederate raiders.[1] Still, over 300 of Morgan's cavalry moved north towards Pittsburgh and Ohio's Mahoning Valley area. Every able-bodied man in the area took up arms and marched south. Panic struck the area, with Pittsburgh and nearby banks moving money to Cleveland. Finally Morgan was forced to surrender at West Point, Columbiana County, about 60 miles from Pittsburgh and 20 from Youngstown (it was the furthest point north of the Confederate Army in Ohio). McKinley had become a "railroad man" during the war and would later befriend George Westinghouse while getting air brakes installed on American trains. McKinley would head up Congress's railroad safety committee as well as chair the powerful Ways and Means Committee in the 1880s.

After the Civil War, railroad business boomed in Pennsylvania, moving oil, glass, iron, steel, and castings out of Pittsburgh and bringing in iron ore and coal. Westmoreland County coke and coal were railed to Pittsburgh. Pittsburgh was also the center of the oil industry with 52 refineries processing Pennsylvania oil from north of the city; and that oil and refined kerosene moved east by rail. Westinghouse would open up his first railroad air brake plant in 1869. Pittsburgh was the largest producer and user of coal-fired steam engines. The air was thick and oily with only a few hours of full sunlight each day. The Pennsylvania Railroad and most of the nation's railroads were expanding west out of the gateway of Pittsburgh. The railroads had taken a poor immigrant, Andrew Carnegie, and made him an investor and industrialist. Andrew Carnegie had teamed up with Pennsylvania Railroad executives, Edgar Thomson and East Ender Thomas Scott, to form Keystone Bridge Company, which further expanded the railroads. A rich and young Andrew Carnegie dreamed of building hundreds of bridges across America's great rivers as well as replacing thousands of old wooden bridges with his super iron structures. Iron bridges allowed for larger locomotives, longer trains, and heavier loads. The Pittsburgh papers were filled with the story of Keystone building the longest span bridge (the Eads Bridge) at St. Louis. Carnegie also had a share of Union Iron Mills, Iron City Forge, and Cyclops Iron Mills, which supplied the needs of the railroads. Railroads were the major users of iron in 1850; and by 1870, railroad iron made up over 50 percent of the production of iron. Carnegie was making wrought iron axles for railroad cars, bridge beams, and rails. His companies were one of the largest users of pig iron to make wrought iron products via

---

1 William H. Armstrong, *Major McKinley*, (Kent: Kent State University Press, 2000), 55

the puddling process. Puddling required the reheating of pig iron into a hot pasty mix to be worked to wrought iron and rolled or forged into beams, rails, and axles. At the time, Carnegie had no blast furnaces and had to purchase pig iron, mainly from Westmoreland charcoal furnaces, requiring rail shipment. Coal was also shipped in from Westmoreland, creating a symbiotic industrial relationship between the railroads and heavy industry.

The iron, coal, steel, and railroad industries were becoming heavily dependent on each other while becoming each other's biggest customers. This interdependence made Pittsburgh the industrial core of the nation. Coal was needed for iron production; iron was needed for steel production; steel was needed for railroad rails; railroads were needed to carry steel products west; and the railroads were needed to carry coal and iron ore into Pittsburgh. What was good for one was good for all. This is why all rails led to Pittsburgh. It was the hub of this industrial network of rails. The world's wealthiest iron, coal, steel, oil, and railroad barons would be found in a few short blocks in Pittsburgh's East End. Not surprisingly, the East Enders had diversified investments in coal, iron, steel, and railroads. They were at the epicenter of the industrial world with investment advice a few doors to either side of them. Decisions made over weekday lunch at the Duquesne Club and weekend neighborhood parties could change the world. It was one of the few times in the history of capitalism that bankers followed the industrialists. In fact, many of the East Enders cared little for bankers or financial men. Only the crafty industrialist, Andrew Mellon, successfully gained the confidence of these capitalists. At the center of this infrastructure was not a banker, but a railroad man, Thomas Scott. The East End was home to the two major executives of the Pennsylvania Railroad — Thomas Scott and Alexander Cassatt.

Tom Scott had aided the formation of Standard Oil in Pittsburgh's East End in 1877 initially with an earlier rate-fixing agreement on shipping oil on the Pennsylvania Railroad; but once Rockefeller took over the Pittsburgh refiners, the table was turned. Rockefeller tried to starve out the Pennsylvania Railroad and force lower rates. The Pennsylvania Railroad was in a real bind, caught in the middle of a national economic depression. This deadly national strike had started in late July as the east coast was in a major heat wave. The nation was still struggling from the Panic of 1873, with high unemployment throughout the nation. The Panic of 1873 represented a period of depression from 1873 to 1879.

The great "Panic of 1873" had started in the fall of 1873 in New York but had spread across the nation by 1875. At the root was an overexpansion or railroad bubble, as we would call it today. The stock market hit new bottoms by November 1873 and had to be closed for over a week. The great post-Civil War railroad and industrial expansion had come to a halt with the failure of Jay Cooke's vast investment house in New York. The panic was starting to break out of New York by early 1874. A young Pittsburgher, Andrew Carnegie, now living in New York, rushed back to Pittsburgh in early 1874 to check the construction needs of his new steel mill being built at Braddock. He checked with Pittsburgh's Exchange Bank about his railroad holdings which were experiencing problems. Carnegie was happy to find that his loans were not being called in as Pittsburgh banks hoped to avoid creating more problems. By late 1874, Carnegie had to put construction on hold for a few months when Pittsburgh money started to dry up. New York had already been devastated by the Panic. Carnegie was said to have trouble getting to his New York office through the lines of men at 34 soup kitchens. By late 1875, gangs and riots had reclaimed many of New York's streets, as unemployment reached 25 percent. The *New York Times* suggested that one buy dogs with good teeth to maneuver the streets.[1] By 1875, the Panic had hit Pittsburgh even harder.

Pittsburgh's banking industry been devastated by the "Panic of 1873," but Andrew Mellon provided one of the nation's steadier hands in this crisis. Mellon would keep his East End industrial neighbors afloat. The panic peaked in 1875, with unemployment reaching 40 percent nationally, and Pittsburgh fared only slightly better. Not only had Pittsburgh's booming iron and foundry industries been stilled, but also its new oil refining business had crashed, with oil falling from $2.30 a barrel to 70 cents a barrel. The coal mining production just east of Pittsburgh had dropped from 45 million bushels to 20 million bushels a year. Half of the nation's railroad bonds were in default. The downward spiral of the railroads quickly pulled down the steel and iron industry which had the railroads as their biggest customer.

Banker Andrew Mellon said he would never forget the "soup kitchens" and the homeless in the streets. Pittsburghers would long remember this period as the "cataclysm of the century," and "the great depression of the nineteenth century." Pittsburgh's smokeless skies reflected the depth of the depression. The over 20,000 laid off workers formed long bread lines in downtown Pittsburgh. Tramps built fires in the streets to keep warm. Never before had Pittsburgh seen so many beggars in the street. Over half of Pittsburgh's forty banks had failed. The real estate market crashed; people just walked away from their houses and mortgages. It was the worst depression the nation had known. With millions out of work, wages were declining rapidly as well. In December of 1875, even Pittsburgh's Mellon Bank was near closing and had to suspend payments on several days. The young company of Heinz, Noble and Company had been one of the area's growth companies since its formation in 1869 and would go bankrupt in 1876. It would nearly break the will of a young H. J. Heinz; but like Pittsburgh, he would rebuild to even larger dreams. Mellon supplied some money to keep the building of Carnegie's first steel mill in Braddock.

By the end of it, over half of Pittsburgh's banks would fail. Thomas Mellon did have to stop payments at times; but unlike other banks, Mellon never closed the doors. The Pittsburgh railroads that didn't fail were unprofitable. Carnegie's great Edgar Thomson steel in Braddock opened in 1877, but struggled, since it had been built to supply the railroad rails. This plant was a $1.25 million investment and had required a personal loan from Thomas Scott. However, in 1875 when New York banker Junius Morgan and his son, J. P. Morgan, called in Thomas Scott's loans for his railroad investment of Texas and Pacific, Carnegie, now living in New York, turned his back on the very man that had made him. Scott's investment had been with his New York friends and was deemed "risky" by conservative East Enders. The story is that it was Carnegie's revenge for a Homewood girlfriend, Anna

---

1 Peter Krass, *Carnegie*, (Hoboken: John Wiley & Sons, 2002), 122

Riddle, stolen by Thomas Scott. There is no question that in business and life Carnegie believed in survival of the fittest, and revenge was part of the struggle.

Carnegie would not be the last of the East Enders changed by moving to New York's Fifth Avenue. Still, this was the Achilles Heel or weaknesses of these Victorian capitalists. Once in the agenda they fought to the death to accumulate money. In their struggle, friendship and loyalty had no value to the East Enders who respected the law and even had an ethical code. This type of financial priority would augur many breaches of friendship such as Carnegie/Frick and Frick/Westinghouse.

Edgar Thomson, president of the Pennsylvania Railroad, made a personal appeal to Carnegie to help Scott, but Carnegie noted that his money was tied up in the building of his new steel mill, Edgar Thomson Works. Carnegie recalled in his autobiography: "I declined. I was then asked whether I would bring them all to ruin by refusing to stand by my friends. It was one of the most trying moments of my whole life. Yet I was not tempted for a moment to entertain the idea of involving myself."[1] Another theory has Thomson also asking Carnegie to talk to Morgan, but Carnegie was trying to build a relationship with Morgan and didn't want to risk it. Carnegie didn't help in this regard either. Yet in his heart, Carnegie knew he should have helped. "I fear Mr. Scott's premature death can measurably be attributed to the humiliation which he had to bear."[2] Carnegie knew well the greatest pain that could be afflicted on an East End capitalist was failure in the financial arena.

Carnegie then became a target of East Ender Shoenberger, who was president of the Pittsburgh Exchange Bank and had been one of the old Pig Iron Aristocrats that had for years been in competition with the young Carnegie. This was an old feud where years before Carnegie had bested the old Pig Iron Aristocrats. Carnegie survived, but the recession had brought out the worst in these capitalists. Scott's biggest sin was his dealing with New York investors. New York banks would never be fully trusted by the East End capitalists that survived.

East End bankers for their part tried to hold the city together from the devastation in New York. Many homeowners in Pittsburgh lost their homes. Judge Mellon noted, "real estate was unsalable at any price." Wages were falling, too, and immigration had been stopped. Labor problems were spreading throughout the iron, coal, and steel industry. By 1875, the recession was global, and at the time it was being called the "great depression." East Enders, who a decade earlier had feared an invasion of the Confederate Calvary, now worried about an invasion of the unemployed in the streets. East Enders pulled their resources to supply soup kitchens and housing for the unemployed. The railroads birthed a new class of drifter that "rode the rails" from city to city. The hobo camps were being built among the major rail centers such as Pittsburgh. Many feared that the violent socialist movement of Europe would come to America.

---

1 Carnegie, p. 172
2 Ibid, p. 174

In 1877, the Pennsylvania Railroad was the largest industrial corporation with over 200,000 employees. The stagnation of the economy had squeezed profits on the nation's railroad companies, and Rockefeller's war with the railroads was squeezing them even further. Over 500 railroad-related companies had gone bankrupt. The Pennsylvania and Baltimore & Ohio railroads had laid off thousands and asked the remaining brakemen and firemen to take a 10 percent pay cut while doubling up on the work. Wages had already been cut in three years from $70 a month to $30 a month. The wage cuts came with the news that the railroad companies were increasing dividends from the prior year. Tom Scott doubled the length of his trains, in effect, doubling the work. The strike would start outside Baltimore at Camden yards on July 16. It moved quickly along the line to West Virginia and west. On July 19, the Pennsylvania Railroad joined the strike, taking control of the Pittsburgh station and the switches. On the morning of July 20, no trains were moving in Maryland, Pennsylvania, West Virginia, Ohio, and Illinois. In Baltimore during the peak of the riots, there were gangs, socialists, and the unemployed who joined the strikers. Heinz would note the dozen deaths that day in Baltimore where he was trying to re-build his bankrupt pickle company.

On July 21st, Pittsburgh erupted in riots, and the state militia arrived. The militia started their sweep in the Irish section of Lawrenceville to push the rioters toward downtown and protect the East End. Tracks were torn up and cars burned. The unemployed, hoboes, and street gangs joined in the riot. Shooting occurred on both sides. By the end of the day, 20 had been killed including the sheriff, with hundreds wounded lying on the sidewalks. Pittsburgh's Catholic Bishop Tuigg walked the streets giving last rites to the wounded, as another nine would die in the streets. Men, women, and children joined into the pillage. The Union Station was torched, and freight cars of products were looted as citizens joined in. In all, 1,383 freight cars, 104 locomotives, and 66 passenger cars were destroyed at Pittsburgh. The fires lit the streets of the East End through the nights and many started to hide their valuables. Damage came to over $5 million. East Enders were cut off from the city, which was under full siege. Some trouble at the East Liberty Station was quickly addressed by the sheriff, forcing the trouble downtown, but the cries of "Give Us Bread" would leave a mark on the East End. Normal people joined in the looting as freight cars were opened. State militia formed to prevent the riot from moving east to the wealthy suburbs. The riot moved as far east as Lawrenceville, where the militia took a stand.

Chicago also had significant riots and property damage. In many cities, the unemployed joined the striking and looting. A mob of over 20,000 terrorized Chicago, and there were even riots in San Francisco. By July 24, the riots had traveled to the entire west coast. With the tracks torn up between Baltimore and Pittsburgh, workers seized the switching stations. President Rutherford Hayes called out the militia. The country had never known such violence except in war and would never see such civil unrest again until the civil rights riots in the summer of 1967. Americans had only read about such work-related violence in Europe in the 1870s, but the European immigrants of the 1840s could well remember the unrest and riots caused by socialists. Heinz had often listened to the stories of his German parents about the European riots in the 1840s. The riots shocked the East

End capitalists who believed such things could never happen in Pittsburgh. At the time, Pittsburgh had few immigrants. They would flood into the city during the next decade. Labor historian Joseph Rayback described the effect best: "The Railway Strike of 1877 thoroughly shocked a large portion of the public. Not since slaveholders had ceased to be haunted by dreams of a slave uprising had the propertied elements been so terrified."[1] It was the perfect storm as the recession, heat wave, and strikers came together on July 21, 22, and 23. It put business and family in perspective for many East Enders. It would also instill a fear and hatred of unions.

A young H. J. Heinz had been caught in the middle of the violence and rioting. Heinz had been on a trip to Baltimore and Washington, D.C. and became stuck in Baltimore. He also feared for his factory and home in Pittsburgh, only a few blocks from the violence. The telegraph lines were cut, and Heinz would not get in touch with the family for days. As he arrived in Pittsburgh, the destruction resembled the pictures of the Civil War. The newspaper and politicians would debate property rights, unionism, and capitalism for months. As George Westinghouse was at his north side factory watching the terror outside, Heinz and Westinghouse took a hard look at the issue and came to believe that people needed to be treated fairly in the workplace. Most capitalists and East Enders blamed the rise of unions and the influx of foreign ideas like socialism. Heinz was also closer to the economic plight of the 1870s than most capitalists of the day. His travels took him to the heart of struggling cities; and his home was in the heart of Pittsburgh, not in the rich suburbs of the time. Heinz and Westinghouse would be committed to paternal capitalism as a necessary element of business.

The Railroad Strike of 1877 had a profound effect on Pittsburgh's capitalists. A future East Ender, young Henry Clay Frick, was in the middle of the strike at his Connellsville Coke Works, unable to ship product to the Pittsburgh mills. It formed their fear and adversarial hatred of unions. The bloody Paris revolution of 1871 where the Marxists took over the government and then were forcibly overthrown was still fresh in the minds of capitalists. In Europe and in the American press, Marxism and unionism were linked. The commercial press throughout the country started to use the terms communism and Marxism in relating the railroad riots. An editorial in the *Pittsburgh Leader* describing the Great Strike noted: "the workingman in Pittsburgh is really a communist, and there is no doubt that communist ideas have spread widely." Many East Enders believed that recent German immigrants were the source of this spread of communism. There had been a Marxist convention in Pittsburgh in April of 1876. Westinghouse and Heinz took leadership in showing capitalism's response by improving working conditions.

In reality, the destruction of Pittsburgh turned many average Pittsburgher against unions and socialism. The typical citizen deemed the destruction and violence over the top. In 1882, the socialists held a convention in Pittsburgh. A violent strategy known as the "Pittsburgh Manifesto" was written, which became the terrorist strategy of the an-

---

1 Joseph Rayback, *The History of American Labor*, (New York: Macmillan Company, 1959), 135

archists nationally. The terrorists targeted capitalists and churches. Most of the nation's socialists were new German immigrants in New York and Chicago. Pittsburgh's older German population had a deep hatred of socialists from the strike. In addition, Pittsburgh remembered the violence and destruction and had no sympathy for radical socialists. Old Germans wanted to rise to the East End, not to destroy it. Germans had a clear path to upward mobility in Pittsburgh and a large middle class German section in the East End. While written in Pittsburgh, "The Manifesto" found almost no support among the Catholic immigrants who worked in Carnegie's steel mills. In particular, the Catholic Church aggressively opposed all branches of socialism while supporting trade unionism. Sunday sermons addressed the evils of socialism aggressively. The famous "Pittsburgh Manifesto" would be better known in Chicago, Cleveland, and New York.

The Great Railroad Riots pushed the city's wealthy to move further east into the suburbs. The migration of Pittsburgh's middle and upper class to the East End in the 1850s created a wealthy political class. The railroad and streetcar lines made the East End the favored location of the elite and middle class who worked in downtown Pittsburgh. Pittsburgh city fathers and politicians were quick to see the shift to the East End. They arranged an annexation in 1867 of the East End and its townships, which added 30,000 inhabitants and 21 square miles.[1] East End politicians soon controlled the city council; and in April 1870, the council passed the Penn Avenue Act, which poured almost the city's entire street budget into the development of the East End. The Act was expanded to improve thirty streets in Oakland, East Liberty, and Shadyside. Eventually over five million dollars was spent on the avenues such as Liberty, Highland, Forbes, and Fifth. During this time a rising East End politician, Christopher Magee, managed to get the construction company of William Flinn, another rising political boss to build a major new waterworks and reservoir in the East End. When the city tried to increase property assessments in the East End, the wealthy residents managed to get the Pennsylvania Supreme Court to find the Penn Avenue Act unconstitutional after all the improvement was completed in 1879!

The amazing development of the East End continued with the formation of the political alliance of William Flinn (1851-1924) and Christopher Magee in 1879. In 1880, Magee appointed his cousin Edward Bigelow as director of the Department of Public Works. Bigelow, like Magee, was a resident of the East End, and the dollars and construction using Flinn's construction company flowed into the East End. Land prices started to rise as East Enders E. Ferguson and Andrew Mellon tipped off young investors such as Henry Clay Frick of the future of real estate in the East End. Henry Clay Frick had become a major landholder in the East End before he was married or joined Andrew Carnegie. Bigelow brought in sewer and water lines. He built an extensive park system for the East End and was the builder of both Highland and Schenley Parks. For all his political ties, Bigelow was a skilled engineer, and his wide boulevards and parks made the East End truly a beautiful spot. It was Bigelow who wrestled the land for Schenley Park from Mary Schenley.

---

1 Samuel Hays, ed., *City at the Point: Essays on the Social History of Pittsburgh*, (Pittsburgh: University of Pittsburgh, 1989), p. 228

The final impact of the railroads on the wealthy East End came in 1911. The railroad tracks that had created this early suburb were now considered a nuisance to its wealthy residents. The problem became critical as railroad magnate families such as Pitcairn and Scott lived in the neighborhood. In addition, most of the Republican Party machine politicians lived in the neighborhood. As the neighborhood became loaded with automobiles, the accidents rose and so did the anger of residents. This wealthy neighborhood commanded the attention of the Pennsylvania Railroad, one of America's largest corporations. Wilkinsburg pushed the issue with ordinances restricting track right of ways. The Pennsylvania Railroad spent an amazing three million dollars (about $55 million today) to raise the tracks going through the neighborhood. A number of pedestrian subways were also built. The completion of this project was celebrated by days of parades and picnics. The Pennsylvania Railroad magazine of July 18, 1916 described it as: "the most remarkable three day celebration ever recorded in American Civic History. The parade was four miles long, was witnessed by 75,000 people."[1] The railroad paid to have floats made, showing how the project was done for the East End. Certainly such a response was lacking in the majority of Pittsburgh's neighborhoods, which had the same problem.

---

1 Harry Gilchrist, *History of Wilkinsburg Pennsylvania*, (Pittsburgh, Private, 1940).

CHAPTER 9. BANKERS AND INVENTORS

Creativity and capital were the main natural resources of the East End. Pittsburgh East Enders seemed to come up with endless inventions and ways to finance their development. Even the smoke and dirt brought out creative genius. East Ender Oswald Werner was one of the first to develop dry cleaning in the 1860s. Werner would make a fortune and build his East End mansion at 830 North Highland Avenue near that of oil baron Charles Lockhart. Inventor George Westinghouse had also come to the East End in the 1860s after making a fortune out of railroad brakes. It was in the East End that a young Thomas Mellon would see the potential of financing this local creativity. The old Indian trail of Penn Avenue brought commerce and the railroads to the East End. Inventors and industrialists were originally drawn to Pittsburgh as a transportation hub, but they stayed because of the available capital. The evolution of the East End wealth went from pig iron to railroads to oil to steel, but it was capital behind all these industries.

The railroads then brought wealth and people to Pittsburgh's East End. The first East End mansions were those of bankers. Most of Pittsburgh's bankers lived in the east's wealthy suburbs, but it would be the king of bankers, Thomas Mellon, and his sons who changed the neighborhood and Pittsburgh forever. Mellon would finance many of the coalmines of Western Pennsylvania, and the crown for king of coke would go to Henry Clay Frick. The Mellon family and Frick would bring the world's art to the East End that would ultimately form the core of the National Gallery of Art in Washington, D.C. The railroads not only brought bankers but inventors such as George Westinghouse (1846-1914). Westinghouse would revolutionize the railroad industry with his air brake. Next, he would drill a gas well on his East End estate and create the natural gas industry. Finally, Westinghouse's alternating electrical current would change the very nature of the world. Mellon and Westinghouse would also supply the two ingredients — electrical power and capital — to create the aluminum industry. After capital, creativity was the other factor behind the growth of industry.

George Westinghouse changed railroads forever with his air brake, which is still used today. His perspective on manufacturing was affected by what some have called the Connecticut River Revolution of the first half of the 1800s. The Connecticut River Valley cuts through New Hampshire and Vermont, but it really encompassed all of New England. The Connecticut Valley was part of the birthplace of the American Industrial Revolution. It was, however, as much a philosophy as an industrial movement. It molded Yankee self-reliance and individualism with an artisan and farming culture, producing machine shops to meet the growing needs of the economy. The spirit of the Connecticut Valley was the same as the Scotch–Irish of Western Pennsylvania. It was this spirit that can be seen throughout Westinghouse's career, combining ethics, self-reliance, and social conscience with diverse manufacturing skills. Westinghouse took this Jeffersonian approach further in applying it to mass production and heavy industry where many believed the Jeffersonian philosophy could not go. Westinghouse represented a wave of Yankee mechanics that came to the Pittsburgh area to expand the industrial revolution. They found the perfect combination of capital and industry in Pittsburgh.

In his father's machine shop in Schenectady, New York, George Westinghouse came up with his first invention called a "frog." The railroad frog was a piece of cast iron switching track that allowed trains to switch tracks. The frog was a permanent switch or piece of track, having a life of only a few months as speeds and car tonnage increased. The term is still used today for a segment of intersecting rail that allows one track to cross to another. These switches had to take the continual impact of trains. Wear and breakage was a constant problem, which in turn clogged rail traffic when replacement was needed. The railroads were purchasing hundreds of these each month. Westinghouse started his work on the frog sometime in 1866. What was obvious, however, was the wear on the device. Cast iron was too brittle and wrought iron too malleable. Steel offered the ideal compromise, but the use of steel was limited by its high cost and difficulty in casting it. Westinghouse hung around the railroads and had heard of steel being used on rails in England. Before he had resolved the materials problem, he applied for a patent calling it an "improved railroad switch" in the fall of 1866. He also started the search for capital to back his idea using a wooden model of his new "switch." He needed a foundry to cast this new steel design as well, and the only steel foundries in the world were in the city of Pittsburgh.

A twenty-two-year-old George Westinghouse went by train to Pittsburgh in December of 1868 just as Mark Twain was finishing one of his famous oratories in Pittsburgh. The Pittsburgh of 1868 was the industrial and metallurgical core of the nation. The Civil War had transformed the town into an industrial giant. Fort Pitt Foundry (formed in 1805) was one of the oldest iron foundries in the country, having supplied cannonballs to the army of Andrew Jackson and the navy of Commodore Perry in 1812. The Fort Pitt Foundry of Pittsburgh had been the major armory of the Grand Army of the Republic. It had pioneered casting techniques that allowed for the world's largest cannons to be produced. By 1868, Pittsburgh was the major iron and puddled steel producer in the nation.

Pittsburgh produced about 45 percent of the nation's total iron production and produced most of the nation's steel. Pittsburgh had six steel foundries and cast more steel than any other place on earth. The casting of steel had only been mastered by a few metallurgists in Pittsburgh and Germany. East Ender Curtiss Hussey (1802–1893) had pioneered the casting of high quality steel, and it was Hussey's work that first attracted Westinghouse to the possibility of casting railroad frogs. Hussey tool steels were considered equal to the best steel of Sheffield, England. Westinghouse headed for Pittsburgh to see if his frog could be cast in steel at Pittsburgh's steel foundries.

Westinghouse arrived at the city's landmark, the four story high Union Depot Building, in December 1868. December in Pittsburgh was a month of almost full "arctic" darkness due to the smoke; still, Westinghouse seemed positively impressed by the industrial city. The city's streets were defined not by geometry but by the geography of the hills and rivers, making it impossible for visitors to find their way. It is a characteristic that modern visitors can still attest to today. It was this urban attribute that might well have helped determined Westinghouse's future success. He was first looking for Anderson & Cook Foundry. The Anderson and Cook Foundry was located on Second Avenue (Blvd. of the Allies) and Try Street. In his search for the firm of Anderson and Cook, he got lost, asked directions, and met and formed a relationship with Pittsburgh industrialist, Ralph Baggaley. Baggaley would be the future financier and manager of Westinghouse's air brake. After arriving at Anderson and Cook, he quickly closed a deal where Anderson and Cook would produce frogs, while Westinghouse would travel to sell them. Westinghouse's wife, Marguerite, remained in New York as George started a year of traveling and missing her. Living in cheap hotels, he saved all he could to move Marguerite to Pittsburgh, at which time they moved into an apartment on Pittsburgh's North side.

Westinghouse's next invention was to address the serious problem of train braking. The hand brake system in place required coordination and muscle power. The locomotive engineer would start throttling down the engine as he signaled the brakemen with the whistle (known as the "down brakes whistle'). A brakeman was assigned between every two cars on the train. Ideally, the engineer had throttled to a coast as it approached the stop. The brakemen would begin the process of applying friction brakes on each car by the turning of a hand wheel known as the horizontal wheel on a vertical post at the end of each car that multiplied the force of his muscles. The needed strength of the brakemen was the source of the term "Armstrong system." The hand wheel pushed brake shoes on each car against the wheels using friction to stop the train. The hand wheel used a chain to transfer the power to the brake shoes. After the brakes were applied to one car, the brakemen jumped to the other car to apply the brakes. Poor coordination between the brakemen could cause "locking" and serious jolting to the passengers. The system inherently caused a series of uneven jolts. Luggage was often thrown wildly inside the passenger cars. Many times brakemen were killed or injured in this difficult task. The danger to the brakemen was unbelievable. He had to race from car to car, often on roofs slippery with ice, snow, or rain. Even on the best days, the swaying, bobbing, and jolting of the cars could cause a loss of footing. Jolting or locking often threw the brakeman off on his way across the car roof to the next car. The average life of a brakeman on the job was estimated at seven years. The statistics of the time were just as unbelievable. It was estimated a thousand brakemen were killed each year with another 5,000 injured![1] While these deaths were horrific, they didn't make the headlines; railroad wrecks were front-page news. These wrecks are what caused the public outcry for safety.

In early 1868, Westinghouse had engineering drawings and models showing the practicality of using compressed air in a braking system. The suggestion of compressed air in railroad braking was not unique to Westinghouse, but a complete engineered system was. By June, Westinghouse applied for a patent of the idea before he had an actual test based on his models. This first Westinghouse brake was known as the straight-air brake. It was simple and primitive. A steam pump on the locomotive using the same steam that drove the engine generated the compressed air. The compressed air was contained in a reservoir located on the locomotive as well. A pipe using flexible couplings was used to connect the individual brake cylinders on each car. These flexible couplings were three-ply rubber, which was available and could handle compressed air (but not the steam of Westinghouse's original idea). When the engineer released the compressed air in the reservoir, it rushed to the individual cylinders which closed the brake shoes on the car wheels. It used friction like our modern car to stop the car. Of course, in today's car, hydraulic fluid is used to apply the force on the brake shoes. The action was solely controlled by the engineer, eliminating all the brakemen, and applying the brakes evenly and simultaneously. On his sales trips to sell frogs for Anderson and Cook, Westinghouse tried unsuccessfully to promote a trial of his air brakes. The board of directors of the Chicago, Burlington and Quincy Railroad was the first to turn down the trial. It was a disappointment because he had successfully convinced the superintendent of the railroad that the application of the air brake would work. The next and more famous rejection was from Commodore Vanderbilt of the New York Central line; but Westinghouse did convince the New York Central to buy his frogs, generating some badly needed cash.

Another meeting was with East Ender Robert Pitcairn, local superintendent of the Pennsylvania Railroad. Pitcairn had even invested with a young fellow employee, Andrew Carnegie, in a number of coal mining ventures. Pitcairn liked the idea and Westinghouse, but he could not approve a trial. Pitcairn brought in the superintendent and assistant superintendent of Altoona, Edward Williams and Andrew J. Cassatt. The meeting was a setback, with the Pennsylvania Railroad refusing to fully finance the trial. One problem was Westinghouse's youthful appearance at the age of twenty-two. Still, they couldn't help but be impressed. The next meeting with W. W. Card, Steubenville Superintendent of the Panhandle Railroad, was successful. Card was almost wildly enthusiastic about the brake, but his board also turned down the financing. Card would ultimately be one of the first investors in the Westinghouse Air Brake. Finally, it was decided that a train would be equipped with the Westinghouse system in September of 1868.[2]

---

1 *The Search for Safety*, Union Switch and Signal Division of American Standard, Pittsburgh, 1981
2 Prout, 29

The *Steubenville Accommodation* of the Panhandle Railroad was equipped for the test at Baggaley's North Side plant, mostly by Westinghouse himself. The trial was with four cars. The last car on the train would carry some special guests including Card and some of the Panhandle directors. Daniel Tate was the engineer, and Westinghouse had trained him personally on how to use the brake. He also gave Tate fifty dollars as the train left Panhandle Station in Pittsburgh on its fifty-mile trip to Steubenville. Westinghouse went to sit in the locomotive cab. Normally, accommodation trains went about a quarter mile through the Grant Hill Tunnel and stopped at Fourth Street to pick up passengers. This reserved train, however, was not scheduled to stop in Pittsburgh that day. It crossed Second Avenue and the Monongahela Bridge and then open track following the Ohio River. The train left the tunnel at thirty miles per hour only to see a merchant and his cart crossing the track at Second Street. It is not clear where the planned stops were that day, but this was an unexpected emergency requiring Tate to use the brake for the first time. He pulled the hand lever, quickly bringing the train to a jarring stop. The guests in the last car were thrown from their seats in confusion. This first successful trial is immortalized in a painting today and verified in personal letters of the engineer and Superintendent Card. This spectacular demonstration launched Westinghouse into the international business of manufacturing railroad air brakes and onto the path to wealth.

By the end of 1860s, Westinghouse had arrived as a Pittsburgh industrialist. He built a beautiful mansion in the East End known as "Solitude." His ten-acre estate was on Thomas Boulevard, Lang Street, and Murtland Avenue. The mansion had a two-story stable. Westinghouse had a membership in Pittsburgh's Duquesne Club. From 1873, it was the private men's club in Pittsburgh of some of America's greatest capitalists. The Duquesne Club was also the haunt of Pittsburgh's Pig Iron Aristocrats as well. Westinghouse's partner, Ralph Baggaley, had become one of the Duquesne Club's earliest members and an officer. For Westinghouse, membership in the club meant little; he preferred to eat dinner at home and would have nightly business dinners there as well. For lunches, he preferred hearty basic meals and often ate at the Allegheny Valley Railway Company diner car known as "Coach No. 2." The bankers dominated the Duquesne Club, which was another reason Westinghouse preferred doing business at home. Westinghouse did feel comfortable with his poker buddies — Henry Clay Frick, Benjamin Jones, and Andrew Mellon — who often met for lunch at the Duquesne Club. Socially, Westinghouse preferred scientists and engineers to businessmen. He was also a member of the Shadyside Presbyterian Church, which was the church of prominent Pittsburgh industrialists and the Scotch-Irish.

By 1880, smoky Pittsburgh was the glass capital of America. These glassworks used cheap coal as fuel. It was an extremely dirty fuel, and this was problematic for glassmakers as well as residents of the city. Pittsburgh was known to have only a few hours of sunshine because of the dense smoke. Rochester Glassworks near Pittsburgh and West Virginia glasshouses had been experimenting with natural gas, and Westinghouse had followed their progress. Several small natural gas companies were struggling in the Pittsburgh area in 1883 and were plagued by many problems. Supply problems to factories caused by pipe leaks were common. Home connections were even more problematic. Cock valves were used to shut the gas on and off. Natural gas is odorless and if cocks are not shut, rooms fill with asphyxiating gas. Explosions were also common, and there were even local laws restricting gas usage. If this wasn't enough, these gas companies had no way to charge for usage; so lacking meters, you were charged for a connection regardless of use. Natural gas was found in 1882 in Murrayville, forty miles east of Pittsburgh. The Murrayville find suggested that natural gas was more abundant than originally thought. Westinghouse even started to study geology and believed the soil around Solitude suggested gas deposits.

Westinghouse hired geologists to explore the grounds at Solitude near Thomas Boulevard. By the end of 1883, Westinghouse had started to drill on his property. He beamed with enthusiasm and spent nights designing drilling tools to amuse himself. He encouraged the drilling crew and spent hours talking and taking notes on drilling. One night the well came in with a major explosion and a hurricane-like hiss disturbed the once peaceful residential neighborhood. To test the well, it was lit, producing a huge column of bright light that could be seen for many miles. The brightness was described as: "The gas lamps of the city dwindled to a little points of light, and persons in the street not less than a mile away were able to read distinctly the finest newspaper print by the light of gigantic natural flambeau on the heights of Solitude." The Pittsburgh fire department had to be summoned to hose down the mansion to prevent it from burning. The tremendous pressure at the wellhead was obvious, and the first step was to design and make a stopcock to cap the well. For weeks, however, the East End had 24-hour daylight.

The problem now became how to get into the business of distributing natural gas. Westinghouse was thinking of a pipeline system. Political opposition was rapidly headed by the Fuel Gas Company which had a public utility charter for the Pittsburgh area. The opposition was extremely stiff as the Fuel Gas Company formed a confederation including the coal gas companies and some banks. His neighbors found a utility company charter in Harrisburg that could be purchased. This charter for "Philadelphia Company" had been set up by East Ender Thomas Scott of the Pennsylvania Railroad for railroad lines but had an open ended charter that could be used for any utility. The Philadelphia Company would be another great company formed in the parlors of Pittsburgh's East End. Westinghouse was able to purchase the charter from Scott for $35,000. On August 4, 1884, the Philadelphia Company was formed with George Westinghouse as president, East Ender Robert Pitcairn as vice-president, and John Caldwell as secretary. Brother Herman Westinghouse and glassmaker John Dalzell were also officers.

The next problem was a fight with the City of Pittsburgh to lay pipe for gas distribution. The politics were problematic, with competing fuel companies arguing that Westinghouse would have an unfair monopoly. Citizen groups argued the danger of major explosions. He laid out all his safety measures to the press. At Westinghouse Machine, he designed new pipe connections to prevent leaks and assure safety. In addition, he offered free gas to the city's fire stations and police stations. The city council was won over by the fairness of Westinghouse in these business offerings. There were also strong political ties, as Henry Clay Frick and Christopher Magee became investors in the new Westinghouse

Company. The city also realized that cheap fuel could rejuvenate industry growth that had slowed from the Panic of 1873. The glass industry was also under pressure as gas finds in more western states were creating a loss of glass houses. Even growth had slowed for Pittsburgh's steel and iron industries.

Westinghouse's Philadelphia Company was profitable within the year. Westinghouse had applied for a patent for his new distribution system. He designed a safety system where a leak in the inner pipe would be captured by the outer pipe and the pressure was diffused. He then devised a system of escape pipes along the street mains to feed leaking gas into corner lampposts or to escape at safe points to the air. High wellhead pressure was great for transmission and smaller diameter increased pressure for line transmission. High pressure made the gas unmanageable at the point of delivery. Westinghouse designed a series of increasing diameters along the line until the point of delivery, which had the bigger diameter to reduce pressure, then reduced pressure, making it more manageable at the point of delivery. For example, the first four to five miles of pipe was small diameter to speed gas into the long distribution pipeline; then every five miles or so, the diameter was increased. Using various diameters from 8 to 36 inches, Westinghouse moved gas up to 20 miles from the well by changing pipe diameters; the pressure was reduced from 300 pounds per square inch to a few ounces per square inch. This simple, yet brilliant engineering system would be used later in his career to solve the problem of AC electrical current distribution.

One safety problem was household explosions, which had been a major deterrent to its use. These explosions resulted because of frequent shutoffs to a house, while the gas flowed to the lights when on unless the household shut the incoming valve. When the distribution line was disrupted and undetected by the household, the light went out; and upon its return, odorless gas filled the house. Westinghouse invented a safety device known as the automatic cut-off regulator. When the gas pressure held below the four-ounce household working pressure, the gas was automatically shut off. Gas heating, cooking, and lighting became very popular in Pittsburgh, but not without some hesitation by the public. One of Westinghouse's first customers was his future neighbor, H. J. Heinz, who converted his Sharpsburg home and north side factory to natural gas. Westinghouse even converted the house of neighbor and coal magnate, Henry Clay Frick. The very fashionable East End would be one of the earliest of the Pittsburgh's suburbs to convert to gas, and Wilkinsburg reported the following:

> Using gas was a new experience to people and most of them were afraid of it, and did not know whether to turn on the gas first and then light it, or just how it should be handled. Many singed eyebrows and burned hands resulted, and even some bad burns. The gas pipes were run to the second floors on the outside of the houses. In grates and stoves T burners were used with broken pieces of firebrick. A can of water was usually set on the stove or hung before grates on account of the dry heat. Gas was plentiful and a six-room house could be heated for about $2 a month [in a time when the typical weekly pay was around $10]."[1] Another small, but

---

1 Harry Gilchrist, History of Wilkinsburg Pennsylvania (Pittsburgh, 1940), 104

revolutionary device for cooks was a temperature control valve. The savings of gas cooking over coal stoves was also substantial, and East End cooks converted quickly. It was assumed the average cost of $12.50 a year for coal; others stated that it took two pounds of coal to cook a pound of meat. Westinghouse had contacted several professors to calculate the savings from gas. It was estimated that for the same amount of coal, a family would use 3,000 cubic feet of gas (at 50 cents per thousand in Boston) at a cost of less than $2 a year.[1] Writer George Thurston noted in 1888, "Mr. Westinghouse's achievement is one at which the wonder grows as time elapses, and the full results are realized."

From 1883 to 1886, gas distribution was Westinghouse's passion as he advanced natural gas distribution to a science. President Grover Cleveland came to Pittsburgh to see the Philadelphia Company's distribution of natural gas and dined on a gas-cooked meal in the East End. Cleveland hailed Pittsburgh's future of natural gas. The growth of Philadelphia Company and natural gas was amazing, having 45 wells and 330 miles of pipe by 1885. Lines reached far beyond Pittsburgh to Homestead, Braddock, and McKeesport. Westinghouse started to convert his Shadyside neighbors, such as Henry Clay Frick's "Clayton" and H. J. Heinz's "Greenwood," as well as their factories. While managing the company, Westinghouse invented meters for household and factory use. The company could now charge by usage. Westinghouse continued to improve the system with the invention of leak detectors and improved drilling techniques. He also invented air-fuel mixing valves to make industrial furnaces efficient. Many of these greatly improved the wasteful distribution of natural gas. Prior to Westinghouse's system, natural gas was vented and lighted to burn every weekend, but Westinghouse valves eliminated the practice. In particular, downtown Pittsburgh was lighted by a battery of stand pipes on the hill over Union Station from Saturday to Monday to burn off surplus gas from the factories, shutting down on weekends. It was estimated that 1,000 cubic feet of this gas was equivalent to 56 pounds of Pittsburgh coal. The cost of 1,000 cubic feet of gas was only 10 cents. In 1887 it was estimated that natural gas had replaced 40,000 tons of coal daily in the Pittsburgh area.[2] Westinghouse's gas industry was starting to seriously impact the coal business of his neighbor, Henry Clay Frick, even though Frick had been one of the first to light his home with gas. The price of coal had fallen 35 to 40 percent by 1887, and estimates of 10,000 miners were being put out of work by conversion to gas.[3]

The amazing change in the Pittsburgh environment in 1889 was described as follows:

> The transition from the use of coal to that of this non-producer of smoke has been simply wonderful. Prior to 1884 the city used 3,000,000 tons, or nearly 80,000,000 bushels of bituminous coal in a year, the smoke from which hung in a black cloud, like a pall, over the city continually, discharging flakes of soot and fine dust in a steady downfall. The black, pall-like cloud has disappeared; the atmosphere is cleaner than that of most western cities, and the temptation to use bright colors in house-ornamen-

1 "Cheap Gas for Heat and Power Purposes," *Scientific American*, April 18, 1896
2 *Handbook of Pittsburgh and Allegheny*, (Pittsburgh: Fisher & Stewart, 1887), 26
3 *Manufacturer and Builder*, January, 1886

tation is steadily growing. The consumption of coal has fallen much below a million of tons annually.[1] For several years, the sun could once again be seen in Pittsburgh, but more growth brought more coal usage. The return of the heavy smoke and dirt in the 1890s most certainly was disappointing to Mrs. Westinghouse, who had always struggled with this feature of Pittsburgh living. The soot and dirt required almost daily cleaning and washing of household linens.

By the end of the 1880s, Westinghouse was one of the famous Pittsburgh millionaires with neighbors such as Andrew Carnegie, Henry Clay Frick, and the Mellons. Mrs. Westinghouse was followed by all the social columns of the day. An 1888 review of Pittsburgh's wealthiest women noted:

> Mrs. George Westinghouse, Jr., of Homewood, lives in greater style, entertains more splendidly and wears more gorgeous, varied, elegant toilets, has more and finer diamonds than any woman in Pittsburgh. Her table appointments are simply superb, the entire service being of solid silver and gold (whose cost it would be idle to attempt to guess), and the cut glass, Sevres, Dresden and other fine porcelains are worth a small fortune. Their whole style of living is after the plan of the household of an English lord. The house is a perfect palace, and the grounds worthy of it. Their stud of horses comprises some magnificent animals. Mr. Westinghouse is blessed with the knowledge that he was married for love, and not for lucre — something rich men cannot usually congratulate themselves on, as when he won his wife both he and she were but moderately well off. Mrs. Westinghouse is notable for splendid charity, both public and private. Her husband's wealth runs well up into the millions, $5,000,000 being an underestimate. Mr. Westinghouse was knighted a few years ago by King Leopold of Belgium as a token of admiration of the master mind that conceived the Westinghouse Air Brake. The brilliant young inventor and his wife would therefore be entitled, did they wish, to style themselves Sir George and Lady Westinghouse.[2]

Still, Mrs. Westinghouse never took fully to industrial Pittsburgh.

During the period of 1889 to 1893, the Westinghouse family was in a state of flux. They built a summer home known as Erskine in the Berkshires (Lenox, Massachusetts). Both George's and Marguerite's families were extremely close, and they loved having family at their homes. As always, family and friends often mixed with the rich and famous at their dinner parties. George moved his elderly parents to Pittsburgh from New York. The Erskine mansion was starting to evolve into their summer home. Mrs. Westinghouse wanted to escape the dirt, heat, and typhoid of Pittsburgh summers. Westinghouse often amused himself in the wiring of the Erskine mansion to the frustration of Marguerite Westinghouse. Westinghouse kept the wires exposed, running along walls and ceilings so he could make changes readily. Marguerite saw an improvement in her health with the Berkshire living. As smoke returned to the Pittsburgh area though, Marguerite struggled

---

1 *History of Allegheny*, (Chicago: A. Warner & Co., 1889), 616

2 Adelaide Mellier Nevin, *Social Mirror: Character Sketch of the Women of Pittsburg*, (Pittsburg: T.W. Nevin, 1888), 94

with the constant soot and darkness and wanted to stay longer at the summer home. Her mood improved as she could wear white dresses and could actually see the sun routinely. When at Solitude, she would have to spend hours cleaning the silverware. Westinghouse continued the dinner parties regardless of which mansion they were using. Guests often included some of the world's greatest scientists such as Lord Kelvin; engineers such as the flamboyant Nikola Tesla; or political friends such as Congressman William McKinley. The dinners had many famous guests such as Henry Clay Frick, Prince Albert of Belgium, European princes, generals from all over the world, and several American presidents. Often he would mix these great guests with the train crew that would be waiting late to take them home. The train station was a short walk, but Westinghouse built a tunnel from the house to the station so he could come and go with little publicity.

We have a further insight into his family life from the family secretary, Walter Uptegraff, who joined the family in 1888. Uptegraff observed the following in his employ at all the Westinghouse's homes:

> After the guests had gone and the family had retired, he would go to his study where he would work on his inventions until one or two o'clock in the morning. During these quiet hours he always liked to have someone with him to whom he could open his inmost self without resistant; to explain what he was trying to accomplish by showing the drawings he was working on; to compliment the listener by inviting suggestions. He required but four or five hours of sleep and would come down to an early breakfast bursting with energy, eager to get at the day's work as quickly as possible.[1]

During the 1880s when Westinghouse was at Solitude, he would eat at 6 A.M. and take the train to his office on Penn Avenue. He would often supervise the daily sweeping of mill dust and soot off the porch every morning. He was behind his desk at 8 A.M. When his plants moved in the 1890s to East Pittsburgh and Wilmerding, he liked to go to the plant first and then take the train back to his office in Pittsburgh. He often rode with his employees on the train and streetcars. As his business increased, Westinghouse would take the express train, the "Pittsburgher," to New York weekly with his personal Pullman car. Most Monday mornings, his train took him to his New York office at 120 Broadway from his personal Pennsylvania Railroad station and returned Tuesday morning.

His special Pullman car on the Pennsylvania Railroad was a true palace. The Pullman car of Westinghouse consisted of a dining room, kitchen, sleeping quarters, and office. The special car was named Glen Eyre and was always ready for a business trip. His journey would start from a tunnel at his mansion that went directly to the train station. His Pullman car, specially built for his comfort, included a drafting desk and engineering office. He had a drawing board in his Pullman, for George still found relaxation in drawing and outlining mechanical devices. Westinghouse was a large man, giving the appearance of a walrus with his Victorian mustache and long coat; he required specially designed chairs

---

1 A. G. Uptegraff, "The Home Life of George Westinghouse," July 1936, page 2
George Westinghouse Museum Archives

in his Pullman. He had designed his train car to be a home, and indeed he spent many hours in that car. He also used it to pick up and entertain politicians such as William McKinley. On winter weekends during the McKinley Administration, he connected his Pullman car to a Pennsylvania express train and went to another home in Washington, D.C. On weekends in summer, spring, and autumn, his destination was his home in Lenox, Massachusetts.

The 1880s brought other problems than just the return of smoke. It would be in 1883 that a ring of Republican bosses took over Pittsburgh led by two East Enders — William Flinn and Christopher Magee. William Flinn (1851-1924) had been elected to the State House of Representatives in 1877 and would be elected to the State Senate in 1890. Flinn's firm of Booth & Flinn was a construction firm with contracts for buildings, parks, and streets. Christopher Magee (1848-1901) was a politician who worked his way from a city cashier in 1869 to Mayor in 1882. Magee was known for his quest of political power. He had spent time in Philadelphia studying political patronage under Pennsylvania political boss, Mathew Quay. On the state level, Matthew Quay was a key player to the Pittsburgh machine. He even studied the fall of the Tweed ring at New York's Tammany Hall, but the Magee ring was a middle class machine. Magee served as treasurer, fire commissioner, and state senator. He owned several transit companies and the *Pittsburgh Times*. Old Judge Thomas Mellon rigorously opposed the Magee–Flinn–Quay alliance in 1883. Judge Mellon would say the following of Magee and Flinn: "Even the desire for fame, which came next to it, is now in a measure subordinated to a groveling desire for office and its emoluments . . . In a corrupt democracy the tendency is always to give power to the worst."[1] Unfortunately, Mellon's son and other East Enders proved to be much more accommodating to the ring.

While East Enders rarely appeared with Flinn and Magee publicly, they did deal with them behind closed doors. They shared one belief that the growth of the East End meant profits in real estate and construction. The Magee-Flinn ring, however, would be as corrupt as Tweed in New York. Its power struggle was the same based on patronage of people needing help and looking for upward mobility. The ring focused on middle class support in saloon owners, storeowners, butchers, and grocers, making it unique from New York and Chicago rings that preyed on poor immigrants. While the ring promoted all kinds of crime, it served the social needs of a rising middle class. From 1880 to 1900, Allegheny County's population went from 235,000 to 451,000. Magee applied the same model used by New York's Tammany Hall to secure the Irish vote but applied it to the middle class. The Flinn-Magee ring secured the German vote. The immigrants of Pittsburgh were in the surrounding river valleys, while the middle class votes of Pittsburgh were the key to political control of the city. Flinn and Magee were in many ways selling upward mobility. Flinn's legacy was in construction where his granite quarry in the mountains was used to pave Pittsburgh streets. Magee focused on transportation. It was transportation that favored the middle class suburbs on the way to the wealthiest of neighborhoods of the East End.

---

1 Burton Hersh, p. 82

Even before the arrival of inventors like Westinghouse and the rise of the banking empire of the Mellons, the East End was home to many pioneering bankers. In 1865, the largest private residence in Allegheny County was the East End mansion of George A. Berry. Berry was president of Citizens National Bank in 1865 and was the grandson of the East Ender ironmaster, George Anshultz. By the 1870s, Pittsburgh was one of the country's largest banking centers with 71 banking institutions. It had a banking tradition going back to the early days of James O'Hara. The bankers tended to locate in the East End because of its rural setting and its transportation system. Many East End families such as the Thaw family, Negley family, Bakewell family, and Wilkins family had banking roots. William Negley (1828–1895) was a director of Thomas Mellon's law firm and Berry's Citizen's Bank, which would be a link in the formation of the Mellon banking empire. Judge Mellon would first enter banking in the 1860s as director of Farmers' Deposit National Bank and as the first president of People's Saving Bank.

CHAPTER 10. THE COKE KING AND THE PRINCE OF STEEL

The railroads would bring Pittsburgh's most famous immigrants to town in the 1850s. The Pennsylvania Railroad and most of the nation's railroads were expanding west out of the gateway of Pittsburgh. The railroads had taken poor immigrants like Andrew Carnegie and Robert Pitcairn and made them investors and industrialists. Andrew Carnegie had teamed up with Pennsylvania Railroad executives, Edgar Thomson and Thomas Scott, to form Keystone Bridge Company, and with Charles Lockhart to form Columbia Oil. These millions of profits would be invested in steel and coke, which would be the core of Pittsburgh's wealth.

Having made big money from his investments in railroads and oil, Carnegie was led by his brother Tom into the iron business. Tom had already borrowed money from Carnegie to enter the iron business. His success led Carnegie to look seriously at the steel industry which was expanding due to the railroad boom. Carnegie had grown up in the railroad industry and was pulled up through the organization by two men — Thomas Scott and Edgar Thomson of the Pennsylvania Railroad. Tom and Andrew first moved into the forging business for railroad car axles. Their Cyclops Mill was built in the East End on the old Denny estate to produce railroad axles. Then they moved into the Union Mills, a rolling mill in the Lawrenceville area of the East End with the help of many East End partners. Now investors were talking about a future in the stronger and tougher material of steel. Carnegie was aware of Edgar Thomson's experiments with steel rails at the Pennsylvania Railroad. He himself tried to develop a new steel "facing" process for iron rails. The process was not successful, but again he found the interest of Edgar Thomson. Carnegie then moved into an iron bridge building to fully utilize his Union Mills.

Carnegie would build his famous Lucy Furnaces in Pittsburgh to supply pig iron for rolling mills and bridge works. The firm of Kloman, Carnegie & Company was formed to build Lucy Furnace (named after Tom Carnegie's wife). The actual furnace was built by

Homewood iron king William Coleman and his company, Coleman Iron. The iron would go to the forge shops of the Kloman Brothers. Andrew and Anton (changed to Anthony) Kloman were two Prussian blacksmiths who had opened a forge shop a few miles up the Allegheny River from Pittsburgh in 1858. The forge was capable of making large wagon axles and heavy railroad axles. The growth was rapid for such a large forge. By the middle of 1859, they needed money to invest in a second trip hammer. This brought in East End money men and friends of Tom Carnegie — Tom Miller, William Coleman, and Henry Phipps. Henry Phipps brought in his east side friend, Henry Curry, to manage the furnaces. These combinations also created a new breed of Pig Iron Aristocrats in the Kloman brothers, Carnegie brothers, Henry Phipps, and Thomas Miller. The new group was in direct competition with the old-line aristocrats of the north side's millionaire row: Oliver, Dalzell, Spang, Chalfant, Jones, and Laughlin who owned the new Isabella Furnace. This new industrial combination would shift Pittsburgh's millionaire row of iron makers from its North side to the East End joining the East End bankers, glass men, inventors, and oilmen.

The battle of Carnegie's new iron men and the Pig Iron Aristocrats would change Pittsburgh. The duel of Isabella and Lucy Furnaces started in June of 1872. The battle became the headlines of Pittsburgh's papers as the furnaces overtook production records of the Struthers Furnace in Ohio. The papers followed the great furnace tonnage battles like a sporting event. For the first year, the weekly tonnage record moved back and forth between the two furnaces. Lucy Furnace ended the year with a 500-ton a week average versus a 498-ton a week average for Isabella. The battle continued for years, as the international press started to follow it. In 1874, Lucy set the daily world production record at 100 ton a day. These records would pale in a few years by the demand caused for pig iron to make steel, and the main demand for steel was railroad rails. It also created a demand for coke, which was necessary for iron and steel production. A young Henry Clay Frick in Connellsville, Pennsylvania was quietly becoming wealthy as the battle raged.

The production of coke required a distillation process which "cooked" out volatile gaseous matter of coal. This is done by heating or "burning" coal with limited oxygen for long periods. The burning or "coking" produced a very hard lump of carbon. The end product, coke, was a high-energy fuel that could be used in iron making because of its strength. Strength was required to support the high column of fuel and heavy iron ore in the blast furnace stack. Coke's smokeless high-energy burning made it popular in the glass furnaces of Pittsburgh as well. A young Henry Clay Frick moved from the coalfields of Westmoreland County to the plush Monongahela Hotel to sell coke to Pittsburgh industrialists.

There were several coke districts in Western Pennsylvania, but the richest and most productive was the Connellsville District, which ran through Westmoreland and Fayette counties. Connellsville in Westmoreland County would become the "Capital of Coke," and Henry Clay Frick was the king of coke. The Connellsville District is part of the rich "Pittsburgh Seam" that is open on the Monongahela and Youghiogheny River banks. The district runs 42 miles and 3.5 miles in width and covers all of Westmoreland and Fayette counties. The richest strip of this coal deposit ran from Latrobe, Pennsylvania, south through Scottsdale, Connellsville, and Uniontown to the Fairchance-Smithfield area. The richest three-mile strip ran by the Overholt — Frick farm in today's Westmoreland County, which is from eight to eleven feet thick. Coke was a hard high temperature fuel that could be used in salt making, steel puddling furnaces, blast furnaces, glass furnaces, forge shops, foundries, and iron making.

Another part of the growth of coke use was by the mushrooming in foundry business which cast steam engines, cannons, stoves, and machinery. Pittsburgh foundries re-melted pig iron in furnaces called cupolas. Pig iron was purchased from Ohio or Pennsylvania charcoal iron furnaces and brought to foundries in Pittsburgh, since Pittsburgh at the time had no charcoal iron-making furnaces. Pittsburgh's appetite for coke in the late 1840s and 1850s could not be supplied by Connellsville coal until river navigation and the railroads opened the flow in the mid-1850s. In the meantime, coal mines started to be opened a few miles up the Monongahela River at Braddock. Judge Thomas Mellon of the East End would team up with the Corey family of Braddock in developing these mines. Thomas Mellon had invested very successfully in a small mine in 1849. In 1856, he became a silent partner in J. B. Corey & Company. Corey was the true expert in coal mining the rich Pittsburgh seam and had brought in expert Welsh miners to mine the coal. The family of Thomas Dickson opened mines in nearby Swissvale and Braddock Hills. Mellon would become one of the East End's wealthiest citizens because of these early coal investments. Mellon would tell his son that he considered the coal business: "one of the best and highly respectable," coal being "the most important article in productive manufacturers."[1] The Coreys, Dicksons, Mellons, and Henry Clay Frick were on the verge of the biggest coal demand boom ever with the development of the iron making blast furnace.

It would be the combination of coke furnaces, steel puddling furnaces, foundry cupolas, and the evolution of the modern blast furnace that turned coal into gold. The development of the blast furnace would become the economic engine of the coal energy. Pittsburgh would not have its first blast furnace until 1859. By the 1850s, river transportation had opened up the Connellsville coal for Pittsburgh use. The Mahoning Valley of Ohio, however, produced most of the pig iron used in Pittsburgh finishing mills. Pittsburgh was merely a user, not an iron producer. By 1870, blast furnaces were using coke faster than it could be produced. Like Thomas Mellon, many an enterprising Pittsburgher would invest in a coal or coke shipment to turn a quick profit. A little known future East Ender, H. J. Heinz, did just that in the coal boom of the early 1870s.

A future East Ender and young Henry Clay Frick was a coke supplier to the new Pittsburgh blast furnaces. Frick needed an additional $10,000 to finance the beehive coke ovens, and he approached Judge Thomas Mellon of the banking firm of T. Mellon & Sons of Pittsburgh. Thomas Mellon, now an East Ender, had originally come from Westmoreland County and knew both Frick's Grandfather Overholt and Frick's mother, Elizabeth Overholt Frick. That tie at least got him in the door, but Frick and his company lacked a lot of experience personally for such a loan. East Ender Thomas Mellon, however, was a well-informed businessman and was in the middle of the pig iron boom in Pittsburgh. What

1   David Cannadine, *Mellon: An American Life*, (New York: Alfred A. Knopf, 2006), p. 29

Frick lacked in experience, he had plenty of hope and business sense to persuade Mellon for the loan. Mellon recognized Frick as "determined, persuasive, and an audacious entrepreneur after his own heart."[1] Mellon also had several investments in coal mines, which had been highly profitable since the 1850s. Mellon had come to believe that the future of industry would be based on coal and coke. The nation in 1871 was experiencing a major business expansion that seemed to have no end, and the future for iron, steel, and coke seemed extremely bright. For these reasons, Henry Clay Frick got his first bank loan.

What raised the old Judge's eyes was when the twenty-one year-old Frick returned in a couple of months asking for another $10,000 to build another fifty beehive ovens! Mellon now called in his friend and coalmining partner, James Corey of Braddock, to take a closer look at Frick's operations. Mellon had partnered with Corey and Thomas Dickson in the 1850s and had a number of mines in Braddock, North Braddock, Braddock Hills, and Swissvale. While they were some of the highest producing mines of the time, most of the coal was used directly in heating and fuel for stream power, lacking the quality needed for coke production. Corey himself was starting to explore the idea of coke production, but the Braddock area mines were small slant tunnels, which did not lend themselves to high volume operations. Furthermore, the Braddock coal was not of the coking quality of the Connellsville area, so it was with great interest that Corey went to look at Frick's operations. Corey would give Mellon a glowing report: "Lands good, ovens well built, manager on the job all day, keeps books evenings maybe a little too enthusiastic about pictures, but not enough to hurt; knows business down to the ground; advise making loan."[2] Frick got the loan with a 10 percent interest rate.

By 1871, Frick was an important Connellsville businessman approaching the status of his grandfather. Frick, however, was far more obsessed with work and reaching his goal of making a million. He had shown an amazing ability to work long hours in difficult environments. He did take time to socialize, and he enjoyed getting dressed up for a social event. He never fully embraced a particular religious creed, but he did readily adopt the vision of a god as a universal creator as defined by the Freemasons. He became the treasurer of the King Solomon Lodge No. 346 in Connellsville. A year later he joined the Urania Chapter No. 192 at Greensburg. By 1880 he would achieve the highest orders of the York Rite — the Orders of the Knights of the Rose Croix, the Knights of the Malta, and Knights Templar. Frick's masonry ties would be very important in getting him accepted by the Scotch-Irish. The Freemasons of the Pittsburgh area had deep roots in the founding Scotch-Irish industrial community of the area. After the Presbyterian Church, no organization had the influence of the Freemasons including men like Thomas Mellon.

Frick's second loan would be the start of a lifetime relationship with the Mellon family and bank. Just as interesting in Corey's report to Mellon were his notes on Frick's living quarters, which Corey called a "shack." Actually, the shack was a small two-room

1 Kenneth Warren, *Triumphant Capitalism*, (Pittsburgh: University of Pittsburgh Press, 1996), p.12
2 Henry Oliver Evans, *Iron Pioneer: Henry W. Oliver*, (New York: E. P. Dutton & Co., 1942), p. 123

cabin. The shack was further described as having a portion for "prints and stretches" in his "half-office and half-living room in a clapboard shack." It is amazing that a struggling businessman living in a shack was then collecting and drawing pictures. Clearly, it would augur his future of art collecting with the sons of Thomas Mellon. With the loan, he built a hundred new beehive coke ovens at Broad Ford along the Youghiogheny River, which could soon be connected by the new branch of the Baltimore & Ohio Railroad. These new ovens would become known as the "Henry Clay Works." The other older beehive ovens were on the Mt. Pleasant and Broad Ford Railroad and then were known as "Novelty Works" (later known as "Frick Works"). In 1871, Frick had 200 out of 550 coke ovens in the Connellsville area and about 1,200 nationwide. By 1872, Frick was the major investor in the partnership, and the company was the largest coke works in the Connellsville area and the largest separate coke works in America, but this would be short lived as over twenty competitors were entering the business and expanding quickly. Connellsville coke was believed by many to be a superior product. Still, Frick had not tapped into the blast furnace market successfully.

The old Pittsburgh Aristocrats looked first to their old coal fields near Pittsburgh. These fields were on the Monongahela River such as Braddock, Pennsylvania, and northeast of Pittsburgh near the Pennsylvania Railroad such as Irwin, Pennsylvania. The fields were bituminous coal but not of the metallurgical high quality of the Connellsville seam. Still, the demand for coke could not be satisfied. Even William Coleman, a partner of Carnegie, had gotten Carnegie money for fifty coke ovens to be built in 1871 at Latrobe, Pennsylvania. This "Monastery Works" was to supply Carnegie's first blast furnace project in Pittsburgh. The company had been supplying Carnegie and had also advanced money for fifty coke ovens at Turtle Creek, Pennsylvania, on the Pennsylvania Railroad, just up the Monongahela River from Pittsburgh. This location became known as Larimer Station and was managed by Carnegie's cousin, Dodd Lauder.[1] Lauder had also built his home in the East End's Homewood area at Carnegie's suggestion. The Turtle Creek operation at Larimer Station did not have the high quality of Connellsville coke and was barely profitable. Carnegie was determined to control his own sources of coal and coke for his blast furnaces, which was part of his overall strategy of vertical integration. Carnegie's trip to Europe in the 1870s to study the steel industry convinced him: "One vital lesson in iron and steel that I learned in Britain was the necessity for owning raw materials and finishing the completed article ready of its purpose."[2] Still, demand for coke was growing faster than even the optimistic forecasts that Frick had suggested, and Carnegie was in no position to control his supply of coke.

As Frick had envisioned, the business was booming, supplying coke to rolling mills, foundries, and forge shops in Pittsburgh, Chicago, Wheeling, St. Louis, and Cincinnati. The real growth for coke, however, was just beginning in Pittsburgh with it new blast furnaces. Two rival groups of Pittsburgh Pig Iron Aristocrats had started large pig iron blast

---

1 Dod or Dodd is a Scotch nickname for George, which Carnegie used
2 Andrew Carnegie, *The Autobiography of Andrew Carnegie*, (Boston: Northeastern University Press, 1986), p. 211

furnaces to supply their rolling mills. The Lucy furnace and Isabella projects battled, driving up coke demand. These furnaces started producing about 250 tons a week each; then in the summer, one of America's greatest industrial competitive battles began between the two companies. The newspapers followed the daily and weekly tonnage production as sports scores are followed today. The furnace managers made personal bets, and the local saloons became betting parlors for the workers and public. These furnaces battled back and forth, breaking new world records weekly. By the end of 1872, the furnaces were averaging 500 tons a week. In August of 1872, Isabella No. 1 overtook Lucy at a rate of 612 tons per week. In October 1873, Lucy took the record back at 653 tons per week. The furnace battle created experiments, which proved that Connellsville coke was the best coke for furnace productivity. Carnegie's partner, Henry Phipps, was an amateur chemist and metallurgist whose furnace experiments demonstrated the superiority of Connellsville coke. The battle went back and forth for years, but at the end of 1873, they were averaging 775 tons per week. At this rate, Lucy Furnace was using 100,000 tons of coke annually. A single beehive furnace could make about 450 tons of coke a year, so Lucy would require a battery of 222 coke ovens to keep it running. Carnegie's partners wanted an assured and unified supply of Connellsville coke. Only Henry Clay Frick had the capacity for such demand. With Carnegie's plans for the world's greatest steel mill, Carnegie needed to bring Frick into his partnership to assure a supply of coke. Carnegie's great Braddock steel mill in 1875 would make fortunes for Carnegie and Frick and their East End partners. The new product of steel would create even more demand. With steel production came the need for larger and more productive blast furnaces. And with steel production came more coke production.

Steel came to Western Pennsylvania in the form of a revolution. Pig iron is the major ingredient in steel, and the area was already the world's "valley of iron." Pittsburgh had the world's largest blast furnaces, producing pig iron for puddling and for foundries to cast cannon and stoves. Steel was being made in "large" quantities in the Pittsburgh area via the slow hand process of puddling. A new commercialized steel process had emerged in the 1850s known as the "Bessemer" process. By the 1870s, Bessemer steel was being made at several locations and the market was flourishing. Andrew Carnegie, a major Pittsburgh iron maker, was hesitant to move into the steel business. Carnegie would often say in his early days, "pioneering doesn't pay." It would be three East Enders who brought Carnegie in to the Bessemer steel industry — Tom Carnegie, Henry Phipps Jr., and an old Pig Iron Aristocrat, William Coleman. This group often rode the streetcar from the East End to their Pittsburgh offices discussing the future of steel. At the time, Tom Carnegie was living with his mother in the family home in Homewood. These three would eventually convince Andrew Carnegie to build the world's largest steel mill and factory in nearby Braddock.

Carnegie hesitated about investing in steel, but Tom and his friend Coleman were convinced a fortune could be made in steel. Carnegie had been slow to see the future of steel, but once he discovered it, Carnegie made steel's future his. On a European trip in 1872, Carnegie stopped in Sheffield to see the inventor, Henry Bessemer, and his marvelous steelworks. Peter Krass, Carnegie's biographer, described the moment: "As Carnegie stood before the dazzling Bessemer converter, the white ingots glowed in his eyes and heat of the blow inflated his five-foot-three-inch frame until he was as big as President Ulysses S. Grant. He felt a surge of power, of enthusiasm, of confidence that steel would indeed replace iron, and he became determined to build a majestic mill." That mill was his Edgar Thomson Works at Braddock, Pennsylvania. Named after Edgar Thomson of the Pennsylvania Railroad, the mill was to make steel rails, replacing wrought iron. Carnegie and his partners endured the Panic of 1873 to see the mill roll its first rail on September 1, 1875. Edgar Thomson Works, in turn, created a huge demand for Connellsville coke, which was owned by future East Ender Henry Clay Frick.

For Carnegie's first steel mill at Braddock, the pig iron pigs were made eight miles downriver at Lucy Furnaces; then the iron was shipped as solid pigs to the Braddock cupola furnaces to re-melt it for the Bessemer converters. Cupola furnaces used air and coke to re-melt pig iron quickly. Even when Carnegie added pig iron blast furnaces to the mill at Braddock, liquid pig often could not go direct to the Bessemer because of timing. It took Bill Jones, Braddock's plant manager of Edgar Thomson Works, to invent a mobile holding (refractory brick lined) tank to hold and mix liquid pig iron in 1879. This "Jones Mixer" allowed blast furnace operations to feed Bessemer converters direct with huge fuel savings by eliminating the cupola furnaces. Carnegie, more than anyone, realized the value of the Jones Mixer, and was at Jones's widow's door to assure the rights to it when Jones was killed in a furnace explosion in 1887. By 1885, a single day's production of steel at Edgar Thomson Works was more than all the world's puddlers could produce in a day. Bessemer steel would change the world, allowing buildings to go beyond five stories high, bridges to span gorges, and trains to carry unimaginable tonnage. The steel industry would give birth to more millionaires than any previous industry, and it would be the root of the East End's second wealthiest resident in Henry Clay Frick.

Jones would not be alone in taking Edgar Thomson Works to international prominence. The designer of the Edgar Thomson Works' blast furnaces was one of the East End's most unusual residents in Julian Kennedy. In the late 1850s, Youngtown blast furnaces in the Mahoning Valley were leading the world in the 1850s. Mahoning Valley pig iron was supplying the rolling mills of Pittsburgh and Wheeling as well as creating new rolling mills in eastern Ohio. Some of this coal was also being used in southern Ohio's Hocking Hills district. Still, the number of charcoal furnaces in southern Ohio allowed it to maintain the larger pig iron tonnage overall. Just as important was the education of the "wizard of blast furnaces," Julian Kennedy, in the Mahoning Valley. Steel demand had created a demand for pig iron in excess of Carnegie's Lucy Furnace and all he could buy on the open market. In 1879, Mahoning Valley furnace wizard Julian Kennedy was brought to Braddock to build a furnace. The basic structure was an old charcoal furnace transferred from northern Michigan. The Kloman brothers had owned the old Escanaba furnace in Northern Michigan. In 1880 this rebuilt furnace set a world record for low coke consumption. Within a year there were two furnaces setting world production records. Julian Kennedy would go on to become the world's foremost steel industry expert. Frick would later hire him to re-organize United States Steel in 1907. Kennedy is also known as the "father of Asian steelmaking," having built the first modern blast furnaces in India and China. He also built a huge mansion in the East End.

The great Braddock mill would create a group of Carnegie executives and millionaires. Charles Schwab was one of Carnegie's superstars and would become the first president of United States Steel. Bill Jones discovered Charles Schwab selling cigars at a Braddock drugstore. Captain Bill Jones hired Schwab to work at Edgar Thomson in the engineering department for a dollar a day. Schwab worked hard at Edgar Thomson Works and took an interest in steel chemistry. Carnegie's partner, Henry Phipps, was an amateur chemist who gave the young Schwab $1,000 for a home chemistry lab. Schwab moved fast to become Jones's assistant. He would become one of many young men known as the "class of 1887" that Jones hired who would eventually become presidents and vice-presidents of Carnegie Steel and United States Steel. These "boys" would include Schwab's friends Alva Dinkey (future vice-president); William Dickson (future vice-president); and William Corey (son of Mellon's old coal partner and future United States Steel president) of Braddock. Bill Jones trained these "Boys of Braddock," and they admired Jones and honored his legend for decades. These friends would go on to manage as much as 40 percent of assets of industrial America in the early 1900s. Several including Charles Schwab and Julian Kennedy would become East Enders. Andrew Carnegie would leave the East End for New York's Fifth Avenue, but he would leave a flock of East End millionaires. It would be the new Carnegie partner, Henry Clay Frick, who would become the East End's most famous and infamous resident.

Frick was a wealthy man even before he joined the Carnegie Empire and moved to the East End. Tom Carnegie did most of the coke supply negotiating for his brother and was a friend of Henry Clay Frick. Frick had also developed a friendship with East Ender Andrew Mellon, the son of Judge Thomas Mellon. Frick had moved to Pittsburgh in 1880 taking up residence at the lavish Monongahela House. He passed his early love of art to Andrew Mellon, and over the years they would become America's greatest collectors, with their paintings becoming the core of America's greatest museums. Frick also increased his reading about art, and he had found a compatriot in Andrew Mellon, another Pittsburgh bachelor. They enjoyed social events, reading, and art discussion trips to the Allegheny Mountains. They also made frequent visits to a small but growing art community in Pittsburgh. Frick and Andrew Mellon were the most eligible bachelors on the social scene in 1881. In early June at one of these social events, Clay would meet his future wife, Ada (Adelaide) H. Childs. Adelaide Childs was the daughter of Asa P. Childs of an old New England family whose roots traced back to the Plymouth colony. Asa Childs had made a fortune in Pittsburgh making and selling shoes. The Childs family had a mansion in the Oakland section of the East End at the present site of Magee Hospital. Asa had also been a leader in the Whig and Republican Parties. Adelaide's brother, Howard, was a major supplier to Frick's company store at his Connellsville mines. The couple would date for three months, with Andrew Mellon and Ada's older sister, Martha, chaperoning. They became engaged in October. Adelaide was just 22 and Frick was 32 years of age. The Childs were strong Presbyterians, but Frick had no trouble switching over (at least briefly) to the faith of Pittsburgh's greatest capitalists at the East End's Bellefield Presbyterian Church where William Holland was pastor. Holland would become one of the East End's most distinguished residents as a future president of the University of Pittsburgh and later director of the Carnegie Museum. Frick would be the first to donate to the new Presbyterian church in Pittsburgh's East End, the First Presbyterian Church of Wilkinsburg, shortly after his wedding.

The wedding of Henry Clay Frick and Ada H. Childs was considered "one of the notable of the season." It took place on December 15, 1881. Andrew Mellon was Clay's best man, and some of Pittsburgh's greatest capitalists and East Enders were present. The *Pittsburgh Gazette* reported: "The scene was one hard to describe. The spacious apartments were tastefully decorated with choice flowers and foliage plants, and soft strains of music from a hidden orchestra served to beguile the time to those waiting. Shortly after five o'clock, louder notes gave warning of the approach of the bridal party; and in a few moments the parlor was filled with elegantly dressed ladies and gentlemen. The officiating clergyman, Rev. W. J. Holland, pastor of the Bellefield Presbyterian Church, and Rev. Dr. W. H. Hornblower took their places, and the bride and groom attended by Miss Martha C. Childs, a sister of the bride, and Miss Overholt of West Overton and Messers. Jacob Justice of Philadelphia and Howard Childs of this city entered the room. The bride was attired in a rich costume of broached cream colored satin, and wore the customary long bridal veil. . . After this a sumptuous repast was served and the balance of the evening was devoted to dancing by the younger portions of the guests. Mr. and Mrs. Frick left on the Fast Line at eight o'clock for the East and will visit the principal cities before their return."[1] The honeymoon included a meeting with Andrew Carnegie at New York's Windsor Hotel. This meeting would bring Frick into the Carnegie partnership. On their return, the newlyweds looked for a home.

Tom Carnegie and Andrew Mellon suggested their neighborhood of Pittsburgh's East End., since Frick was already well acquainted with it. Frick's wealthy first partner, Edmund Ferguson, had a beautiful home in the fashionable Shadyside section, and Frick had spent many enjoyable hours there. Frick and Ferguson had been making investments in real estate in the East End for a couple of years, believing in its growth potential. The East End had a railroad station on the Pennsylvania Railroad which connected this beautiful area to downtown Pittsburgh, New York, and the South Fork Club in the Alleghenies. The East End was considered a future real estate boom and many investors were getting in on the development. In 1882 some of the first horse drawn streetcars became available in the East End, making it a suburban paradise. Frick would enjoy riding the streetcars to his downtown office. Residents could make the commute to their Pittsburgh offices by train or streetcar. Frick purchased a two-story, 23-room, Italianate and chateau-type house beside George Westinghouse's home known as 'Solitude" in April of 1882. A few years later, H. J. Heinz would move in on the other side. Frick's new house went back to 1876 and was

---

1 *Pittsburgh Gazette*, December 16, 1881, page 4

located on a 5.5-acre lot at Penn Avenue and Homewood Avenues and had originally been owned by Carnegie's partner, John Vandevort.

John Vandevort was a close friend of both Tom Carnegie and Henry Phipps. The Vandevort family was part of Pittsburgh's original industrial elite. The original house was known as "Homewood" and had a stable and greenhouse. Carnegie had originally met John Vandevort at his visits to the East End mansion of Judge Wilkins in the 1860s. In 1864, Carnegie was looking for a companion to travel to Europe with him and asked Vandevort, "If you could have three thousand dollars would you spend it in a tour through Europe with me?"[1] Carnegie included Vandevort in one of his oil investments and turned the necessary profit. In 1865 Carnegie, Henry Phipps, and John Vandevort left for Europe. Carnegie made Vandevort a partner in his steel and coke works where Vandevort met Frick. In 1882 the firm of Carnegie Brothers consisted of the following seven shares of East Enders: Andrew Carnegie with $2,737, 978; Tom Carnegie with $878,097; Henry Phipps with $878,097; David Stewart with $175,319; John Scott with $175,319; and John Vandevort with $50,000. Vandevort's success had him searching for a new home.

Frick also wanted a bigger home than Vandevort's original mansion, and Frick hired Andrew Peebles, a prominent Pittsburgh architect, to expand and bring the house up to standards of the wealthy. He named the homestead "Clayton." He had telephones installed, which were some of the earliest in Pittsburgh residences in the suburbs. The wealthy businessmen in the East End required mail to be delivered as often as five times a day. So business could be transacted, telephone calls were limited to a few miles in the Pittsburgh area. Telephone service from the East End to downtown banks was an important attribute to businessmen. The house was located on a special line of the Pennsylvania Railroad designed by George Westinghouse. The private station would allow for direct entry on the train to New York and points east. Frick had officially arrived on "millionaire's row," which stretched on Fifth Avenue from Neville Street through the Shadyside area to Point Breeze.

The Fricks had started decorating the house with furniture from many trips to New York. They purchased fine horses and carriages for the house as well. The couple found a common love of art and paintings and started what would become one of the nation's greatest art collections. Frick, the workaholic of early years, seemed to have been tamed by money and Adelaide. They had moved in at the end of January, and Adelaide gave birth to their son, Childs Frick, on March 12, 1883. Frick's friendship with Andrew Mellon deepened, as Andrew was often a dinner guest. On weekends the two might play cards and talk art into the night with Andrew staying over in the guest house. Frick established a neighborhood poker game that often included Andrew Mellon, George Westinghouse, Philander Knox, Edmund Ferguson, Benjamin Jones Jr., Henry Oliver, Tom Carnegie, Andrew Carnegie, and many of the Carnegie's partners. There were certainly nights that the men sitting around the table would represent over 60 percent of America's industrial assets.

---

1 Carnegie, p. 137

Frick and Andrew Mellon would meet for lunch at the Duquesne Club to discuss art and personal investments. Frick and Mellon were active in Pittsburgh real estate, banking, and coal companies. The two loved to invest in small coalmines, looking for potential capital appreciation. The little lunch group grew into a type of wealthy man's investment club. Andrew Mellon joined Frick in buying the Overholt Distillery which Frick's grandfather had owned. These business meetings at the Duquesne Club would always include a bottle of Old Overholt, a Monongahela rye liquor with roots going back to the area's first Scotch-Irish settlers and its early roots to capitalism. This younger luncheon core group of Frick, Mellon, Jones Jr., and Westinghouse soon became as famous as the "Room # 6" of the old Pig Iron Aristocrats. The luncheon group grew over the years and became the basis of the "Union Trust" company, a kind of investment mutual fund. It was made up of East End neighbors who worked downtown. While "Room #6" group created industrial Pittsburgh, the "Union" group created industrial America.

Andrew Mellon and Frick discussed and purchased small coal, steel, and railroad companies as well as Pittsburgh real estate. Frick was brought in on several banking deals of Mellon including Fidelity Title & Trust (a Mellon company) and Union Trust. In the early 1880s, both men put personal funds into small railroads such as Fort Smith and Western Railroad. Many railroad executives would lunch with the two young friends as well. Like both their fathers before them, they enjoyed making deals in the coal industry outside of Frick's company. Frick would be one of the first investors in George Westinghouse's natural gas company and Pittsburgh political boss William Magee's street car company. Mellon taught Frick about banking and finance, while Frick taught Mellon about art. Frick had a well-diversified personal investment strategy, and during his future partnership with Carnegie, Frick became an expert in corporate financing.

Tom Carnegie had never stopped negotiating with Frick about his coke operations, including the day of the wedding, and laid the groundwork for a final deal. Tom Carnegie even made arrangements for Frick and his new wife to meet Andrew Carnegie at his suite at the Windsor Hotel in New York. Carnegie struck a deal with Frick. The initial deal arrived at was very favorable to Frick. It was a type of partnership in which Carnegie purchased 4,500 shares of H. C. Frick Company for 11.25 percent ownership. The deal required Frick to supply all of Carnegie's coke needs, including supplying the best Connellsville coke for Carnegie's furnaces. The distribution of shares on January 31, 1882 was Frick holding 11,846; the Ferguson brothers holding 23,654; and Carnegie holding 4,500 shares. Frick would become a partner with Carnegie in his steel business as well.

In October of 1886, Tom Carnegie died of pneumonia and hard drinking. This was a real blow to Andrew Carnegie who had allowed Tom to basically run the day-to-day operations of his steel company. Frick had also lost a neighbor and ally in the steel company. Tom had remained in Pittsburgh's fashionable East End, maintaining key local political ties for Carnegie Brothers, while Andrew had moved to New York's Fifth Avenue. Carnegie had no real replacement for Tom. East Ender Henry Phipps had been a loyal friend and partner, but he lacked the executive skills needed. Now he had to turn to Frick as a possible replacement. In November Carnegie allowed Frick to become a stockholder in

Carnegie Steel. Carnegie slowly allowed Frick to enter into the organization, realizing he needed long-term help, but he feared Frick's involvement after Tom's death and developed a legal document known as the "Iron Clad Agreement." The agreement protected against an internal takeover from the partners. The agreement assured that on the death of a partner, his shares would be purchased by the partnership. It also provided a means for securing the removal of a partner. Frick proved he was up to the management task as he started a crash course on steelmaking through a reading campaign. Frick's knowledge would soon overtake that of his master.

Frick continued to meet with Andrew Mellon and other neighbors weekly for lunch at the Duquesne Club. These lunches became an exclusive club within a club. Frick became involved in business clubs such as the Union Club that combined social and business in this period, and in many ways they were natural environments for Clay Frick. The Duquesne Club, which had a group predominately of Pig Iron Aristocrats such as Henry Oliver and Frank Laughlin, was always a favorite of East End capitalists. Frick was a charter member of the Duquesne Club along with Henry Oliver, Ralph Baggaley (who had originally bank rolled George Westinghouse), and Frank Laughlin. The Duquesne Club would combine Scotch–Irish Presbyterianism, Monongahela Rye, Masonic principles, and business. It would grow into a castle of pig iron capitalism, and later steel capitalism. At the Duquesne Club, the Pig Iron Aristocrats met daily in "room number 6." These old-line industrialists included Benjamin Jones, Henry Oliver, Henry Phipps, C. B. Herron, J. W. Chalfant, and C. H. Spang. Oliver had helped found the Duquesne Club. Such meetings would border on illegal today. As a new young capitalist, Frick had to slowly work his way into the inner circle in "room number 6." His involvement was limited early on; but in 1881, Frick was a charter member of this august club of capitalists because of his coke works, which they all required. On a given day, one might see Andrew Carnegie, H. J. Heinz, George Westinghouse, Henry Clay Frick, Benjamin Jones, Thomas Mellon, Henry Phipps, John Chalfant, E. M. Ferguson, and many others at these meetings. It was often said that more pig iron was made in the bar of the Duquesne Club than in Pittsburgh's seven furnaces. Frick learned to relish the capitalistic Duquesne Club.

While most of the old Pig Iron Aristocrats had opposed the upstart steelmaker Carnegie, they formed new alliances with men like Frick and Andrew Mellon. Having moved to New York, Carnegie was considered more and more an outsider; and with Tom Carnegie's death, Carnegie lost business ties to the East End elite. Benjamin Jones and his son, Benjamin Jones Jr., were part of this new alliance. Jones was the owner of Pittsburgh's second largest steel empire of Jones and Laughlin Steel. Benjamin Jones Jr. was active with Andrew Mellon and Henry Clay Frick in their Duquesne Club lunches that evolved into Union Trust. Benjamin Jones Jr. became a director of Mellon National Bank and was also a senior member of the Republican National Committee which allowed him to coordinate the millions contributed by his East End neighbors.

In the meantime, Frick's business partners, friends, and neighbors were helping him break not only into Pittsburgh's social world, but its financial world. Frick's business partners, the Ferguson brothers, were wealthy and had connections in the banking world, as did Frick's best friend, Andrew Mellon. Frick had become a trustee of the Mozart Club which promoted the appreciation of classical music. Mrs. Frick was also involved in the Mozart Club, which often sponsored struggling musicians. Frick became a director of the Pittsburgh National Bank of Commerce. It was common for neighbors to drop in on Frick for advice on corporate finance.

In addition, he continued to expand his real estate investments in Pittsburgh's East End along with Andrew Mellon and Edmund Ferguson. In the 1880s, Frick became a major landowner in the eastern suburbs. He invested with mayor and political boss, Christopher Magee, in utilities and streetcar companies to support real estate development in the East End, although political bosses such as Magee were never part of the Duquesne Club's inner circle. Frick personally took the streetcar each day to his downtown office. Another important directorship of Henry Clay Frick was in the Philadelphia Gas Company of his neighbor, George Westinghouse. The company was supplying natural gas to homes and industries in the Pittsburgh area. Natural gas was a new concept in the 1880s, and George Westinghouse had made it competitive with coal by developing a delivery system. By 1887, natural gas would cut the usage heating coal in Pittsburgh by 30 percent.

CHAPTER 11. A BIBLICAL PLAGUE

The rich East End of Pittsburgh was as distant as the Garden of Eden for most Pittsburghers. Its wealthy neighbors had lived free of any press attention for decades. To their credit, they were a peaceful group without the wild parties of their eastern counterparts. They were big community donors to the poorer communities of the area and had built a social safety net for many. They built hospitals, churches, fire stations, libraries, and funded soup kitchens in hard times. They enjoyed the lives of earthly princes with Bourgeois virtues. Many had been founding members in an exclusive club in the mountains around Johnstown, Pennsylvania, which allowed neighbors to make a two-hour trip by Pennsylvania Railroad. The organization was known as the South Fork Fishing and Hunting Club, which would be mired in the famous Johnstown Flood of 1889. Frick had been a founding member of this rich man's resort. A dam on a small mountaintop created a lake for this fishing and sailing resort. It became known by Carnegie as the "glorious mountain," and reporters talked of sailboats on a mountain. The faulty dam that was built would burst in May of 1889, creating one of America's worst disasters. Even by today's standards, the Johnstown Flood has statistics on the level with the Twin Towers. The official death count was 2,209 with hundreds missing. Wherever the blame belonged, the press pinned it on the wealthy members of the club, and the name of Frick was the most prominent in the newspapers. Of the club members, Frick gave $5,000, Andrew Mellon gave $1,000, and Carnegie gave $10,000 to help the victims, while most of the club members gave nothing. The Johnstown Flood would forever mar the reputations of many East Enders. Unfortunately, for most of them, it was guilt by association.

Henry Clay Frick had been a charter member in the South Fork Fishing and Hunting Club near Johnstown, Pennsylvania. The Queen Anne clubhouse was actually located at Cresson Springs, forty miles from Pittsburgh, which had its own Pennsylvania Railroad Station. This was not surprising since many of the members were Pennsylvania Railroad executives. For years Cresson Springs had been a resort area for wealthy Pittsburghers such as the Carnegie family. The South Fork Fishing and Hunting Club was initially a group of young industrialists who were rising up in Pittsburgh's circle of capitalists, but it quickly spread to the old East End capitalists. The club was built on a mountain top lake known as Lake Conemaugh which had been artificially created in the 1870s by an earthen dam. This area of the Alleghenies was a short trip on the Pennsylvania Railroad from Pittsburgh, yet it offered a slice of true wilderness. The initial forest had been lumbered out to fuel the charcoal iron furnaces of the 1700s, which had made many East Enders wealthy in the 1800s. The area had returned to its former wilderness in the 1870s by this same wealth. Black bear and wildcats were still common in the area as well as eagles, geese, vultures, hawks, and turkey. Huge flocks of passenger pigeons darkened the skies for hours at a time. The Mountain View Hotel had a clientele of wealthy from Pittsburgh and Philadelphia, and well-to-do families rented cottages in the summer.

Tom and Andrew Carnegie had built a cottage in the area next to the Mountain View Hotel and the South Fork Club. The club was a bit stark, and meals were usually taken at the hotel. Carnegie had built there because he believed in the restorative powers of the air and water in the Alleghenies. He suggested that summers in the Alleghenies might help Frick's very sick daughter, little Martha, and to at least avoid common Pittsburgh complications of thyroid and pneumonia. Carnegie's cottage was a beautiful two-story home, but it did lack central heating, cooking facilities, and servant's quarters. He would often rent a small cottage for his traveling staff of a coachman, cook, maid, and a nurse for his mother. Carnegie usually made his staff available to Frick when he and his family vacationed there. The hotel offered many family events and activities and attracted the wealthiest families of Pittsburgh and Philadelphia in the summer. The industrialists could fish in the summer and hunt in the fall. The men could spend the evening at the nearby South Fork Club playing cards. Carnegie often had guests at his cottage. The nearby springs (Cresson Springs) were believed to have medicinal properties for typhoid sufferers. As a precaution, the wealthy of Pittsburgh had often fled to Cresson when typhoid epidemics hit Pittsburgh. Typhoid knew no class barriers and had taken the wife of East Ender H. J. Heinz.

The creator of the South Fork Club was Benjamin Ruff, a Pittsburgh businessman and coke broker, who purchased the mountain lake resort from Altoona's Congressman John Reilly for $2,000. He used the fact that Andrew Carnegie had a nearby vacation cottage to promote the club. Ruff pulled in a young Henry Clay Frick in 1879 for a major share. Initially, members were young and upcoming industrialists such as Frick and C. C. Hussey. Within a few years, the club had a galaxy of capitalists including well established East Enders such as Andrew Carnegie, B. F. Jones (Jones & Laughlin Steel), Edgar Thomson (Pennsylvania Railroad), Henry Phipps (Carnegie Steel), Thomas Mellon, Andrew Mellon, William Thaw, Joseph Horne (Horne department store), and Philander Knox (future Secretary of State and Senator), to name but a few. The club built a dam to improve its mountain top lake, and members built cottages near the clubhouse. The club became known as the "bosses club." David McCullough described the East End members as: "They were an early-rising, healthy, hard-working, no-nonsense lot, Scotch-Irish most of them, Freemasons, tough, canny, and without question, extremely fortunate to have been in Pittsburgh at that particular moment in history. They were men who put on few airs. They believed in the sanctity of private property and the protective tariff. . . They trooped off with their large families regularly on Sunday mornings to one of the more fashionable of Pittsburgh's many Presbyterian churches. They saw themselves as God-fearing, steady, solid people, and, for all their new fortunes, most of them were. Quite a few had come from backgrounds as humble as Carnegie's."[1] This new crowd of capitalists was a lot different than the old guard of New York's Fifth Avenue such as the Vanderbilts and Astors. The club would come to end with the failure of their mountain dam and the famous Johnstown Flood of 1889.

Nearly all of the South Fork Club members were from Pittsburgh's East End. They could take the Pennsylvania Railroad from the East Liberty or "Westinghouse" station to the club above Johnstown. The full membership list was: Edward Allen (founder of Pacific and Atlantic Telegraph); D. Bidwell (owner of mining explosives company); James Brown (treasurer of Hussey Company and future U.S. congressman); Henry Brunot (Pittsburgh lawyer); John Caldwell (Westinghouse partner); Andrew Carnegie; C. A. Carpenter (freight agent); John Chalfant (Pig Iron Aristocrat, steelmaker, and banker); George Christy (Pittsburgh lawyer); Thomas Clark (Pittsburgh lawyer); Charles Clarke (Pittsburgh investor and Frick neighbor); Louis Clarke (son, inventor, and car manufacturer); A. C. Crawford (lawyer); William Dunn (building supply executive); Daniel Euwer (lumber baron); John Ewing (real estate baron); Aaron French (manufacturer of railroad springs); Henry Clay Frick; Walter Fundebburg (dentist); James McClurg Guffey (oil and gas magnate); A. G. Harmes (machinery manufacturer); John Harper (banker); Howard Hartley (manufacturer of industrial products); Henry Holdship (industrial investor); Americus Vespecius (banker); Durbin Horne (owner of Horne department store); George Huff (industrial investor and future U.S. congressman); Christopher Hussey (owner of Hussey metal company); Lewis Irwin (lawyer); Philander Knox (lawyer, future Secretary of State, and U.S. senator); Frank Laughlin (manufacturer); John Lawrence (paint manufacturer); John Leishman (Carnegie partner); Jesse Lippincott (baking powder manufacturer); Howard Lash (president of Carbon Steel and founder of ALCOA); Sylvester Marvin (founder of National Biscuit Company — Nabisco); Frank Oliver (merchant); Walter McClintock (merchant); James McCord (hatter); James McGregor (lawyer); W. A. McIntosh (president of Cleveland Gas Coal Company); H. S. McKee (banker); Andrew Mellon; Reuben Miller (steel executive); Maxwell Moorhead (iron manufacturer); Daniel Morrell (president of Cambria Iron Company); William Mullens, Edwin Myers, H. Patton (glass manufacturer); Duncan Phillips (glass manufacturer); Henry Phipps (Carnegie partner); Robert Pitcairn (superintendent of Pennsylvania Railroad); D. W. Ranking (doctor); James Reed (law partner with Knox and future federal judge); Marvin Scaife (Pig Iron Aristocrat); James Schoonmaker (coke producer); James Schwartz (president of Pennsylvania Lead Company); Thomas Scott (branch president of Pennsylvania Railroad); Robert J. Scott

---

1 David McCullough, *Johnstown Flood*, (New York: Touchstone, 1968) p. 61

(Carnegie partner); Frank Semple (banker); Christian Shea (Horne department store executive); Moses Suydam (industrial manufacturer); F. Sweet; Benjamin Thaw (Pig Iron Aristocrat and coke and iron manufacturer); Colonel Elias Unger (hotel owner and president of club); Calvin Wells (president of Pittsburgh Forge and Iron Company); James White (manganese ore producer); John Wilcox (civil engineer); James Willock (banker); Joseph Woodwell (hardware baron, artist, and Frick neighbor); William Woodwell (hardware baron); and H. C. Yeager (dry goods).

The lake resort was built on a mountain overlooking the town of Johnstown in a deep valley. The valley gorge was one of the deepest east of the Rocky Mountains. The lake dam was built in the 1870s and had required many patches over the years. The lake was two miles long and sixty feet deep and had been stocked with black bass for the club members. There were several steam yachts and many sailboats docked on the lake. During the summer there were theatricals and musical performances. Many nationally known artists performed there in the summer. The club had not built the original dam but had repaired it over the years. There had been some concerns voiced early on about the dam and lake. The mountainous region around Johnstown, Pennsylvania, is even today prone to flash flooding when creeks might rise twenty feet in a matter of hours. The town of Johnstown had a population of 25,000 in 1889, and one of the country's largest iron works — Cambria Iron Company.

The Johnstown Flood would be a perfect storm that would create a "500 year" flood. Western Pennsylvania had just experienced a winter of record snowfall in 1888–1889, and the rains continued throughout the spring of 1889. The spring floods of the Monongahela River and Allegheny River in Pittsburgh had been some of the worst on record. Downtown Pittsburgh had suffered some of the worst floods in recent history in the spring, and many East Enders were unable to get to their downtown offices for days. The dam at South Fork had suffered problems every year, but this year the record snow and rain would put an additional strain on the dam. The rains of May 30 and May 31 had caused the streams to overflow and some localized flash flooding. The poor weather had deterred many East Enders from going to the club that week, and less than half a dozen members were at the club. The rain seemed endless that morning when the winds accelerated.

On Friday morning, May 31, things were peaking, with the river at Johnstown rising a foot an hour and filling with trees and debris. That morning, lake rain gauges recorded five inches in a couple of hours, and the lake was rising an inch every ten minutes. The water input was a century event that would test even the best engineering of the area. The citizens of Johnstown had worried for ten years about the dam and such an event. Johnstown was a main switching yard for the Pennsylvania Railroad and had towers in the hills to monitor traffic. The track up the line had been washed out, and east and westbound trains were being held with passengers. A little after noon the tower telegraphed the yardmaster that "South Fork Dam is Liable to Break: Notify the People of Johnstown to Prepare for the Worst."[1] Amazingly, no one at the telegraph office took it seriously, although the

---

1 McCullough, p.87

downpour was the hardest many had seen. Creeks and runs that were usually only a few inches deep were now up to four feet deep. Around three o'clock in the afternoon the dam burst, and 20 million tons of water was unleashed on the Conemaugh Valley and Johnstown. It took 40 minutes for the lake to drain. The wave crashed into Johnstown like a tidal wave. The valley passage from South Fork to Johnstown was a narrowing gorge of about twelve miles, which created a wave 75 feet high! The wave reached Johnstown 57 minutes after the dam collapsed and it took ten minutes to fully pass through Johnstown. The waiting trains full of passengers, many of them immigrants, were overwhelmed. The disaster would result in over 2,200 deaths with many others missing. The Johnstown Flood remains number 3 on the list of U.S. natural disasters (Galveston Hurricane of 1900 is number 1, Hurricane Katrina is number 6, and San Francisco Earthquake is number 7). It remains America's worst flood. Almost 1,600 homes were completely destroyed. The statistics were just as grim with 98 children losing both parents, almost 400 children under the age of ten died, and 99 entire families killed by the wave. Many of the bodies were never found, and over 700 bodies were unidentified. After the killer wave, oil tanks caught fire, and the town burned for another day. The stories of death were unbelievable, including stories of a whirlpool of screaming men, women, and children. The property damage would reach $17 million.

Word of the catastrophe reached Pittsburgh within a few hours, even with telegraph lines down. It was America's largest natural disaster at the time. Reporters from all over the nation rushed to Johnstown. Surviving townspeople pointed to the South Fork dam and its mysterious capitalist members — a perfect story. Like Hurricane Katrina of 2005, the initial headline was "10,000 Dead." This was a number that no one could image at the time. A few days later the *New York Sun* headline — "CAUSE OF THE CALAMITY — The Pittsburgh Fishing Club Chiefly Responsible" appeared. The *New York Times*' headline of June 9, 1889 was "An Engineering Crime — The Dam of Inferior Construction — According to Experts." Such reporting launched a search for culprits. As the reporters searched for the club's highly secret membership, the name Henry Clay Frick stood out; but it would take years for all the names to be revealed. Frick's name had been on the incorporation papers, while most members were never noted in print records. A total of 61 members paid a membership fee of $800 in 1889. Carnegie's membership remained secret for another year.

The night the dam broke, the East End members of the club met at the East End home of Charles Clarke, and a Pittsburgh Relief Committee was proposed. It is believed that the members had taken a secrecy pact that night before looking at the aid needed. An executive committee was founded that included Henry Clay Frick, Henry Phipps, Robert Pitcairn, and James B. Scott. The committee dispatched an army of volunteers, which included Edgar Thomson Works steel plant manager, Bill Jones, and 300 Braddock steel workers. Scott and Pitcairn arranged endless rail cars to deliver supplies. With Frick's approval, Jones shut down Edgar Thomson at a cost of $15,000 a day to assure fresh relief workers. The Pennsylvania Railroad sent special trains of aid. But even as the estimates approached 2,000 dead, the pictures of destruction were overwhelming.

Frick worked his financial magic as well. The money flowed from many sources to the Pittsburgh Relief Committee. H. C. Frick Company donated $5,000, and Carnegie Company donated $10,000 (about $185,000 today). The Pennsylvania Railroad gave $5,000, and T. Mellon & Sons gave $2,000. The South Fork Fishing and Hunting Club gave $3,000 and emergency goods. Robert Pitcairn held a meeting at the Pittsburgh's Old City Hall and collected $48,000 in less than an hour. Citizen collections from cities were impressive — Pittsburgh $560,000; Philadelphia $600,000; New York $516,000; and Boston $150,000. Capitalists added tens of thousands such as Benjamin Thaw, $3,000; John Astor, $2,500; Jay Gould, $1,000; George Westinghouse, $1,000; and Joseph Pulitzer, $2,000. The New York Stock Exchange gave $20,000; Macy & Company, $1,000; and Tiffany, $1,000. Foreign aid came as well with Germany giving $30,000 and the London Stock exchange giving $1,000. Buffalo Bill Cody held a benefit show at the Paris World's Fair, which Carnegie was attending at the time. School children added thousands in pennies and nickels. It was the first major relief effort by the American Red Cross; in all, $3.7 million (about $68 million today) in cash was donated from over 20 countries. Non-cash donations were just as impressive with 20,000 hams from Cincinnati and sixteen carloads of flour from Minneapolis. In general, food and supplies clogged the rails and roads, and the army was needed to distribute the supplies. Unfortunately, the heroic work of the East End executive committee was lost in the search to blame.

The blame came to rest on the rich club members. For all their crimes, this was the one they probably had the least fault in, however. The Johnstown Flood filled the papers for months. Myths were created as hundreds of reporters searched for news stories. Bodies were said to have been found floating in Pittsburgh 40 miles away. The publicity was one thing the East Enders hated. Their silence was often interpreted as uncaring. A number of suits were filed, but none proved successful. The Carnegie and Club lawyer Philander Knox always argued that there was no negligence, only an act of God. History continues to research the question of involvement, but the only issue appears to be the silence of the club members. Flood historian David McCullough may have best summarized the issue: "For to prove that any living member of the club had been personally negligent would have been extremely difficult. And in all fairness, it is quite likely, as the *Boston Post* suggested, that the clubmen themselves knew no more about the structural character of the dam than did anyone in Johnstown."[1] The biggest problem for the club remained its secrecy and silence. It took years for the press to forget Johnstown. The media was now interested in the industrialists of the East End and its ties to big business. Carnegie Steel executives came under new scrutiny. Any problem reported in the future would often reference their connection to the Johnstown Flood. The members were cleared in court cases over damages, but the press never relented in its blame. Even an awesome Carnegie Library for Johnstown did nothing to remove their guilt.

The Flood would be one of two events that would haunt Henry Clay Frick for his entire life. The year 1890, however, was a prosperous one for East Enders. Frick had launched

---

1 McCullough, p. 259

a renovation of Clayton in the late 1890, using Pittsburgh's best-known architect, Fredrick Osterling, and decorator, A. J. Kimbal. Osterling had designed a number of East End homes including H. J. Heinz's "Greenlawn." The Frick project began in the winter of 1891, and the Fricks moved to a temporary home in Shadyside. Frick's library and office were to be expanded but so were the children's rooms. A solarium and portico were added. The renovations cost $131,300. The house had some of the first machine-made carpets, curved glass windows, and tooled leather as well as some machine-lathed wood decorations. One of the more interesting improvements was the use of aluminum foil as a wall covering. Aluminum foil at the time was novel and as expensive as gold. The music room had velvet on the walls, and the dining room was paneled with mahogany with a dado of painted leather. The Mellons were investing millions in the production of aluminum, but this special foil came from France. Later a bowling alley was added to the cottage house, turning it into a playhouse for Frick's children.

The real struggle for Frick had been the illness of his youngest daughter, Martha. Martha's illness tore Frick apart for years. She continued to worsen during 1891. A famous homeopathic doctor and neighbor, Doctor McClelland, began visiting her daily, but there was little that could be done. In the spring of 1891, Frick had taken the children to New York to shop on the "Pittsburgher" express to New York. Frick bought Martha a tricycle and Helen a doll, but Martha would soon be unable to ride the tricycle. Frick tied to cheer up the children; but Martha's slow decline was heart breaking for the whole family. As her condition worsened, Martha had the full-time assistance of a caretaker. On a short walk to Philander Knox's home with Martha, Frick noticed the limp had returned. Adelaide and little Helen became extremely anxious. For Frick, early summer of 1891 was the most difficult as the decline could be seen daily. Martha Sanger described the struggle: "As June warmth began to turn into July heat, the final stages of Martha's long, slow death from peritonitis and septicemia began. Bacteria had claimed Martha's abdominal cavity and bloodstream. Her vital organs, starved for nutrients and oxygen, were now on the verge of collapsing, one after another, like dominos."[1] Frick and Adelaide established a nightly routine of sleeping in Martha's room. Frick stayed in the room to around three o'clock every morning. During the day he commuted to the Pittsburgh office.

In late June Doctor McClelland and Carnegie recommended that Martha visit Cresson Springs and the Mountain House Hotel near the old South Fork wreckage. Cresson Springs had always been hailed for its restorative air and water. The Carnegie cottage was prepared for Frick as well as four rooms at the hotel. A full staff of servants, nurses, doctors, and helpers were brought in. They remained there through July, with Frick commuting by the Pennsylvania Railroad to the Pittsburgh office. Frick would bring Martha a gift every time he returned to the cottage. He took the fragile child outside to enjoy the fresh air and her dog, Brownie. In late July, Carnegie sent for his personal doctor, Jasper Garmany from New York's Bellevue Hospital, but there was little that could be done. The struggle would end on July 28, 1891, with the family around and Frick holding his daugh-

---

1 Sanger, *Henry Clay Frick*, p. 138

ter's hand as she passed. Robert Pitcairn sent his private railroad car to return the family to the East End. The family was devastated and accepted an invitation of neighbor and old friend, E. M. Ferguson, to stay at his vacation home on the Connecticut coast. Carnegie had even suggested a European holiday at his castle, but Frick needed to return to work.

The impact on Frick could be seen throughout his entire life. Martha was buried in Homewood Cemetery, about a tenth of a mile from Clayton, and Frick had the trees cleared so his could see the grave from Clayton's second floor. Frick had to spend more time with young Helen, who may have felt the impact most. He would commission sculptors and painters to recreate Martha in art throughout the years. Mrs. Frick never fully recovered from the depression that struck her after the death of Martha. Frick returned to his routine of taking the streetcar to his office and returning home for a family dinner. Helen, the older daughter, remembered how the once jocular father changed to one of quiet thought at the dinner table.

CHAPTER 12. THE BEST OF TIMES AND THE WORST OF TIMES

The mid-1880s to early 1890s were probably some of the best years for East Enders such as Frick, Mellon, Westinghouse, Pitcairn, Jones, Knox, and many others. These rising titans of industry were approaching mid-career with America on the eve of its greatest expansionary period. The East End had beautiful but not extravagant homes. The skies were clear again thanks to Westinghouse's national gas systems. Children enjoyed the rural nature of the suburb. There were still farms and farm animals for their enjoyment, and endless bridle paths for horses and ponies. Families like the Fricks and Westinghouses often had weekend picnics in the nearby vast woods that would become Frick Park, Swisshelm Park, Highland Park, Schenley Park, and Swissvale. Westinghouse even institutionalized the weekend family picnic by giving his employees Saturday off and often inviting them to join his family picnic. Those picnic baskets included "Marvin's Upper Crust" biscuit manufactured by East Ender Sylvester Marvin. The "Upper Crust" was a picnic cracker. His bakery business in 1888 was the largest in the United States, and Marvin was known as the "Edison of Manufacturing" for his innovative automation of the bakery business. Marvin's company became The National Biscuit Company (Nabisco).

Another common item in the picnic baskets was a jar of Heinz pickles. Heinz didn't invent pickles, but he was one of the first to put them in glass bottles in the 1880s. Relishes such as chow-chow were popular on Marvin's biscuits. The late 1880s saw a major expansion of the Heinz product line into relishes. Relish is a mixture of chopped vegetables or fruit in a pickling sauce. Relishes go back to the late 1700s, but they had gained popularity in Victorian picnic baskets. Chow-chow was a relish that Heinz had been producing since the 1870s. In 1885 Heinz started producing a celery relish. At the time, celery was an extremely popular vegetable believed to have many health benefits. Celery sauce had been one of Heinz's first products, so it was an easy expansion to other celery-based products such as pickled celery pieces and celery relish. This product was typically more American than other competing products in that it was based on sweet pickles. In 1888, Heinz started the production of a sour pickle relish known as "Piccalilli." Piccalilli was a mixture of green tomatoes, gherkin pickles, cabbage, cauliflower, onions, turmeric, mustard, vinegar, and spices, having a bright yellow color. Legend has its origin with Napoleon's chef. Heinz started the production of "India Relish" and "Chutney." These were closer to the true Indian dishes of Asia. Indian pickles were much different than those of America and Europe. Pickles in India could be very spicy and were often stored in oil. Pickle relishes in India contained a similar mix of American relishes with additional additives of sesame oil, lemon juice, ginger, and garlic. Chopped mangoes were also in most Indian relishes. Chutney is similar except with the addition of chili peppers and tomatoes. Heinz introduced his "India Relish" in 1889 and his "Tomato Chutney" in 1890. His India relish was a secret recipe but was close to that of Indian relishes with additions of cinnamon and allspice. The basic Heinz ingredients were pickles, green tomatoes, cauliflower, white onions, red bullnose peppers, vinegar, celery, and mustard seed. Interestingly, Heinz baked beans (a common picnic item today) was popular only in England in the 1880s among the wealthy as an exotic food.

Recreation became important as the families grew. Frick built a special playhouse for his kids, which included a bowling alley. The 1880s saw a surge in neighborhood bicycling with many clubs being formed in the East End. Horse trails became overpopulated with cyclists. In the winter, ice skating and horse-drawn sleighs were the mode of recreation. Outdoor recreation even became big business with Christopher Magee and his Public Works Director, Edward Bigelow, planning an extensive park system for the East End to serve Pittsburgh. This would lead to a recreation growth of the 1890s, starting with the East End "Casino," which was the nation's largest ice skating rink and dance center. After a fire, Christopher Magee replaced it with "Duquesne Gardens" to attract Pittsburgh's middle class to the East End. As an ice arena, it was the world's largest, modeled after a 20,000-square foot one in Paris. The Gardens was also for concerts and sporting events. It was one of the first places outside Canada where hockey became a popular sporting event. It was always a first class event palace for the local wealthy and Pittsburgh's middle class who rode on Magee's Duquesne Traction Company street cars to reach the Gardens. Political bosses, Christopher Magee and William Flinn, would develop Highland and Schenley Parks as well as the zoo and aquarium.

In 1900, Howard Heinz, H. J. Heinz's middle son and heir to the corporate throne, met a beautiful graduate of the elite Ogontz School for Young Ladies in Philadelphia at a skating party of a mutual friend. The skating party was at Magee's Duquesne Gardens. Elizabeth "Betty" Granger Rust was the daughter of Charles Rust, a Saginaw, Michigan, lumber baron. She seemed a perfect fit for the Heinz family with her reputation as an outstanding horsewoman. The wedding on October 3, 1906 was one of the nation's noted social events. The best man was Henry Sloane Coffin, a Yale friend of Howard and heir to the Sloane Furniture Company of New York. The ceremony took place in Saginaw, but H. J. shut down the plant in Pittsburgh for a party for all his employees. The employee reception and dinner was held in the company auditorium which was decorated with

East End flowers. Part of H. J.'s $100,000 wedding gift was used to build a home in the rich Pittsburgh suburb of Sewickley. After a brief honeymoon in Virginia, the couple took a two-month trip to Europe.

The neighborhood itself had blossomed into a true Garden of Eden with many large gardens and conservatories. Frick raised world-class orchids and roses, and H. J. Heinz grew pansies and chrysanthemums. Richard Mellon's garden at 6500 Fifth Avenue could rival Versailles. Neighborhood competitions were held in the 1890s. Heinz also had trees transported from all over the area for his "Greenlawn" mansion grounds. Not to be out-done, Westinghouse planted exotic trees such as Siberian elm, gingkoes, and amur cork at neighboring "Solitude." Henry Clay Frick often set up neighborhood flower contests with $50 awards. Neighbors always supplied flowers for weddings, parties, and major social events. The East End formed a number of flower and plant societies. Henry Clay Frick even became an expert mushroom grower. The neighborhood conservatories had many exotic flowers and exotic trees, and these were opened to the public on weekends. Middle class visitors would come by streetcar to enjoy the grounds of their wealthy neighbors. Eventually in 1893, East Ender and Carnegie partner, Henry Phipps, built Phipps Conservatory for the public in the East End.

Heinz added 12 conservatories and stables, both of which he continued to expand over the years. In his later years, he opened these conservatories to the public. The large estate allowed him to purchase Shetland ponies for all the kids. Heinz had numerous horses for riding as well as for his carriages. He replaced the hardwood floors and added stained glass windows throughout. Heinz commissioned George Carpenter, who had worked on the Waldorf-Astoria Hotel in New York, to paint several murals throughout the house. He renovated the fourth floor to be a museum of his curios and watch collection. He added additional space for his evolving collection of hand carved ivories and curios. He also opened his museum of curios to the public. Expensive tapestries were purchased to cover the walls. The mansion included a stable and tennis court. Heinz was the envy of one of America's richest neighborhoods.

Part of William Magee's East End neighborhood beautification program included the development of Schenley Park in 1896. The main part of Schenley Park was over 300 acres donated by Mary Schenley. The park entrance was bordered by the Carnegie Museum and Phipps Conservatory. City director Edward Bigelow and British landscape architect, William Falconer, designed it. At the time, the park was considered one of the nation's finest. It included the world's first permanent electrified fountains which included dancing waters. George Westinghouse had been personally involved in its set up, and modeled it after the fountains of the 1893 Chicago Fair. Westinghouse also helped with a fully lit music pavilion using 189 incandescent lights, another first. Today, Schenley Park has a beautiful memorial to George Westinghouse built by his employees at the original "Lily Pond." The park included ponds, a man-made lake, and pools as well as extensive bridle paths. The Oval Racetrack, a half-mile track, was where the East End elite such as H. J. Heinz raced their thoroughbred horses. In the early 1900s, a young Howard Heinz formed automobile races at the Oval, one of a kind in the nation. Henry Clay Frick helped add a small private golf course and club to the park, but the city won a court case to make it the public Schenley Park Golf Links in 1910. The park was clearly America's finest city park. A nine-foot bronze statue of Edward Bigelow was erected in 1895, proclaiming him the "Father of City's Parks."

Schenley Park had the city's first zoo, but in 1899 the 350 animals were sent to the other East End park. The larger Highland Park was also part of the East End and the land had been set aside since 1895 by Edward Bigelow. Highland Park was centered on two large reservoir lakes in the East End. One entrance was at the William Flinn mansion on Highland Avenue. The park encompassed the lands of Alexander Negley and oil pioneers — Charles Lockhart and James McCully. Both Schenley and Highland Parks created thousands of middle class riders for streetcar companies owned by Andrew Mellon, Henry Clay Frick, George Westinghouse, Christopher Magee, and William Flinn. These streetcar lines tied in the middle class surrounding neighborhoods but not the steel mill neighborhoods. However, in the 1890s, the working-class citizens did use the parks on weekends. Later the Mellons expanded city's streetcar system and opened these amazing parks to all Pittsburghers.

The other city park that bordered the East End was the extensive Frick Park, which was developed in the early 1900s. Frick Park was a large tract of land going from the back of the Frick mansion to the Monongahela River. Its dense woods were the playgrounds of the world richest citizens. The extensive woods were a rich nature preserve. These woods defined Childs Frick's career as a famous paleontologist. Henry Clay Frick purchased a small shotgun for Childs Frick, and Childs took up taxidermy. He loved to trap and keep animals at Clayton including foxes, squirrels, and snakes. His parents purchased additional pets such as a baby alligator. Childs was a fun loving kid who pursued his own science interests over those of school. He collected the famous seashell fossils common in the Pittsburgh area Ames limestone deposits in the park. They were the same limestone fossils that had interested a young Andrew Carnegie in natural science. Childs formed a group of cadets who paraded and marched. They played "cowboys and Indians" in the woods with many famous sons and daughters. The Heinz, Hunt, Reed, and Westinghouse kids also enjoyed horse riding in this deep ravine cut by nine-mile run. It was a young Helen Frick inspired by the conservationism of Teddy Roosevelt, who asked her father to make it a park in 1904. In his will Henry Clay Frick left an amazing two million dollar bequest for Frick Park.

Childs Frick and other East End kids also found much inspiration in the Carnegie Museum in the East End's Oakland section, only a short streetcar ride away. On November 5, 1895, Carnegie opened what he called the "cathedral of civilization" in Oakland. Being on the main street car lines, it was perfectly set up to readily serve the East End neighborhoods and downtown. Carnegie, a proud Scot, chose Guy Fawkes Day to showcase his $25 million achievement. Guy Fawkes had tried to blow up the British parliament in 1605. The great Italian Renaissance building originally housed a 250,000-volume library with a science, art, and music wing. It would make the East End the cultural center of Pittsburgh. The new director of the museum was the East End's most accomplished Renaissance man

— William J. Holland. Holland was a minister, naturalist, painter, linguist, chancellor of Western University of Pennsylvania, and renowned lepidopterist. As minister of Bellefield Presbyterian Church, William Holland had performed the marriage ceremony for a young Henry Clay and his bride. Holland himself had married the daughter of East End iron manufacturer, John Moorhead, who had one of Oakland's largest mansions. Like many East Enders, the Hollands summered in Cresson near the South Fork Club, where they got to know Andrew Carnegie.

Holland's collection of Lepidoptera and his *Butterfly Book* were world renowned. East End iron masters Henry Oliver and Henry Phipps were financial supporters of the book. As Director of the Carnegie Museum, he would make it the world's showplace for dinosaurs. With Carnegie's money, Holland backed one of the nation's greatest dinosaur digs in the American west. The largest dinosaur and a new species was found and named *Diplodocus carnegii* in 1899, which captured the imagination of the world. Newspapers all over the world ran endless articles on "Dippy." The great dinosaur would eventually be featured in the Dinosaur Hall of the Carnegie Museum in 1907. Carnegie, however, had cast copies made and gave them to the British Museum, the Russian Museum, as well as casts to museums in Spain, Germany, and Mexico.

The East End of the 1890s was a beautiful Eden even with the increasing smoke and soot of the mills. The Carnegie executives in the neighborhood were at the peak of their careers. Westinghouse and Frick were dedicated neighbors until business would force them to New York. The 1890s started with a recession that would lead to depression. The so-called Panic of 1893 created the greatest economic setback the nation had seen. The Panic had started as a financial crisis in New York but had moved within months to cancel the enormous backlog of steel orders. Like most railroad centers, Pittsburgh was filled with a new class of unemployed known as "Hobos." Hobo towns lined the great railroads leading into the city, and the streets were filled with beggars. Immigrants in tent cities struggled to stay warm and eat. The rich suburbs lived in constant fear of looting or attack. The city had emptied its coffers to supply relief. Andrew Carnegie kicked in an equal amount of about $125,000, and other capitalists including Frick chipped in another $100,000. The money was used for city work projects. Mrs. Frick and the East End wives became active in children agencies to help the poor children of the city. Still even with this outreach, their wealth had a way of isolating them. Years earlier, Carnegie had left the East End for New York's Fifth Avenue and had clearly lost his touch with the reality of the men who worked in his Pittsburgh steel mills, but he still sent large sums of money to Pittsburgh charities.

H. J. Heinz poured in more time in the development of children's Sunday schools. Even in his darkest business days, Heinz would show up to teach on Sundays; and when traveling, he always found a Sunday school to visit. Heinz gave of his time, talent, and treasure. He belonged and was an executive director of the Allegheny County Sabbath School Association, the Pennsylvania State Sabbath School Association, the International Sunday School Association, and the World Sunday School Association. He always combined Sunday school visits with his world travel; and in later years, he traveled the world to spread the application of Sunday school. Heinz tried to stay close to the people he worked with, but he knew wealth distorted one's perspective. He even lamented the days when he could visit his huge north side complex and know everyone's name. During this recession, Heinz often welcomed street beggars to his company lunchroom, remembering how the last recession had bankrupted him personally and how he lacked money to feed his own family.

Mr. and Mrs. Frick became financially involved with the social outreach project of Kingsley House in these tough times. Mrs. Frick and her daughter, Helen, became personally involved as well. Kingsley House was the ideal type of Frick charity. It was the idea of Frick's pastor, George Hodges at Calvary Episcopal Church, and Father Sheedy of Pittsburgh's St. Mary's Church in the poorest area. Kinsley House was a type of YMCA and YWCA, both of which Hodges was active in along with George Westinghouse. The purpose of the house was to address the "ethnic, social, and economic conditions" of children. The Kingsley House provided clubs for youth as well as a variety of classes. Classes stressed skills for future employment such as typewriting, needlework, and manual arts. It had a kindergarten for poor children and a nursery for working mothers. The Kinsley House inspired neighbor, H. J. Heinz, to open a similar operation (the Sarah Heinz House) on the North side of Pittsburgh. Originally Kinsley House was located at 1707 Penn Avenue but moved closer to the city on the suggestion of Mrs. Frick. Frick donated $50,000 (almost $1 million today) to purchase a new house and expand it. Mrs. Adelaide Frick often took young Helen Frick to help distribute clothes and food. One tradition was the Christmas party for orphaned girls, which was a tradition that Helen Frick carried on for decades. Frick was particularly enthusiastic about funding these Christmas parties. He served on the Pittsburgh Free Dispensary Board, which was like a local emergency room for children and young mothers. Throughout his life, Frick made quiet donations of expensive equipment to area hospitals in memory of Martha. Another charity which Frick quietly supported his whole life was the Salvation Army. This would be the hallmark of Frick's type of giving (as well as most East Enders) as opposed to Carnegie's press releases calling attention to his giving.

Westinghouse was expanding the YMCA and its social services to help poor boys. Westinghouse and his friend, Ohio Congressman William McKinley, were national supporters of the YMCA. Westinghouse infused money into YMCA programs to integrate immigrants into American society. These efforts included English language courses, citizenship courses, and tax courses. Like his neighbor H. J. Heinz, Westinghouse did everything he could to keep employees on the payroll in the downturn. Westinghouse believed this was philanthropy. Carnegie, on the other hand, continued to open libraries as thousands were laid off in the slow period. Many of them lived in the slums of Braddock and Homestead and would argue that the East Enders didn't do enough for the welfare of their workers.

During 1892, Carnegie had two companies — Carnegie Brothers & Company with Frick at the head and Carnegie, Phipps & Company headed by East Ender William Abbott. Frick's flagship at Carnegie Brothers was Edgar Thomson Works, which mainly produced rails. Abbott's flagship plant was Homestead, which produced structural steel and steel plate but had suffered endless labor problems. While the companies had the same ownership, the administration of the two was separate. Carnegie had learned to count on Frick's advice while William Abbott had lost favor. By the end of 1891 with Frick's help, Carnegie had completed months of study about bringing the two companies together. Carnegie wanted to get Frick in charge for the upcoming negotiations with the Homestead union. In January of 1892, the deal was cut to bring the assets of Carnegie Brothers and Carnegie, Phipps & Company together as the Carnegie Steel Company. H. C. Frick Company was kept as a separate company with Thomas Lynch as General Manager. Frick would become CEO of all, and Abbott would be removed from active management. Charles Schwab would be General Superintendent of Edgar Thomson, John Potter General Superintendent of Homestead, and Thomas Morrison (a Carnegie relative) General Superintendent of Duquesne. The partners had evolved over the years as Carnegie rewarded his key managers with shares. The shares and partners (most of which were East Enders) of Carnegie Steel were as follows:

Andrew Carnegie	$13,833,333
Henry Phipps	$2,750,000 [oldest partner and boyhood friend]
Henry Clay Frick	$2,750,000
George Lauder	$1,000,000 [a cousin of Carnegie]
Henry Singer	$500,000 [joined when Carnegie bought American Bessemer]
Henry Curry	$500,000 [Manager of Lucy Furnace, joined as partner in 1886]
Henry Borntraeger	$500,000 [started as clerk in 1878, mgr. 33 Street Mill, joined in 1886 as partner]
John Leishman	$500,000 [joined in 1886, became US ambassador]
William Abbott	$250,000 [started as employee in 1871, partner in1886]
Otis Childs	$250,000 [Frick's brother-in-law]
John Vandevort	$200,000 [one of the original six and friend of Tom Carnegie]
Charles Strobel	$166,666 [Carnegie bridge designer from Carnegie's Keystone Bridge — started as employee in 1872]
F. T. Lovejoy	$166,666 [Carnegie Company secretary, joined in 1881]
Patrick Dillon	$166,666 [started for Carnegie in sales]
William Blackburn	$125,000 [started as sales clerk, became regional sales agent]
William Palmer	$83,333 [sales manager]
Lawrence Phipps	$83,333 [Henry Phipps's nephew]
Alexander Peacock	$83,333 [Carnegie sales Vice-president]
J. O. Hoffman	$83,333 [Carnegie sales agent]
John Fleming	$83,333 [Carnegie sales agent]
James Simpson	$62,500

Henry Bope $27,777 [started as sales clerk and worked up to agent]

Pittsburgh and its nearby river valleys had gone through a tremendous change with the opening of Carnegie's first steel mill in Braddock in 1875. Tens of thousands of immigrants had flooded western Pennsylvania to man the steel mills. These immigrants poured in because of a labor shortage created by the massive industrial boom. Henry Clay Frick had been one of the earliest to bring in eastern European immigrants to man his coal mining operations. Coal and steel companies advertised and sent agents to Europe to recruit workers. The workers came because of the higher pay in American factories; yet to native workers, these immigrants seemed to work for little pay. Initially many immigrants were young and single, hoping to work but a few years and return home or at least send money home. They packed into poor housing to save money; still conditions were often better than what they had known in Europe.

These immigrant workers took the lowest level unskilled jobs in the industrial hierarchy. The unions, which represented the skilled workers, had nothing to do with these immigrants. The union denied them membership, and the union workers often isolated them socially. They were often in no-man's land in strikes. If they supported the union, they lost work and received nothing in the pay raises won in the strikes. Often they broke into better jobs by becoming strikebreakers. They rushed in as technology created a demand for more unskilled workers and displaced skilled workers. In the early era of nineteenth century, the union workers tended to be highly paid crafts workers, being paid far above the national average wage. These unionized crafts and skilled workers, however, were increasingly becoming the minority as technology eliminated skilled crafts. This is where the workers at Homestead found themselves in 1892. The Homestead Strike has now become legendary. From its earliest reporting, it was viewed as an act in a morality play with black and white hats; a struggle of good versus evil; rich, uncaring East Ender Henry Clay Frick against the poor immigrant workers. In reality, the unskilled immigrant workers were actually caught in the middle of the titanic struggle between the crafts union and management.

From Carnegie and Frick's standpoint, the rules and control of the crafts union was unacceptable. The crafts union set the working rules, the wage scale, and membership. Carnegie in steel and Frick in coal had a long history of union battles. For Carnegie, it was more his obsession with lower costs; and for Frick, it was more about management control. They were not alone in their hatred and fear of unions. The growing population of European immigrants was anti-union or neutral since they feared the union's policy of restricting immigrant labor. In fact, many of these immigrants as well as American blacks had come to Pittsburgh as strikebreakers. Even worker-friendly East End owners such as Westinghouse and Heinz harbored the same hatred of organized unions; and in general, German, Welsh, Scotch, British, and native born Pittsburghers at all class levels were anti-union. Industrial crafts workers represented the core support. The difference was the treatment at the Westinghouse and Heinz plants. Workers had little motivation to form a union. Unions in America were not a socialist movement as in Europe but one of necessity to protect jobs, wages, and control of the craft. To some degree, American crafts unions were really fighting the advance of technology and the decline of the crafts system. Lastly, the great Homestead Strike was a political battle for the votes of the union workers.

Ignoring over 2,000 unskilled immigrant workers, the Homestead battle centered on the wages of about 300 skilled workers. These skilled workers made about $2,500 year (compared to $425 a year for the average American worker and $200 a year for the un-skilled Homestead worker) based on the tons of steel processed. The company demands were: (1) reduce the minimum sliding wage scale in the rolling mill to $22 per ton, which could mean a pay cut as high as 30 percent; (2) reduce the tonnage rate paid in the open-hearth furnace departments; and (3) change the contract date from June 30 to December 31. The justification for the tonnage rates was the installation of new equipment, which boosted production. The date change was to put the company in a more favorable posi-tion for contract negotiations because workers would not have their gardens for food and would need fuel for heating. The unwritten goal was to eliminate the Amalgamated Union because of its control and work rules. Carnegie wrote to Frick to note this strategy: "As I understand matters at Homestead, it is not only wages paid, but the number of men required by Amalgamated rules which makes our labor rates so much higher than those in the East. . . The chances are, you will prepare for a struggle in which case, the notice (i.e. that the works are henceforth to be non-union) should go up promptly on the morning of the 25th [June]"[1] Frick was just as interested in getting his foreman system to replace the master craftsman as the managers of the operation. Still, Frick and Carnegie seemed to waffle on the idea of breaking the union as the contract expiration date approached. Frick seemed more willing to deal, sensing that breaking the union might be unachievable.

The dollar amounts earned by Homestead workers ranged from about $12.00 a day (skilled) to $1.40 day (laborer) in the operating departments. The highest tonnage union man was paid $3,280.00 a year and the lowest $378.00 a year. The average skilled worker at Homestead made $50.00 per week ($2,500.00 per year); the average American workers made $8.50 a week ($425.00 a year).[2] An average unskilled laborer at Homestead made around $200.00 a year. A laborer made from 75 cents to a $1.40 a day or around $180.00 a year. A foreman made about $6.00 to $8.00 a day or $1,900.00 a year. The average work days for the year were 270 days, and the average day was twelve hours. Poverty level for a family was considered $300.00. Entry into the middle class probably required an annual salary of $800.00. Walt Whitman put the middle class test at $1,000.00 per year. The press framed the Homestead Strike as labor against capital; but in reality only the highest workers would benefit, and these were some of America's highest paid workers. There was a clear aristocracy in the union jobs. Rollers in the slab and billet mills made around $9.00 a day ($2,400.00 a year); a melter in the open-hearth furnaces made $4.14 to $3.10 a day ($1,200.00 a year to $850.00 a year). First helpers in the open hearth made $2.80 a day. The lowest man on the crew made $1.40 a day or $380.00 a year. The proposed contract

1 Schreiner, p. 73
2 Richard Sheppard, "Homestead Steel Strike of 1892," *Susquehanna*, February, 1988

at Homestead said nothing of the laborer making less than a dollar a day. To the tonnage workers, the proposed cut was around 20 to 30 percent, a significant cut to be sure. For Carnegie, the cut was the saving of a few cents a ton of steel rolled, making it a public relations nightmare.

One of the bigger problems for the Homestead strike threat was the build-up of national press in Pittsburgh. This was being billed as a momentous clash between labor and management, and reporters poured into Pittsburgh that summer. The buildup had started a year earlier at the steel union's national convention, predicting they would make their stand at Homestead. It was estimated that most of the available rooms in Pittsburgh were taken up with reporters. Socialists and radicals of the period were attracted to the build-up of tension in Pittsburgh as well. Socialists and anarchists came in trains from Chicago and New York to seize any opportunity. Even the political parties got involved with the Democrats, using it as an example of abuse of the McKinley Tariff Act of 1890, and the Republicans standing strong. President Harrison, a Republican, was in the White House, and a Democrat was Pennsylvania's governor. If things weren't bad enough, politicians headed for Pittsburgh to make public appearances. As July of 1892 began, Pittsburgh was struck first with a major heat wave as final negotiations broke off. Carnegie and Frick closed the plant to force the issue. Andrew Carnegie left for Scotland, leaving Frick in charge with orders to break the union. Both men would stay in close contact via telegraph.

Carnegie and Frick had decided to bring in Pinkerton guards to protect the mill property and equipment. Pinkerton Company had been advertising in Western cities for armed guards at five dollars a day plus food and lodging. They mustered the raw recruits in Chicago. They were a mix of college students, drifters, and laid-off workers. The union similarly prepared their forces, which included the unskilled workers. The union expected the mill to be taken over. They patrolled the river, railroad tracks, and the bridges, assuming scabs would be sent in. Scouts on horses were sent up and down the river to warn the town of any approaching company men.

Things had reached the breaking point in Homestead as the saloons filled up, and effigies of Carnegie, Frick, plant manager Potter, and others were hung on telegraph poles. At his office in Pittsburgh across the Monongahela River, Frick called in Sheriff McCleary, politician boss William Magee, and company lawyer and neighbor Philander Knox. The sheriff committed to work with Frick and Pinkertons. Frick laid out his plan to have the Pinkertons enter the works, turning it into a fort. They would enter via the Monongahela River at the mill's back entrance. Meanwhile the workers were meeting at the Homestead opera house. They had managed to gain the support of the unskilled workers, which surprised Frick and Carnegie, but it was a weak alliance with the unskilled having nothing to gain. The unskilled were caught in the middle and could only hope for a quick settlement. By July 1, both sides had their plans as an uneasy calm descended on Homestead. Frick had spies in the mill and town and was the better informed. By July 4, the workers had gotten word of men being hired by Pinkerton in Chicago. On July 5 the workers pushed down the fence and surged into the mill. Local authorities were overwhelmed and the deputies ran. The die was now cast, and the union went to full alert, posting workers up and down the Monongahela River.

The hired Pinkertons were moving by the Pittsburgh and Fort Wayne Railroad from Ashtabula, Ohio, where plant manager Potter had met them. They would muster at Bellevue on the Ohio River, a few miles from Homestead. The sheriff met them with his deputy, Joseph Gray, who would travel with them and deputize them if necessary. Frick was able to bring the necessary political pressure on the sheriff through East Ender and political boss, Christopher Magee. Deputizing these outsiders would put the responsibility on the county and make things legal. Carnegie was cabled in Scotland as to the movements. The Pinkerton landing was planned for two o'clock in the morning of July 6. The hope was to slip into the works under the cover of darkness. The Pinkertons moved by two river barges from Bellevue to the Homestead plant. The barges had been purchased and converted to cover troop carriers in Allegheny City (Pittsburgh's North side). These were floating forts described as "Noah's Ark" equipped with dining halls and kitchens. They had a hired steward and twenty waiters. Winchester rifles were in closed boxes to be opened only by command.

As the barges moved toward the plant, fog helped cover their approach. Pittsburgh was experiencing a July heat wave and an air inversion, making it hot and humid. The Smithfield Bridge on the Monongahela River was lined with watchmen as were the riverbanks. A horseman was sent to wake Homestead. At 2:30 a.m. the Homestead Electric Works sounded a whistle alarm. Residents and workers, like the minutemen of old, got out of bed and picked up old family guns. As the barges approached the mill landing at 4 a.m., they faced the guns, men, women, and children. Old Civil War cannon monuments were worn from their mountings and loaded for action. The Pinkertons started to land, armed with new Winchester rifles. There was some pushing and then shots rang out. Three steelworkers were killed on the spot and dozens wounded. An old twenty-pounder cannon was fired from the Braddock side of the river, missing the barges and hitting and killing a steelworker. The Pinkertons had wounded as well and retreated to their floating forts. Telegraph sent the word to the hotels of Pittsburgh, and an army of reporters flew into action. The word was now moving out to the world. Pittsburghers and valley residents started to assembly on the Swissvale hills across the river to view the battle.

Frick had received the message of the Pinkertons on the move and took a carriage to the Pittsburgh office. Chris Magee and the sheriff were at their offices. As the shooting started, the sheriff telegraphed the governor to send troops, which he refused. Governor Robert Patterson was a Democrat, and the Homestead uprising played into politics to break the Republican support by the workers. The huddled Pinkertons in the barges had some protection but lacked air conditioning, and the barges were becoming sweaty iron furnaces. They were not professionals, so they doubted the value of their lives in this strange action and a dollar a day with meals. Many were from Midwestern towns. In Pittsburgh, Frick, the sheriff, and Magee tried to use the courts to put pressure on the governor to send troops. Press reports to Washington brought calls to repeal the tariffs that had helped Carnegie Steel, as the struggle played into the politicians. Meanwhile the

Homesteader poured oil on the Monongahela and started a few surface fires. By 7 p.m. the Pinkertons had had it and raised a white flag. The count was 13 dead and 36 wounded.

The Amalgamated Union Advisory committee accepted the surrender but lost control of the crowd. The crowd of men, women, and children were half-crazed by this point. The Pinkertons in their blue uniforms became prisoners of the crowd. They were forced to run the gauntlet of angry workers and townspeople and were beaten and stoned by the crowd. The sheriff arrived by special train at 11 p.m. to remove the beaten Pinkertons. Homestead continued to celebrate as the train moved out of town. Frick returned to Clayton protected by personal bodyguards for the first time. Prior to the strike he had often taken the streetcar to the mill. Frick made arrangements to have his older son, Childs, go to Fisher's Island. On July 8, Adelaide gave birth to a very sick Henry Clay Frick Jr. at Clayton. Helen would remain at Clayton to be with her mother. Frick had major concerns for his family as the press turned extremely negative, arousing old enemies and rogue anarchists.

The sheriff struggled to find deputies and to regain control of the town. Lookouts were still posted as the town took the next couple of days to bury their dead. The struggle degraded to a political one, with Carnegie's unionized mills in Beaver and Pittsburgh offering support. Union men in Chicago talked about sending men and guns. The United States Congress debated daily. The governor finally sent troops after political bosses, Magee and Flinn, pulled every string possible; still the troops were not greeted in Homestead. Rails were torn up to slow the trains, but the troops were in place by July 12. With the town under military control, Congress sent a special committee to hold hearings. With Homestead peaceful and under martial law, the advantage passed to Carnegie Company. The union called unsuccessfully for a national boycott of Carnegie steel product, and Samuel Gompers came to help support the unsuccessful boycott. The union continued to work the press and congress, which now was the best hope. A strong-willed Frick, however, refused, sensing he had a victory. On July 17, Homestead union officers went to New York to try to win over the Republicans, who were counting on the labor vote for high tariffs in the fall election. Frick started to advertise for scabs on July 14, according to the long-range plan. On July 21, Frick tried the old strategy of opening the mill and allowing men to return on an individual contract. The move failed, making the lockout a true strike.

Things changed again as the socialists and anarchists entered the crisis. The socialists and anarchist movements in the United States had been following the action at Homestead. The most radical left fringe were the anarchists, who even rejected the minor organizational bent of Karl Marx mainstream socialists. The anarchists had always looked for opportunities to get involved in labor stifle. They were best known for the Haymarket riots in Chicago. For them, the capitalists were the evil of the world. The anarchists approached the religious homicide bombers of today. They believed the greatest political accomplishment was to die creating a scene for the cause. Dying was the highest form of propaganda for them. Homestead was now the ideal location for creating propaganda. Their philosophical leader was the orator, Emma Goldman, whose boyfriend was Alexander Berkman. Years later, the young Emma Goldman would be called "the most dangerous woman in the United States" by J. Edgar Hoover.[1] On July 23, a clean-cut Alexander Berkman in a suit entered Frick's office at the *Chronicle-Telegraph* Building on Pittsburgh's Fifth Avenue.

Berkman had arrived alone in Pittsburgh around July 16 with little money, a gun, and wearing the suit Emma Goldman had suggested. Pittsburgh had a small anarchist community in Allegheny City. Berkman responded to a newspaper ad that Frick had placed for scabs and set up an interview at Frick's office. The first visit was more to check on the routine and guards. Frick was without bodyguards and was following his routine of taking lunch at the Duquesne Club and then returning to the office. At the Duquesne Club, Frick lunched with his friend, Andrew Mellon, and Mellon's younger brother, Richard. Frick lunched late often and returned to the office by himself without guards.

Berkman was forced to wait until a telegraph boy delivered a message to the office. Frick was in the office with partner, neighbor, and second in command John Leishman. Berkman rushed in and fired, hitting Frick in the shoulder. Frick fell and Berkman fired again hitting Frick in the neck. He took aim for the third shot but Leishman intervened, forcing the shot to go wild and hit the ceiling. Leishman wrestled Berkman to the ground. Frick jumped in, and Berkman took out a sharpened file dagger and struck Frick in the leg and knee. The office boy got a sheriff's deputy who took aim, but Frick called him off, only wanting to see his face. The struggle with the deputy found Berkman with an explosive pill in his mouth but it failed to go off.

Doctors were called for immediately and performed an operation to remove the bullets. Frick refused anesthesia while the bullets were removed. Then amazingly, he seemed revived. He wrote a short telegram to his wife, to Carnegie, and to the press. He even talked of returning to the office on Monday. The doctors stayed with him for some time. Finally an ambulance was called to take Frick to his home in the East End. Now a crowd had gathered at the office building and hospital. Frick returned home bloodied and weak, but the first thing he asked about as he saw his wife was the health of his newborn son. Adelaide's bed was moved from her room to Frick's so they could be together. It was six days before the first anniversary of the death of their first child, Martha. Twenty years later Frick admitted to a reporter that when Berkman first aimed at him he saw Martha at his side.[2] Frick would always contend that it was the spiritual light of Martha that blinded Berkman, who had reported sunlight from the window, which caused him to miss the head.

Berkman's entrance into the crisis changed things. The union wanted no part of Berkman's act. While the press continued to villainize Frick, they also hailed his courage and nerve. Frick's courage and resolve was amazing. He continued to refuse to have guards at Clayton and the office. He continued his routine of taking the trolley from Clayton to his office. The Pittsburgh public seemed split. A New York reporter stated: "those who hate him most admire the nerve and stamina of this man of steel whom nothing seems to be

---

1 Standiford, p. 213
2 Sanger, p. 199

able to move."[1] Still, union papers continued to demonize him. Public opinion did turn a bit in favor of Frick, but to this day he is still the poster boy of union oppressors. Pittsburghers had no love for socialists and anarchists after the Great Railroad Strike of 1877. The religion of the workers was Catholicism, and the local priests and press saw more evil in anarchists than capitalists. The *Pittsburgh Catholic* noted: "The attempt on Frick's life is an eye opener. We are no better, no safer, no securer, than the people residing in France, or Germany, or Russia. Our lax laws have given the Anarchists a foothold here."[2] An editorial in the *Catholic World* in 1893 noted: "The distribution of wealth is frightful in its very inequalities. Still I do believe that the social system is radically and hopelessly wrong. I do believe that the American workmen can right their wrongs by the machinery at their disposal and without violating of votes any law human or divine."[3] After that, capitalists, religious, and particularly Catholic priests were on the European socialist's hit list. Personally, the crisis was far from over for Frick, and the personal toll was enormous.

Frick had extra telephone lines installed to Clayton to better manage Carnegie Steel. He took daily reports from the plant superintendents. Frick had newspapers from all parts of the country coming in. He also stayed in close contact with Carnegie by telegraph. Frick seemed determined to recover to keep Carnegie from returning and taking over. Meantime, the newborn baby, Henry Clay Frick Jr., struggled for life. The baby had a fulltime nurse, Adelaide's sister, and daily visits from doctors. Still, little could be done; and on August 3, the child died. Adelaide was devastated, and Frick felt more pain than that inflicted by Berkman. Frick made the funeral arrangements, but both he and Adelaide remained in their room during the actual service in the house. The baby was buried beside his sister, Martha, in Homewood Cemetery. Adelaide Frick slipped into a depression and needed to be at Frick's side. She would never fully recover.

The greatest loser of the Homestead Strike was the union. By October the strike was over and Frick was hiring new workers. The Amalgamated union was smashed and the Carnegie mills would not be unionized until the late 1930s. The membership of the Amalgamated dropped from 24,000 to 14,000 after the strike. The Amalgamated union lost power and members after the Homestead Strike. It eventually morphed into a finishing mill organization — the National Amalgamated Association of Iron, Steel, and Tin Workers. Many workers ended up blacklisted by the company and union. Most of these workers moved on to cities like Cleveland and Detroit to find work.

The biggest winner of the Homestead Strike was the Democratic Party. The Homestead Strike was used as a political hammer to pay back the Democratic defeats funded by Pittsburgh East Enders. Frick and Carnegie had helped to defeat the Democratic Speaker of the House, John Carlisle, and others in 1888. The democrats in Congress moved for hearings to highlight the strike. The Congressional inquiry into the strike was filled with questions about protectionism. Clearly, the fight over protectionism was a factor at least in the amount of publicity. For years, Homestead would be pointed to as an example that

1 Schreiner, p. 102

2 Standiford, p. 214

3 John Conway, "America's Workmen," *The Catholic World*, January 1893, vol. 56

profits from tariffs did not help the worker. It was a wedge Democrats could use to break worker loyalty to the Republican Party. It was a populist cry; but the facts showed that tariff-generated profits were poured into plant expansion, consistent work and jobs, although the union would argue it did not create high-paying jobs.

The Harrison Administration lobbied Frick to recognize the union for the good of the party. Neither Frick nor Carnegie would bend to the political pressure. For Frick, it was a difficult stand since he realized it would mean a Democratic victory. Frick realized this would impact his strong belief in tariffs, property rights, and American exceptionalism. Carnegie, on the other hand, felt Cleveland differed little in reality from the Republican candidate. The Homestead Strike played well nationally but not in Pittsburgh. Grover Cleveland won by over 100,000 votes and carried the Electoral College 277 to 145. There were Democratic majorities in the House (218 to 127) and the Senate (44 to 38). Amazingly, the Republicans carried Western Pennsylvania, but most other industrialized areas went Democratic with Democrats controlling the White House and Congress.

CHAPTER 13. PICKLES, KETCHUP, AND ELECTRICAL POWER

The 1890s were the golden years for two of the East End's most prominent citizens — pickle king H. J. Heinz and master inventor, George Westinghouse. This newfound wealth for both of them was found, not in Pittsburgh but in Chicago. It would be at the Chicago World's Fair of 1893 known as the Columbian Exposition. Interestingly, the symbol of the fair was a giant Ferris wheel built by Pittsburgh inventor George Ferris. Pittsburgh East Enders and their companies dominated the fair, and the Pennsylvania Railroad set up special direct trains from Pittsburgh to Chicago. The Chicago Fair would be the ultimate triumph of the Westinghouse alternating current system over Thomas Edison's direct current system. It was a triumph of Westinghouse over the nation's most powerful banker, J. P. Morgan, as well. The Fair would be bathed in the light of the Westinghouse lighting system. Westinghouse was not alone, as East Ender companies had many exhibits. H. C. Frick Company had a well-financed exhibit. A small start-up East End aluminum company (ALCOA) with a bright future won a medal. Gulf Oil of the Mellon family also had an exhibit. One of the most popular exhibits, however, would be that of H. J. Heinz. The famous pickle pin would be the most wanted souvenir of the fair.

Pickle king Heinz came to the East End neighborhood in 1889. At the time pickles were the main product of the H. J. Heinz Company. He had started selling horseradish and preserves, but his fortune was built on pickles. The new Heinz mansion was a four-story French Renaissance style house with thirty rooms. His immediate neighbors included George Westinghouse and Henry Clay Frick. Not far were the Carnegies and many of Carnegie's millionaire partners. There could be no doubt that the pickle king was on par with America's greatest industrialists. Heinz's factories were models for the new era, pioneering electricity, material handling, employee benefits, and continuous production before Henry Ford. Carnegie produced tons, but Heinz's profit margins did not require volume on an industrial scale. The Heinz estate cost $50,000 (almost a million today) and took up a full block, rivaling the steel barons of the neighborhood. The renovations told even more of the booming business in ketchup and pickles. Heinz hired the use of the first tree-moving machine to move 32 trees to the somewhat barren lot that Heinz named "Greenlawn." Like his neighbors, George Westinghouse and Henry Clay, Heinz focused on the grounds as much as the house.

Heinz's mansion was heated and lighted initially with natural gas, which had been one of the first in the Pittsburgh to convert to it, using Westinghouse's natural gas distribution company. Heinz was always an early adopter of technology both at home and at the factory. Heinz loved to attend lectures on new technology such as electricity, telephone, and natural gas heating. Heinz was one of the first in Pittsburgh to apply all three technologies. He led the home conversion movement of the 1880s from dirty coal to natural gas with the Westinghouse system. In 1883, Westinghouse came to Sharpsburg to sell his natural gas system and talked to Heinz. Heinz was convinced natural gas would be the primary source of Pittsburgh fuel and signed up for his home and factory. An early explosion in 1883 in Sharpsburg had originally caused much hesitation, but it didn't stop Heinz. Heinz added his parents' home and Sharpsburg Grace Methodist to the list of gas users. Gas heating, cooking, and lighting did become very popular in Pittsburgh by 1886 but not without some hesitation by the public. A few years later, Heinz would be one of the first to convert to electricity (again his neighbor Westinghouse's system) with his East End neighbors.

Heinz added a conservatory and stables, both of which he continued to expand over the years. At his death the estate would have ten conservatories. His conservatory, like that of his neighbor Frick, would be opened to the public. Heinz and Frick would sponsor neighborhood flower shows as well. The large estate allowed Heinz to purchase Shetland ponies for all the kids. Heinz had numerous horses for riding as well as for his carriages. He replaced the floors with hardwood floors and added stained glass windows throughout. Years later, like Henry Clay Frick, he would have an extensive collection of automobiles. Heinz's son, Howard, would have one of Pittsburgh's first automobiles. It was a fast bright red Panhard-Levassor from Paris. This auto would be one of a handful on the Pittsburgh streets but would be best known as the "Red Devil." Howard drove the car daily from the Greenlawn mansion to the north side Heinz factory, often at high speeds, creating clouds of dust. It was the most advanced car in America, having aluminum parts and pneumatic tires. Heinz commissioned George Carpenter, who had worked on the Waldorf-Astoria Hotel in New York, to paint several murals throughout the house. He renovated the fourth floor to be a museum of his curios and watch collection, which are now in the collection of Pittsburgh's Carnegie Museum in Oakland. The space for his evolving collection of hand carved ivories and curios seemed to be part of his motivation to move to the East End's Point Breeze section in the first place. He joined the East Liberty Presbyterian Church, a congregation of America's richest capitalists, but remained a parishioner at Grace Methodist in Sharpsburg.

H. J. Heinz was a native born Pittsburgher from German immigrant parents. Like most East Enders, he came from modest means. Heinz's story is typical of many East Enders.

Like his neighbors, Heinz had started as a young boy selling vegetables from his mother's Southside garden. He then moved to selling his mother's prepared horseradish in glass bottles. Before his 21st birthday he had made money in brick making and coal distribution; but vegetable selling remained his passion. His business expanded and grew, but it would be bankrupted by the Panic of 1873. With help from his mother and family, Heinz re-invented his business on Pittsburgh's Second Avenue; however, Heinz soon wanted to expand into pickles, vinegar, and sauerkraut.

Heinz built a new plant on Pittsburgh's north side (then known as Allegheny City) to have direct access to the railroad, something he lacked at his Pittsburgh Second Avenue plant. Allegheny City was happy because its textile industry had been lost, and the Heinz plant joined the large Westinghouse Air Brake operation in Allegheny City. Heinz wanted to add vinegar manufacturing to his company because it was becoming a major needed raw material for his pickles and sauerkraut, and he wanted to compete better in the vinegar barrel market. Vinegar by the barrel was a huge business in Pittsburgh and throughout his sales network. Most homes in the country had a couple barrels of vinegar in their cellars, and all grocers had vinegar barrels. Heinz was also interested in producing crystal clear distilled vinegar for his pickle operation. Apple vinegar and even wine vinegar imparted some flavor to pickles and sauces. Heinz also was the first to package vinegar in bottles for table use. The use of table ready products in glass bottles had been the heart of Heinz's revolution in the food industry, beginning with his bottled horseradish. Prior to Heinz's pickles, vinegar, sauerkraut, and other products were sold out of barrels at the local dry goods store. Heinz's bottled distilled vinegar had proved a market success, and Heinz planned to dominate that market by mass production. The vinegar plant on the north side cost $20,000 and would become the core of a future manufacturing complex. The other innovation of Heinz was mass marketing, which created an expansive market nationally for his products. Heinz was said to paste his name on any blank wall in the city.

Heinz had always been a Republican and supported the party, which was now starting to pay off, as the Republican tariffs expanded in the 1880s. Like his East End industrialist neighbors, Heinz would also get a major boost in his pickle and ketchup sales from the protectionist Republican administration of 1883. Congress passed a tariff bill in 1883 to help protect domestic producers, including vegetables. The Tariff Act of 1883 put a 10 percent duty on vegetable products. Heinz's sales increased 23 percent from $359,055 to $442,581 in the first year of the tariff, and sales doubled to $1,235,184 by the end of the decade. Heinz penetrated more East Coast markets with the help of the tariffs and even started to export pickles. The tariff included tomatoes and pickles which were technically fruits of the vine. Importers challenged the tariff on tomatoes and pickles, but the Supreme Court ruled the tomato and the pickle a vegetable for tariff purposes. Because of the court's decision, the mistaken identity of the tomato remains today. Ultimately, the McKinley Tariff of 1890 would take the pickle tariff to 40 percent. The tariff and railroads made Heinz into a major national pickle manufacturer by 1889. Men like Heinz made the Republican Party's protectionist policy a huge success by investing profits back into the business and increasing employment. To their credit, Republican capitalists of the period

— Heinz, Westinghouse, Carnegie, and Frick — poured the windfall profits of the tariffs into factory expansion and job creation. The Republican tariffs would lead to a great expansion for Heinz and the East End.

By the end of the 1880s, Heinz needed and started building the world's largest processed food factory. The buildings represented the factory of the future but appeared more like an industrial fortress. The style was the rich brick design of Georgian and Palladian architecture. Heinz had started as a brick maker and loved the look of brick. Oak panels and the best-fired bricks were used throughout the new factory, regardless of cost. Heinz personally inspected every load of brick before using. The outside design of Romanesque highlighted the beauty of the brick, which would be washed weekly. Heinz built it to be completely fireproof with steel beams and concrete fill between floors. The infrastructure was structural steel from Carnegie Steel. The architectural details added to its beauty. The "Time Office" where employees clocked in was modeled after Thomas Jefferson's design for the Library of Congress. The entrance portico was made of polished red Swedish granite, which was cut and polished in Scotland. The interior had an Alhambra tile floor, Italian marble walls, and red mahogany woodwork. The ceiling consisted of eight specially designed stained windows with various Heinz sayings such as "Labor sweetens life; Idleness makes it a burden." He contracted artists to design stained glass windows and paint murals. The center window was a picture of the Sharpsburg home considered his first factory. There was an iron-reinforced dome with inlaid gold. The entrance and plant would be one of the earliest to use full electric lighting and electric motors for machinery. The electric system was supplied by the local Westinghouse Company; and his East End neighbor, George Westinghouse, visited the electrical work often. The Heinz powerhouse used mammoth Westinghouse generators and steam engines. The power plant was a cathedral of machinery with Alhambra tile floors, mahogany walls, oak staircases, and burnished brass decorations. The heating was by steam radiators. Westinghouse Air Brake was a neighbor plant to the Heinz plant, and during the plant building, Heinz would become Westinghouse's neighbor as well.

The factory itself would be state-of-the-art as well with electric cranes, automated packaging systems, electric lighting, gravity-fed material handling systems, and electric equipment. The plant's technology was ahead of the Carnegie steel mills that dominated Pittsburgh. Engineers and engineering societies from all over the world came to visit the Pittsburgh Heinz plant. The technology was perfectly blended with paternal factory practices. Heinz employed mainly Pittsburgh women, and he pioneered a better treatment of the worker. Lunchrooms, restrooms, and factory floors were washed and cleaned daily. The restrooms included running water, something few employees had in their homes. Women were supplied clean uniforms. There was daily availability to doctors and dentists for the women and their families. Heinz was one of the earliest to believe that dental care and general health were interrelated. Heinz would be one of the first in the United States to use pre-employment physicals. He took his paternal approach far beyond what he had seen in his trips to German factories. Heinz had many social and educational programs for the women as well. Widowed, abandoned, and divorced women were given special help. Lunchtime carriage rides were available as well as concerts.

It was truly the first "green" factory with gardens and energy efficiency motors. Heinz was the chairman of Pittsburgh's smoke abatement committee, and he converted his generators from coal to natural gas. Roof gardens and relaxation areas included music, plants, picnic tables, and refreshments. For many women, the Heinz factory was far superior to the homes they returned to in the evening. Heinz saw his factory as a new ideal in manufacturing. His work on smoke abatement drew mixed results, however. Smoke had been a symbol of Pittsburgh's economic might. The smoke problem was a result of coal burning and the topology of deep valleys. Coal had been the source of Pittsburgh success, and its use powered its great mills employing over 70,000. Coal mining was also the second biggest industry in the Greater Pittsburgh Area, so smoke abatement would be a tough fight for the Heinz coalition of progressive Republicans. Westinghouse's natural gas system did bring clean skies to Pittsburgh for a brief period in the late 1880s.

The technology and application of scientific management was far ahead of later industrialists such as Henry Ford. Heinz borrowed from the friendly workplace designs of early Pittsburgh capitalists such as Jeffery Scaife and his iron working plants of the early 1800s. Heinz's blend of human work with automation was revolutionary and was similar to East End neighbor George Westinghouse. The installed material handling systems predated the modern assembly line. Pickling stations and rail connections were designed for efficiency and ease of handling. Heinz even had specially designed tank cars built to support overall materials flow in his new factory. Heinz was one of the first to use refrigerated rail cars for his vegetables, which opened up the southern states for supply. His Westinghouse power station was the best in America at the time. He set up mini-assembly lines for sealing, corking, and vegetable sizing. Conveyors and chutes were used to move material between floors. His continuous flow system and assembly techniques were twenty years ahead of the auto industry. He used stainless steel and silver coated steel tubes to move material. The level of the design and automation would rival anything in the world prior to the building of Henry Ford's Highland Park assembly plant in 1907.

Heinz's mechanical and electrical machines were years ahead of industry. Heinz patented a machine to size and group pickles for packaging in glass jars. He had always stayed close to the concerns of grocers and housewives for new ideas on how to better serve them. One frustration of grocers and housewives was sizing of pickles. Grocers preferred to sell pickles at a price per pickle, but this required uniformity in pickle size in the barrel that was not always there, requiring customers to fish for big pickles. Grocers purchased pickles by the barrel by price per barrel; and again pickle size uniformity was important for customer satisfaction. Having been fermented in the barrel in the ship, imported pickles had major size variation. Heinz realized that uniform sizing could give him a market advantage. He started to hand size and pack in glass jars or bottles, which allowed both the grocer and consumer to see the uniformity. Heinz employees painfully packed the pickle jars for size and presentation. The uniform pickle size in barrels and glass jars delighted grocers and consumers. Heinz even built a glasshouse to produce glass jars and bottles.

He was one of the first industrialists to apply the automated bottle-making machine of Michael Owens.

Heinz was a true pioneer in the use of Westinghouse's AC electrical distribution system. The new factory buildings were lighted by electricity, having a state-of-the-art Westinghouse generator on site at his power station. The generator was a steam driven Westinghouse dynamo and was one of the biggest applications of the Westinghouse system in which Westinghouse had personally supervised the installation. The lighting system was state of the art as well. This was in a time when all homes and factories were lit by natural gas flames. Another steam generator was used for heating. The plant had an electric ventilation system, which again was one of the first in Pittsburgh. Parts of the plant had electric trolley cranes. Heinz also had an electric fireproofing system to close iron doors and sound alarms, which was the world's first. Since Heinz had over 200 horses to pull his famous delivery wagons, his stables were critical to him. He had a four-story brick stable for his many horses; he had electric brushes for his horses as well as electric feed systems. Electric buttons operated the horse water troughs. Electric lighting was used throughout. The stable in general was an early highlight of the complex. It was a four story "equine palace" of Romanesque design and had turrets and towers, which rivaled most churches in its beauty. All of the buildings were adorned with stained glass windows. Heinz visually reinforced the corporate vision with murals reflecting the "world is our field." There were special heated footbaths for his horses. The Heinz horses lived far better than the steelworkers of Carnegie Steel.

Heinz was also a pioneer in fireproofing with good reason. As new immigrants, Heinz's parents had witnessed the "burning of Pittsburgh" in 1845. This devastating two-day fire completely destroyed the city of Pittsburgh including most of the bridges. The memory of this full leveling of the city was passed down to the next generation. Fire insurance had become a major cost of doing business. Heinz's stables for so many horses were also a major investment, even more than the equipment. Besides brick he used steel in place of wooden beams. Heinz designed his factory to be totally fire resistant. He built a water storage tower on top of his buildings. One factory tower supplied water via fire hoses for fire protection. Heinz used a cell approach also to block any fire from spreading. His use of iron, concrete, and brick with preventive fire systems enabled him to carry no insurance on the building. The factory, in general, gave Heinz efficiencies and productivity advantages beyond any factory in the world.

Heinz's treatment of his workers was every bit as revolutionary as his factory. Heinz provided musical entertainment for the lunch hours. All workers in the 1880s were on day-rate, so the pay remained the same as they attended these lunchtime events. The women usually got a half-hour lunch, but it was expanded to an hour for major events such as concerts. Horse carriages were available for women to take a lunchtime ride in the city. The locker rooms and lunchrooms were spotless and cleaned three times a day. The men and women had separate lunchrooms. There were reading rooms and libraries for employees and family. There was a gymnasium and a swimming pool. There was also a small hospital with full-time doctors, which Heinz opened up for family members. Finally, a large auditorium with massive stained glass windows was used for free lectures, employee Christmas parties, and company-sponsored dances. Visitors entered a huge marble rotunda in the administration building that exceeded those of the most fashionable hotels of the time. The factory had a waiting room and sampling room for visitors, which Heinz encouraged. By 1905, the factory was getting 50,000 visitors per year to see this wonder of the industrial world.

The five-story auditorium was every bit as amazing. It was believed to be the first auditorium in the country built for employees. When finished, it had over 2,000 incandescent light bulbs. It had a stereopticon slide projector for slide shows, a pipe organ, and a Steinway Grand Piano. It was said to have inspired fellow Pittsburgh industrialists and neighbors, George Westinghouse and Andrew Carnegie, to build their own. Heinz even hired a musical director for the 1,500 seat auditorium. The auditorium was used for lunchtime talks, singles dances, and a wide variety of after-work and family events. The administration building approached the decor of a palace. It also had special rooms for visitors. The high point of the season was the Christmas Party given for families by Santa Claus and Mr. Heinz.

The sales to support Heinz's manufacturing fortress would come from his 1893 Chicago Exposition success. While Heinz did not introduce any new products, the fair would be remembered for the introduction of Cream of Wheat, Juicy Fruit Gum, Pabst Beer, Aunt Jemima Syrup, Shredded Wheat, and the hamburger. Heinz would introduce his famous pickle pin which would become a marketing icon. The Heinz exhibit at the fair would be one of the best remembered with that of Libbey Glass and Pabst Beer. The Heinz exhibit was on the second floor of the Agricultural Building and had the most floor space of the food and beer manufacturers. Heinz had designed it out of polished hand-carved oak. The display included free samples and the Heinz pickle pin. Beautiful women from several countries were hired to act as guides and hostesses. Heinz built a working pickling line where women sized and bottled pickles for visitors. He even had a parade float for two women to demonstrate pickle bottling. There was one problem. The Heinz exhibit was on the second floor while the European firms such as Crosse & Blackwell and Lea & Perkins were on the first floor. Due to the enormous size of the fair and amount of walking, visitors were reluctant to walk up the stairs of the large Agricultural Building. Heinz also had a ground floor small exhibit in the Horticultural Building, which he used to hand out coupons for a free souvenir of his pickle pin. Actually these were watch chain ornaments, which Heinz had first introduced in 1889. He also hired boys to pass out free coupons. The green pickle was made out of the natural plastic gutta-percha. Heinz noted that over one million of these pickle charms were given away. Foreign food exhibitors claimed, to little avail, that Heinz was using unfair practices. The large crowds visiting Heinz's second floor exhibit required strengthening parts of the building. Still, the *New York Times* reported the building sagged around the Heinz display. Fairs and advertisements like his Atlantic City pier and Times Squares electric billboard (the first electric one) were all part of what would later become known as branding.

The Columbian Exposition was to celebrate the 400th anniversary of Columbus's discovery of America. The fair would be a triumph of the electric lights, with George Westinghouse winning the contract to light it up. The fair would need three times the power used for the whole city of Chicago. Almost 93,000 incandescent lights and 5,000 powerful arc lights would light the Chicago Fair. Edison used a patent to block Westinghouse from using his bulb, but Westinghouse called on Pittsburgh glassmakers to develop a special bulb for his use. Most of these bulbs were made at Westinghouse's glass plant, a few blocks from the Heinz factory in Pittsburgh. The dominant symbol of the fair was to be fellow Pittsburgher George Ferris's invention, the "Ferris Wheel." Henry Clay Frick Company presented a working model coal mine, which was very popular with the crowds. The fair would have over 28 million visitors. General admission to the fair cost 50 cents for an adult and 25 cents for children. The Pennsylvania Railroad set up special trains and fares to make the fair accessible to all Americans. In addition, several express trains were set up for Pittsburgh's East Enders.

Heinz's greatest advertising effort came later in 1898 when he purchased the Iron Pier in Atlantic City. With the pier, Heinz found a way to extend his 1893 Fair success. It was particularly popular as a summer vacation spot with residents of Western Pennsylvania and Ohio. The cost of the pier was $60,000 (about $1.2 million today) which represented a considerable amount for the times. It would be comparable to a Busch Gardens of today. Heinz always found high paybacks at world and regional fairs, and Atlantic City offered a similar opportunity. After Niagara Falls, Atlantic City was the number one vacation spot for the eastern United States at the time. The Heinz Pier took in thousands daily during the summer. Tens of thousands of Pittsburghers and Ohioans alone flocked every summer by train to Atlantic City, making East End railroad executives even wealthier. It offered the ideal spot for a permanent exhibition. It would be lit with power from the Westinghouse power plant at Niagara Falls. The pier, which would become known as the Heinz Ocean Pier, extended 900 feet into the ocean. Heinz's renovation was ostentatious as was his style. The pier was adorned with giant pickles and eventually large electric signs. The pier was a tourist attraction in its own right; no one could go to Atlantic City without visiting the Heinz Pier. The pier also functioned as a personal museum for H. J.'s many curios from his numerous travels around the world. The curios included the mummy he had purchased on his trip to Egypt, a Buddhist shrine, ship models, carved ivories, and a chair of General Grant.

The World's Fair launched another East Ender into name recognition. While Thomas Edison was building neighborhood DC power plants in New York, Westinghouse changed the very core of the industry with his revolutionary AC power system. Westinghouse produced AC current at his downtown Pittsburgh power plant and sent the current an amazing three miles to the Lawrenceville section of the East End to light 400 bulbs — a distance far beyond that achievable from DC current. One of the major differences between AC (alternating) and DC (direct) current is how it can be delivered. High voltage (pressure) AC current can be distributed over very long distances. The characteristic that measures the pressure of the current is voltage. DC current is, by its nature, low voltage and lacks the push to deliver it long distances. One mile was about the practical limit for DC current. AC current is, by nature, produced at a high voltage that can push it many miles. Practically, a transformer must step down high voltage AC current to a lower voltage for use. This simple engineering principle is analogous to the gas delivery system designed by Westinghouse in which high-pressure wellhead gas is stepped down in pressure by increasing the delivery pipe diameter. The secret to Westinghouse's success lay in this very principle. Westinghouse's use of AC current earned it the name "Westinghouse current." AC offered major cost advantages, not only requiring many fewer power transmission stations, but a third less copper wire. It was only Edison's stubborn belief in DC and J. P. Morgan's early backing of Edison that slowed AC use. Westinghouse's amazing demonstration of electrical power launched a battle between Edison and New York banks against George Westinghouse, which would become known as the "war of the currents." The great banker, J. P. Morgan, was the financial backer for Edison Electric. J. P. Morgan's first approach was to buy out Westinghouse.

The first three years of the 1890s would, to a large degree, define Westinghouse's legacy as well as Westinghouse Electric's destiny. In 1890 Westinghouse had rebuffed the House of Morgan in refusing to join a trust, only to see Edison General Electric merge with Thomson-Houston to become General Electric. J. P. Morgan would wait to take down his only competitor and an industrialist who would not join a monopoly. At the time the new company of General Electric dominated the market with its DC power system; however, Westinghouse was gaining in the most rural and less densely populated areas with his distance advantage. Thanks to Nikola Tesla, Westinghouse had General Electric blocked from entering the AC power generation. Tesla had left Edison to join Westinghouse in Pittsburgh. Tesla added the needed technology in AC motors and transformers to make AC competitive. Tesla's transformer work would make AC transmission possible over many miles, but Edison held to his belief in DC current. Edison hated Tesla's science and his high living. Tesla worked all day in the lab and then partied all night in New York's best clubs. He often owed large sums of money because of his high living.

Tesla found that both Edison and Morgan were terrible managers of scientific research. Nikola Tesla noted the difference in approaches: "If Edison had a needle to find in a haystack, he would proceed at once with the diligence of the bee to examine straw after straw until he found the object of search. I was sorry to witness of such doings, knowing that a little theory and calculation would have saved him ninety percent of his labor." Westinghouse's knowledge and use of science saved him months over Edison's approach. Westinghouse was rare in his ability to dream, design, and build devices. His brother Herman, a trained engineer, always admired George's engineering skills. Westinghouse's "Solitude" was buzzing with dinner parties, of which George proudly showed his plans for the upcoming fair and a future power plant at Niagara Falls. It became a nightly routine to retire with his guests to his study and spread out the drawings on his billiard table. Nikola Tesla had become a favorite of Marguerite and George during these challenging times. They shared their dislike of Pittsburgh's smoky and dark days, but Tesla found intellectual nourishment in Pittsburgh's East End. Tesla loved rich living in Pittsburgh's

East End, and he often recalled this as the best time of his life. For his years in Pittsburgh, Tesla maintained a suite at the exclusive Monongahela House, but Pittsburgh lacked the nightlife of New York. Still, Tesla found a home in the mix of entertainment and work at the Westinghouse dinners. He was also known to join in Henry Clay Frick's poker games; and when in New York, Frick and Tesla would have poker games with the Astors at the Waldorf-Astoria. Engineers Benjamin Lamme and Albert Schmidt were also frequent dinner guests, reporting on activities and progress. Even international scientists such as Lord Kelvin came to Westinghouse's famous East End dinners. In George and Marguerite, Tesla found the type of parental supervision he needed, and Westinghouse found the genius he needed.

Westinghouse's winning of the world's fair contract would be the first big victory for the superior AC current system. George Westinghouse was excited about the prospects, having enjoyed himself at the Philadelphia Fair of 1876. The 1876 fair had been a major marketing success for his air brake, and he believed this fair could do the same for AC current. He was locked in the "War of the Currents" with Edison's direct current system. Edison had also been triumphant at the Paris Exposition of 1889. The Paris Exposition had used Edison's DC system to power 1,150 arc lamps and 10,000 incandescent lamps. The bid specifications for Chicago called for 5,000 arc lamps and over 90,000 incandescent lights. The power requirements were ten times that of Paris. The technical requirements would be challenging to both Edison General Electric and Westinghouse Electric. It was assumed that the newly formed General Electric would win because of the financial demands and because its major investor was J. P. Morgan. George's brother, Herman Westinghouse, argued against George entering the competition, realizing that even with loans this could bankrupt the company. His brother, who lived nearby in Edgewood, was the operating manager of the company. George was determined to make it work, against the advice of his brother and others. Marguerite seems to have been an important supporter of this project, even offering to make any personal financial sacrifices. Bids opened in April 1892 after Westinghouse had put together his financial syndicate with Morgan competitor, August Belmont; but Westinghouse was facing an even bigger technical challenge.

Thomas Edison was battling Westinghouse on a very personal level. Edison was using fear to destroy the use of AC current. Morgan forced Edison out of General Electric. At General Electric now, Morgan realized that the future could include AC, and he wanted to hedge their bets. Still, Edison continued his campaign against Westinghouse's AC current. A horse and cow were electrocuted for the press. At one point Edison was searching for a circus elephant to electrocute. Edison even went to the *Times* to challenge Westinghouse to an electrical duel, running the two currents through their bodies. As the state of New York considered AC for executions, Edison devised a cap and shoe to do the job, using Westinghouse AC dynamos. Westinghouse failed to stop the use of his generators. In August 1890, William Kemmler, a convicted murderer, was electrocuted. The system bungled the job and turned it into a cruel spectacle. Westinghouse said, "They could have done better with an axe." Still, the overall campaign had been extremely successful in putting fear in the general public. The White House had been wired with an AC system, but President Harrison and his wife were afraid to use the switches. Westinghouse even stopped work on his AC motor because of the public hostility to Tesla. Edison and Morgan had taken the opportunity to "repay" Tesla for his defection to Westinghouse. One positive part of the campaign was that it forced Westinghouse to move to the 60-Hertz (cycles) frequency, which was considerably safer than the 133-Hertz system.

December of 1892 brought a new attack by General Electric. On December 15, the courts handed down a decision on the incandescent light that prevented the use of the Edison-type bulb by Westinghouse. Westinghouse did own an old bulb patent known as the Sawyer-Man stopper lamp. The Westinghouse Sawyer-Man lamp remained outside the court decision, so Westinghouse was satisfied that he could meet the fair requirements with the stopper lamp. George and family went to New York on the "Pittsburgher" express to do a little business and shop a few days before Christmas. While there, Westinghouse learned that General Electric lawyers had left for Pittsburgh. If they could stop Westinghouse bulb production for even a few weeks, it would cause Westinghouse to be unable to light the fair. Since Westinghouse had the contract, this was a direct attack to hurt, destroy, and embarrass Westinghouse Electric. The General Electric lawyers were ready to file for an injunction to stop the production of the Sawyer-Man lamps by Westinghouse. Westinghouse immediately called his neighbor, Pennsylvania Railroad executive Pitcairn, to ready his Pullman car and line up an express to return to Pittsburgh. Westinghouse reached his East End lawyer by wire to get over to the United States Circuit Court in Pittsburgh. Westinghouse was able to shock and surprise the General Electric lawyers at the courthouse. He first got a postponement until after Christmas. Westinghouse never could understand the nature of the attacks; he had always been open to a compromise. Westinghouse had been known to think little of bankers, and Morgan was out to teach him a lesson. But just as important, Morgan had wanted Westinghouse to join his "Electric Trust;" but Westinghouse refused, telling Morgan he would never enter such an unethical trust. Few men had ever stood off J. P. Morgan; even the president of the United States had to kiss his ring. The judge ruled no basis for any infringement until after Christmas. Precious time had been saved, yet General Electric would continue to harass Westinghouse, fortunately to no avail. Westinghouse immediately pulled in Pittsburgh glass expertise to start a bulb manufacturing plant. The Westinghouse bulb was an inferior bulb, and Westinghouse would hire hundreds of workers to constantly change bulbs at the fair.

George, Marguerite, and George III (son) attended the opening day festivities of the Chicago Fair. As was his style, Westinghouse stayed in the background, spending the day with family. It was a day of triumph; only a few weeks before, he had received a telegram that the International Niagara Commission had selected AC current for the Niagara Falls power plant. This would be the final victory of alternating current over direct current. No doubt the fair's use of AC had turned the tide; but in reality, alternating current was the superior power transmission system. General Electric would now be on the other end of a patent feud. Westinghouse owned the AC patents, but he was well aware that General Electric had also developed an AC power system to compete. Even more disturbing for

Westinghouse was the recent discovery of spying at his Pittsburgh operation. This happened two days after the Commission decided on AC current. Initially, Westinghouse thought the leak might have been with the Commission with so many Morgan people around, but a search warrant showed that General Electric had corporate spies involved. A draftsman was fired for selling blueprints to General Electric as well. General Electric argued they were protecting against patent infringements by Westinghouse. The Niagara Commission certainly leaked some through the normal course of comparing and visiting the plants involved. Once Morgan saw that AC current was going to win out, he forced the overextended Edison out of his own company. Morgan next looked to corner Westinghouse.

For years Niagara Falls was being called "white coal," as the energy of the falls was enormous. The Niagara power project really goes back to 1890 with the formation of Cataract Construction prior to the formation of General Electric and Westinghouse Electric and Manufacturing Company. Edison was one of the early investors in Cataract Construction because of the problems in lighting New York City. The cost of building steam powered DC power plants to light New York was impractical. DC power could only be transported a few blocks from the power station. Edison's DC system would require thirty-six power stations to service all of New York City. He was far from that goal of 36, as citizens were complaining about the noise and smoke of his steam driven central power stations. Vibrations were being felt in nearby buildings. Threats of lawsuits were rising, and even available land for these stations was in short supply. Edison, of course, was hoping for a DC power plant at Niagara. On the other hand, with its high voltage, AC could be transported many miles. J. P. Morgan came to the realization that Edison and DC power were the problems, and he forced Edison out. Westinghouse would win the Niagara contract, but he had to mortgage Solitude and much of his assets. J. P. Morgan tried to lure Westinghouse into an electrical trust, but Westinghouse rebuffed him. Morgan had been after Westinghouse since 1890 when he tried a takeover and then tried a merger attempt. Westinghouse had been on the ropes after the cash layouts for the fair and almost went under, but rival New York banker August Belmont saved him. Now Morgan would lay in wait.

The first power came on at Niagara on August 26, 1895. The initial power went to the electrochemical plants nearby, which would create a new opportunity for another group of East End inventors and investors. Full power didn't come on stream until September 30, at which time the directors of Cataract and Westinghouse plus assorted millionaires came to celebrate. Two important figures were not present. One missing was J. P. Morgan who was licking his wounds and would come in late October. One of the great results of the Niagara Power station was the rise of the American electrochemical industry. The two biggest customers of Niagara were the East End-owned Pittsburgh Reduction Company and the Carborundum Company. Pittsburgh Reduction Company (the future ALCOA aluminum) contracted for 5,000 horsepower of the 15,000 available. The Pittsburgh company, prior to the Niagara power plant, lacked the power needed for commercial scale aluminum production. Within a year, a massive electrochemical industry grew up around Niagara including sodium, soda ash, sodium peroxide. Calcium carbide plants followed. By 1897, 12,500 horsepower of the 13,500 horsepower available for local consumption was for electrochemical plants.[1] Westinghouse enjoyed visiting these plants since he always had a fascination with metallurgy. The aluminum industry owes a great deal to George Westinghouse and his East End neighbors.

Westinghouse and Heinz were also unique in the East End because they were mavericks. Heinz was a good neighbor, but his temperance beliefs left him out of the famous Thursday night poker games and the Frick-Mellon lunches at the Duquesne Club. Heinz also cared little for bankers and investments outside the food business. Like Heinz, George Westinghouse cared little for bankers, which put him at odds with fellow poker players — Andrew Mellon and Henry Clay Frick. In 1890, Westinghouse had approached Judge Mellon for a loan to support his expansion into electrical power. Westinghouse needed $300,000 and the Judge was willing. But Westinghouse refused to meet the Judge's terms of an equity position. Westinghouse would not have bankers on his board making technical decisions. He refused Mellon and went to the New York banking house of August Belmont. Mellon was a Pittsburgh banker and despised New York bankers as much as Westinghouse hated bankers in general. The Mellon/Westinghouse break would divide the loyalties of East End neighbors. Westinghouse's hatred of bankers would also strain his friendship with Henry Clay Frick, but both Frick and Westinghouse had an amazing ability to remove business from friendship.

Westinghouse even supported Democrat Glover Cleveland. Westinghouse's view of capitalism could be seen in his somewhat unique politics. Certainly, for most of his life he was a Republican, but he had crossed over for Democrat Grover Cleveland in 1892. Cleveland's pro-business approach had even gotten the support of the Pittsburgh local Republican Party. Westinghouse's Republican roots went back to abolition and Lincoln. Cleveland had offered an anti-boss, anti-trust approach that had won over many Republicans in 1892. His political crossover, however, isolated Westinghouse from his neighbors. Cleveland believed also in a full employment approach; it was a popular movement that the Republicans would later adopt as their own. Westinghouse would return to the Republicans with the presidential campaign of William McKinley. Westinghouse's close friend in the Senate had been Republican Chair of the Railroad Safety Committee, William McKinley. McKinley came from Canton, Ohio, an industrial town with many railroads. He had worked with Westinghouse on railroad and industry safety. They both favored a soft government hand to keep business ethically straight. McKinley was a "lunch pail" Republican as were most of the East End capitalists. McKinley wanted full employment and was willingly to take whatever measures needed. Like Westinghouse and Frick, he favored tariffs only when proven to be needed to foster job creation. Both McKinley and Westinghouse opposed the trusts and unethical behavior, while being pro-business. Both believed in a stronger application of the 1890 Sherman Anti-trust Act that had been nulli-

1 Passer, 293

fied by the courts. Both men felt unions were to be opposed but more as a reaction to poor management. Both were always anti-union but pro-worker. McKinley believed in tolerance among religions while being a somewhat independent believer like Westinghouse. He was also one of the first supporters of women rights.

During the McKinley Administration, Westinghouse purchased a secondary Washington home in fashionable and powerful DuPont Circle. He purchased the former mansion from Republican kingpin, former Speaker of the House, and former Republican presidential candidate James Blaine. Blaine himself had been a close friend of Andrew Carnegie and other East Enders. McKinley and Westinghouse had shared dinners at "Solitude" and were good friends. They often shared Westinghouse's special Pullman railroad car for trips to and from Washington. Both were national supporters of the YMCA. President McKinley often visited Westinghouse at his Berkshire Hills summer home, and Westinghouse was a visitor at the White House. The McKinley administration was the highpoint of East End capitalism. McKinley would have the seat of Jupiter in the East End pantheon of capitalism. Interestingly, Henry Clay Frick would finance a real pantheon of East End bronze busts at the McKinley Memorial in Niles, Ohio years later.

CHAPTER 14. PITTSBURGH'S STEPCHILDREN — THE ALUMINUM CAPITALISTS

During the McKinley administration a new commercial metal came on to the scene, and no metal would change the world more. It was a strong metal and much lighter than steel. Its commercialization had been dreamed about for years. Science fiction writers such as Jules Verne and H. G. Wells hailed it as the future of metals in the 1880s in science fiction books that a young Andrew Mellon had read. Jules Verne used it in fictional boats, buildings, aircraft, and a space capsule for the moon (all came true) in many of his novels such as *To The Moon and Back*. Wells used it for his Martian spacecraft in *War of the Worlds*. Baron Von Zeppelin in Germany awaited commercial aluminum to use in his air ships. In 1914, Pittsburgh Reduction Company would ship his dream order of aluminum. Even Charles Dickens was fascinated by the strange metal and wrote of it. Aluminum was rolled into foil for wall decorations of the rich. An example of such wall decorations can be seen in the nineteenth century mansion of the East Ender and steel magnate Henry Clay Frick. This wall decoration was rolled in France to a fine fold, costing ten times that of gold fold, and used only on the walls of the world's richest people. Frick was quite proud of this aluminum fold decoration and showed it to his neighbor and best friend, banker Andrew Mellon. Frick's aluminum wall covering was in his poker room where the Mellon brothers and Westinghouse would meet on Thursday nights. Interestingly, Frick made his only investment mistake a few years later in failing to invest in the start-up aluminum company of East Ender Captain Hunt. East Ender Andrew Mellon, however, would become the company's major backer and make a fortune in doing so. Besides Hunt and Mellon, another East Ender, George Westinghouse, would supply the final piece of the industrial puzzle.

Captain Alfred Hunt is truly one of the "lost" residents of Pittsburgh's East End. Hunt and his East End neighbors would commercially make aluminum and form the Aluminum Company of America (ALCOA). Pittsburgh has been known over the years as the "Glass City," "Iron City," and the "Steel City." Yet it was not glass, iron, or steel that was first commercially made available in Pittsburgh. It was aluminum that was commercially birthed in Pittsburgh. It was even the different spelling of aluminum in the company name that changed the American spelling (aluminum in most of the world). But even when aluminum was only available in limited quantities and more expensive than gold, it adorned the walls of the Frick and Mellon estates in the East End and castles of the kings of Europe. The first structural use of aluminum would be in the East End home of Andrew Mellon. Mellon would also have the world's first aluminum car at his East End mansion. Commercial scale aluminum production was the result of three East End neighbors. Alfred Hunt built the manufacturing process needed, financed by Andrew Mellon. Hunt was the first to use aluminum pots and shoe his horses with aluminum horseshoes. However, the miracle of mass-produced aluminum awaited the opening of the Niagara Falls electrical plant by East Ender George Westinghouse. Westinghouse himself had been an early adopter of aluminum applications. No area deserves the tile "Aluminum City" more than Pittsburgh's East End.

Aluminum is the earth's most abundant metal. Yet aluminum oxides and silicates are extremely stable oxides that are not easily smelted to aluminum metal. Most clay contains aluminum oxide; thus, it is known as "silver from clay." The metal did not become commercially available until the twentieth century; yet there are some intriguing stories and legends of its use in ancient times. One story is from the ancient Roman historian, Pliny the Elder, who tells of its existence over 2,000 years ago. The story is that Roman Emperor Tiberius had a cup of an extremely light, silvery metal. The inventor claimed he made it from clay. Fearing that this new precious metal would devalue his gold and silver reserves, he had the inventor beheaded and his workshop destroyed. Thus the technology disappeared for two thousand years, only to surface in Pittsburgh's East End in the 1880s. Amazingly, a metal ornament was discovered in the tomb of Chinese military leader, Chou-Chu, which was 85 percent aluminum. Chou-Chu would date back to the third century. The use of aluminum compounds such as alum was common in the Middle Ages in the manufacture of paper, dyes, and leather production.

One of the earliest, although probably not the first to produce pure metallic aluminum, was Danish chemist, Hans Christian Oersted, in 1825. He used chemical reducing agents and electrical current. Two years later German chemist Frederick Wohler perfected the process, but the methods could produce, at best, a few buttons. These aluminum buttons were stored in bank vaults with guards. Industrialist Saint Claire Deville displayed these few buttons at the 1855 World's Fair in Paris. The simple display of "silver from clay" inspired Emperor Napoleon III of France. Along with Deville, the emperor invested in aluminum plants. The cost was $522 a pound or about $10,000 a pound in today's dollars. Napoleon III had aluminum tableware produced for his best guests, while lesser guests used gold and silverware. Napoleon III even planned to produce aluminum armor for his army. In the 1870s, aluminum remained more expensive and precious than gold. With the completion of the Washington Monument in Washington, D.C., it was decided to cap the monument with a pyramid of precious aluminum in 1884.

Before the commercial breakthrough of aluminum, a young Alfred Hunt had published a paper predicting aluminum buildings, airplanes, and pots. Hunt even believed that aluminum horseshoes might give his racehorses a competitive advantage. Horseracing and gambling had become a popular East End pastime for many like Captain Hunt. The real breakthrough to the commercial production of aluminum came in 1886 by Charles Hall. Hall was an Oberlin College student in Ohio working in a makeshift laboratory. He was an obsessed "Edison" type chemist whose endless experimentation had unlocked the secret. Today a beautiful aluminum statute of Charles Hall commemorates the discovery. Motivated by the possibility of making a fortune, he continued endless experiments on aluminum making, even as he discovered an electrolytic method to remove aluminum from its oxide. Hall had tried many different oxides, taking his Edison-like experimentation approach to extremes. Finally he discovered that cryolite, a mineral from Greenland, would work. The Hall process was an electrochemical, requiring an electric current; and like Edison, Hall used a series of batteries to supply the electricity for his laboratory.

About the same time a French student, Paul Heroult, developed the same process of Hall using chemical electrolysis. The process used a huge amount of electrical current, limiting its use until George Westinghouse opened the Niagara Falls generating plant in the 1890s. Commercialization would, however, get its start in Pittsburgh. Neither Charles Hall nor Paul Heroult had the energy source to take their process beyond the laboratory. One drawback to aluminum smelting with the Hall process, even today, remains its consumption of electrical power. The amount of energy needed to smelt just one pound of aluminum would keep a 40-watt light bulb burning for 10 to 12 days. To state it another way, today aluminum smelting takes 4 percent of the world's electrical power. Only one city in the world, Pittsburgh, had electrical power sources on that level in the late 1880s. East Ender Captain Alfred Hunt, however, would take a first step in manufacturing aluminum in his Pittsburgh plant, using a Westinghouse steam powered electrical generator. It was even more interesting that the development of aluminum can be traced to the old Pig Iron Aristocrats of Pittsburgh.

Alfred Hunt was one of the country's first true metallurgists. His mother was a chemist who encouraged him in the study of metallurgy. Metallurgy, however, was not a discipline of its own. Hunt went to the Massachusetts Institute of Technology to study metallurgy in the chemistry department. After Hunt graduated, a friend of the family and Pittsburgher, James Park Jr., asked Hunt to come to Pittsburgh and work for Black Diamond Steel of Park, Brother & Co. The Park family was part of Pittsburgh's old Pig Iron Aristocracy since 1804. The original Park factory had been one of the first to morph from a blacksmith shop into an iron manufacturing plant. The Park mansion was close to William Thaw and B. F. Jones on the north side of Pittsburgh's millionaire row. The Park family had been the first investors in Pittsburgh baseball, the Allegheny Observatory, and the University of Pittsburgh. James Park Jr. was the founder of the Chemistry and Mineralogy Department at the University of Pittsburgh in the 1860s. Later James Park's fight to support the patent battle of Pittsburgher William Kelly over Bessemer would result in a victory in 1898, although Kelly would be lost to history. Hunt's relationship with James Park opened many doors for the young Hunt. He would be accepted in the core of Pittsburgh's aristocracy which included the Masons, Presbyterianism, the pig iron industry, and large sums of East End capital.

When Hunt joined Black Diamond Crucible Steel, it was making specialty steel that was considered on a par with those of Sheffield, England. East Ender Curtiss Hussey had developed the American crucible process earlier in the 1870s. Hunt rented an apartment in the upscale boarding home of the Negley family in East Liberty near Hussey's mansion. He joined the Presbyterian Church and the Masonic Lodge as he rose through Black Diamond. Hunt had positioned himself as a young and upcoming East Ender. He opened his own company of Pittsburgh Testing laboratory, which offered expertise to many Pittsburgh steel companies. Hunt gained expertise in the special crucible steel process, which manufactured expensive tool steel. He built a beautiful home on Shady Lane (Shady Avenue) in East Liberty. Early on, Hunt had become interested in the possible use of aluminum in tool steelmaking. Aluminum could be used to stabilize and produce a sound steel structure; the steel industry would need tons, not pounds, of aluminum on a daily basis. The problem was that aluminum could not be supplied in the quantities needed to apply this to steel making. At the same time, metallurgist Hunt began to experiment with aluminum making and practical uses of aluminum.

One of the metallurgists that Hunt had on the aluminum smelting project was Romaine Cole, who left shortly afterward to work for Cowles Electric Smelting and Aluminum Company. At Cowles, Cole met Martin Hall who was trying to sell his aluminum smelting process. In the meantime, Cole returned to Pittsburgh Testing. On July 31, 1888, Romaine Cole, Alfred Hunt, Howard Lash (president of Carbon Steel), Millard Hunsiker (sales manager of Carbon Steel), Robert John Scott (a Carnegie partner and superintendent of Union Mills), and W. S. Sample (Chief Chemist – Pittsburgh Testing) held a meeting at Hunt's home at 272 Shady Lane (Shady Avenue) in East Liberty. This organizational meeting resulted in the formation of Pittsburgh Reduction Company (future ALCOA), whose name would be the commercialization of the Hall process. Martin Hall took up residence in an East Liberty apartment house owned by Hunt. A few months later, two other old time East Enders would invest — Andrew Mellon and William Thaw. Captain Hunt had come to Andrew Mellon for a small loan to help with the operation. Andrew Mellon, liked so many of the Gilded Age, was captivated by this silver-like metal. He offered a much larger loan and bought $6,000 worth of stock. It was the beginning of an historic relationship.

The new company started operations on Pittsburgh's Smallman Street. Yet another East Ender, George Westinghouse, supplied the two powerful Westinghouse dynamos to produce the needed electrical current. The 1,200 amperes and 25 volts of each stream-driven dynamo was beyond any laboratory battery and offered the potential for a continuous operation. George Westinghouse himself supervised the installation. Westinghouse had been experimenting with aluminum parts for several years and looked forward to the availability of aluminum. On Thanksgiving Day 1888, the plant, under the supervision of Martin Hall, produced its first commercial batch of aluminum. By mid-1889, the Smallman plant was producing about 1,000 pounds of aluminum a month at around $5 a pound. By the end of the year, the price was about $2 a pound, but the problem was now lack of demand. Still the company enjoyed profits. For Captain Hunt and his family, they started looking for a bigger home in the East End. The Hunts acquired a three story stone house at 4916 Wallingford Street, which was within walking distance for their son, Roy, to Shadyside Academy, which had been founded by East End capitalists such as Westinghouse, Frick, and Heinz for the education of their sons.

The year 1893 would prove the turning point. While Hunt and Hall had made rapid progress on the development, there was a major patent challenge from Cowles Electric Smelting and Aluminum Company. Cowles had a weak case but, as in most inventions, the Hall process was a confluence of prior discoveries. The trial had dragged on for years, but a decision came on January 20, 1893. The Judge was William Taft (future president of the United States and a friend of the East End). The 1,500-page decision was clear that Hall was the inventor. Pittsburgh Reduction now controlled the patent to the only commercial process of aluminum production. The aluminum capitalists now joined their neighbors with an exhibit at the Chicago World Fair in 1893.

Alfred Hunt and Charles Hall would join East End exhibitors — George Westinghouse, H. J. Heinz, and Henry Clay Frick — at the 1893 Chicago World Fair in stealing the show. The Pittsburgh Reduction Company was an award winner at the fair with its educational exhibit. The exhibit included some of the original small pellets made by Hall at his Oberlin laboratory. There was a scale model of the Hall process and aluminum samples. The short preparation time limited the number of uses that could be shown at the fair. However, a year later at the Pittsburgh Exposition, the company demonstrated an aluminum bicycle and kitchenware such as pots and pans. The potential use of aluminum in bicycles attracted the Wright brothers who would use an aluminum crankcase in their first plane. The company had also built a new aluminum-making plant at New Kensington, Pennsylvania, on the Allegheny River. This plant would use coal to fire the steam-driven Westinghouse generators and could produce 1,000 pounds of aluminum a day. The year 1893 brought Westinghouse the Niagara Falls power project, and the Pittsburgh Reduction Company signed a contract to be the major customer of the new Niagara Falls plant. This new plant would have the capacity to produce 10,000 pounds of aluminum a day. Westinghouse's Niagara project and ALCOA's new aluminum plant would realize the dreams of science fiction writers of the previous hundred years.

Interestingly, one of the first commercial users of aluminum would be George Westinghouse. George Westinghouse was extremely excited about the new availability of aluminum that his AC system had created. Westinghouse anticipated that cheap power would mean low cost aluminum, and he and his engineers were looking at potential uses. Aluminum additions to Babbitt bearing metal showed superior results at Westinghouse Machine and Air Brake Companies. These engineers were also using aluminum bronze in corrosion applications. Westinghouse soon became a customer of Pittsburgh Reduction experimenting with aluminum parts. One of his first applications was a valve in his air brake. He also found uses of it as a shim for machinery. Westinghouse's foundry even looked to it as a casting metal to replace cast iron. Another application that Pittsburgh Reduction Company was the first to use was aluminum foil. Westinghouse had studied the production of aluminum foil in France and had suggested its manufacture to Pittsburgh Reduction. Westinghouse and a number of his Homewood neighbors like Henry Clay Frick used aluminum foil on walls when it had a price higher than gold. The aluminum wall decoration of that period can still be seen today at the Frick mansion.

Alfred Hunt was an eccentric and a passionate metallurgical engineer. He had aluminum sinks and bathtubs installed at his Shadyside home as he tried to market these new applications with his East End neighbors. Andrew Mellon, a major investor in the company, would also install aluminum bathtubs and sinks. The aluminum foil in the Thursday night poker room at the Frick home had always fascinated Mellon. Andrew Mellon had become a believer in aluminum and backed the company loans in very difficult times. Interestingly, Frick would turn down the aluminum investments that Mellon brought to their weekly Duquesne Club investment meetings. It would be one of the few times that Frick passed up a successful investment. By 1894, Mellon owned 12 percent of the company and controlled all the loans. In later years, Mellon converted many decorations in his mansion to aluminum and ordered the first all aluminum cars to be made. Mellon had achieved a foothold in a Pittsburgh company that his father had failed to do with Westinghouse Air Brake. Westinghouse would not have allowed a Pittsburgh banker on the board. This model of banking and industry became known as the "Mellon System." Brother Richard Mellon also became a major investor with his brother.

Alfred Hunt would characterize the East End's love of community and country. Hunt, like Henry Clay Frick and all the East Enders, was extremely patriotic. The sinking of the U.S. battleship *Maine* in Havana took the United States into the Spanish-American War. Hunt would volunteer and command an artillery unit. He had training in artillery at MIT. Aluminum would make its first war appearance thanks to Hunt as well. War applications had been the dream of Germany's Count Von Zeppelin and France's Napoleon III, but those countries could not produce the volume needed. Teddy Roosevelt charged up San Juan Hill with an aluminum canteen. The army was using aluminum tent pins. It was a short war, and after a year Hunt returned, marching in victory down Pittsburgh's Fifth Avenue. Hunt would return to steer Pittsburgh Reduction Company forward. He would also lead many civic efforts in the area, including the effort for clean water in the area.

The growth of the company after the Spanish-American War was phenomenal. By 1899, a larger production plant was needed. The decision of locating at New Kensington on the Allegheny River was heavily influenced by Andrew Mellon and his brother. T. Mellon & Sons owned large amounts of land on the Allegheny and were investing in land development companies. The Mellons offered four acres of level ground on the river and a $10,000 cash bonus to locate there. The New Kensington plant was specifically designed to manufacture sheet aluminum to make cooking utensils. In 1901, Pittsburgh Reduction Company organized The Aluminum Cooking Utensil Company to sell to housewives. The company developed a novel plan to sell its Wear-Ever brand. College students were re-cruited to sell door to door by demonstrating aluminum cookware.

ALCOA continued its amazing growth, but in 1912 it ran up against the new anti-trust laws. The anti-trust progressive movement was sweeping the United States. The 1912 election was one of the first election setbacks for the East End. Frick, Heinz, and Mellon poured money into the Republican effort as their old nemesis Teddy Roosevelt left the party to run as an independent. The East End was solidly behind the Republican can-didate Howard Taft, but Roosevelt was a popular figure and split the Republican Party. The end result was the election of Democrat Woodrow Wilson. Wilson pushed through new tariff reductions, which reduced those on aluminum. Wilson also brought anti-trust pressure on Pittsburgh companies and restricted bank involvement in corporations. East Ender Philander Knox, now back in the Senate, mounted a strong defense of Pittsburgh industries. The last political efforts of East End lions such as Frick and Heinz were to defeat the Democrats in 1920. The East End mounted an unequaled $400,000 in Allegheny County (most of it from East End neighbors). Mellon put his own organization directly into the campaign. Republican Warren Harding won handily. For both Frick and Mellon, the election was beyond business as both opposed Wilson's League of Nations (forerun-ner of the United Nations). In 1918, they started a fund to support members of Congress known as the "Irreconcilables" who opposed the league.

CHAPTER 15. CAMELOT

The McKinley presidency represented the peak of the Republican Party in the Pittsburgh area. Two East Enders and old Carnegie partners would serve in the McKinley administration: John A. Leishman as Minister to Switzerland and Philander Knox as Attorney General. While McKinley came from Canton, Ohio, his family had roots and shared values with the East End. His Scotch–Irish grandparents had lived and manufactured iron in Western Pennsylvania before moving on to Youngstown and then Canton. Like most of the East Enders, McKinley was pure Scotch–Irish and an active Mason. He was educated on the *McGuffey Readers* and even taught Youngstown students using the *Readers*. The 1896 presidential election unified the East End, and it was the greatest geographic financial contributor to McKinley. The McKinley/East End relationship became symbiotic over his administration. As a young Civil War officer, McKinley had been part of the army assigned to protect the strategic iron industry of Pittsburgh, and he realized its importance to nation building. His relationship over the years with George Westinghouse had often taken him to the East End, and he respected these capitalists. With the nation suffering from the depression of 1893, McKinley needed the East Enders to lead the nation back to prosperity.

The presidential campaign of 1896 was between free trader William Jennings Bryan of Nebraska and protectionist William McKinley of Ohio. Frick had always been a strong supporter of protectionist tariffs and of Ohio Congressman McKinley. McKinley's manager, Mark Hanna, approached Frick for help. Hanna obtained $250,000 donations each from Frick, Carnegie, Rockefeller, and J. P. Morgan. Of the four, only Frick was an enthusiastic supporter. Carnegie, Rockefeller, and Morgan were concerned about McKinley's weak support of the gold standard. For Frick, however, the issue was tariffs, jobs, and industrial growth. Frick was the most active in his support, following up with calls to others for financial support. Heinz, Westinghouse, Jones, Knox, Mellon, and many East Enders poured in major amounts. The huge backing of Pittsburgh's East End allowed McKinley to run free of the east coast and New York political bosses. Of course, many argued that he eliminated political bosses in favor of industrial bosses, but they shared the fundamental belief of McKinley in the protection and building of American industry. Frick truly had his heart in this election, believing it was critical to the very future of the nation. Frick's son, Childs, named a pet rabbit after presidential candidate McKinley. Even before McKinley started the campaign, he was pulled into personal bankruptcy; Frick helped pay off his debt and allowed McKinley to purchase a new suit for the swearing-in ceremony. Frick had another motive in the election. He and Carnegie both hoped to have East Ender and corporate lawyer, Philander Knox, be selected as attorney general and soften the growing anti-trust movement of the federal government.

The campaign was a tough one, with McKinley running his famous "front-porch" campaign. McKinley was the first Republican since Lincoln to reject the East Coast political bosses of men like Teddy Roosevelt. Eastern blueblood Republicans and bosses gave weak support, leaving the victory in the hands of the industrialists and the grassroots labor support. East Ender Benjamin Jones, the Pittsburgh Republican Party head, unified with Ohio industrialist, Mark Hanna, to build a worker-management political alliance centered on tariffs. Frick paid for steelworkers to get active in the campaign. Train fare was supplied to Homestead and Braddock workers to take their families to Canton, Ohio, on the Pennsylvania Railroad (a two-and-half hour trip). The families were also supplied a picnic style lunch at the McKinley home. Actually, McKinley found substantial labor support because his protectionist policies meant steel jobs. Steelworkers poured into Canton, not by the thousands but tens of thousands. Carnegie's rail mill at Braddock sent thousands alone. East Enders and the Pennsylvania Railroad offered special trains weekly for workers and families from the Pittsburgh and Youngstown areas. Braddock's Edgar Thomson was one of the largest factories, producing most of the steel rails for the booming railroad expansion. The mill had started in 1875 and owed its very existence to the Republican tariffs. Over 90 percent of rails were imported at the time Edgar Thomson started up in 1875. Thanks to tariffs, it survived and thrived, overtaking the domestic rail market by 1882. In 1889, British steelmakers hailed Edgar Thomson Works as the most productive mill in the world. By the end of the 1890s, Edgar Thomson Works would have made more steel rails than the rest of the world combined.

Support was not only coming from the mill at Braddock, but a huge delegation from the troubled Homestead Works came in September by 33 special train cars furnished by Henry Clay Frick. McKinley avoided any reference to the 1893 labor lockout, which had generated Democratic criticism, as McKinley had no direct ties to that strike. Even though Carnegie and Frick paid for the Homesteader visit, McKinley was very popular with the steelworkers and grassroots labor. Steel tariffs had been the source of their income, and they were thankful to the politician who had made a career out of the tariff issue. The Homestead steelworkers presented him with a gold-plated piece of steel armor plate. Charles Schwab headed the delegation. A large parade was organized to march the Homesteaders from the train station to McKinley's home. The mile path from the railroad station was lined with food and souvenir stands. The Homestead speech exemplified the model of the front porch campaign. McKinley used what would later be called the "rhetoric of silence." McKinley avoided the local issue and keyed in on a national and future path. Mrs. McKinley served the workers lemonade during the speech. After the speech, the workers were escorted to a tent for lunch.

The McKinley presidency would offer an expansion of American jobs through steel tariffs. Frick was a firm believer in nationalistic capitalism using tariffs versus free-trade capitalism. McKinley won the election by 51 percent to 47 percent over Bryant. The Republicans took the house back, but Congress was hesitating to take on increased tariffs. Frick went on to suggest a specific review of specific metal product tariffs by Congress. Frick argued not for arbitrary higher tariffs but focused tariffs to promote American business. The East End was now in a position to control the political forces. Pittsburgh industry was growing in many directions thanks to the McKinley tariffs of 1890. In Pittsburgh, the great labor-management alliance gave McKinley 70 percent of the Pittsburgh and Allegheny County vote, exceeding the previous Republican vote record given to Abraham Lincoln. From 1876 to 1890, the Pittsburgh mean Republican percentage had been 53 percent. The East End became the financial engine for the Republican Party. East Enders such as Frick, Jones, Westinghouse, and Heinz were said to select presidents in secret neighborhood meetings or over lunch at the Duquesne Club.

Senate leader Nelson Aldrich consulted secretly with Frick on how to proceed with the tariff bill.[1] Frick wrote a fair and balanced response, not asking for huge increases for steel tariffs; in fact, he suggested only the status quo, feeling the industry's protection was adequate. In 1897, McKinley and Aldrich pushed through a bill based on Frick's suggestions, which ushered in one of America's greatest industrial booms. Frick got another favor from McKinley. After the election, Frick wrote McKinley suggesting his partner, neighbor, and fellow poker player Philander Knox for Attorney General. McKinley did select Knox, replacing industrialists for the eastern political bosses of previous administrations. Frick would commission a portrait of McKinley as a present for his election. Frick would commission another picture of McKinley after his 1900 re-election. While not close friends, McKinley was one of a few politicians that had the respect of Frick. Both McKinley and Frick were strong supporters of protecting all American industries. They did share a strong belief in the principles of Freemasonry, America first, and the importance of the YMCA and YWCA in developing America's youth. Frick never fully understood McKinley, who had the same love of capitalism but had none of the benefits of wealth. East Ender Westinghouse, another friend of McKinley, would vacation with McKinley that summer.

The McKinley presidency was the industrial Camelot of America. It was a presidency that Henry Clay Frick was initially reluctant to support but came to admire. Personally quite different, Frick and McKinley shared a common belief in capitalism. In the five years of the McKinley presidency, America rose to world leadership in economic might and Pittsburgh to national prominence. America led in the manufacture of steel, iron, coal,

---

1 Harvey, p. 295

---

oil, glass, electrical equipment, tools, machinery, and pickles. The growth spurred a massive influx of immigrants as jobs went unfilled in a massive economic boom. The government's biggest issue was what to do with the surplus. The government coffers overflowed, not from taxes (there was no income tax!), but from tariffs on incoming imports! To the modern reader, this appears as a bizarre world where things are reversed. America had created a manufacturing utopia. Some might argue that many problems would follow, but the manufacturing success also covered many evils and fed many immigrants and their families. From McKinley's standpoint, his East Enders were capitalists behaving correctly. McKinley cared little for the New York bankers and financiers. The East End capitalists poured their profits into building steel mills, factories, museum, hospitals, and social organizations. They muted the constant claims that the savings from tariffs went into the pockets of the rich. The industrial surge of Pittsburgh put money into the worker families and made class differences less aggravating. Industrialists like Frick, Heinz, and Westinghouse had much influence in the McKinley administration.

Westinghouse and McKinley went back to the 1880s. Westinghouse's biggest supporter in Washington of his railroad projects had been William McKinley, then head of the Ways and Means Committee in Congress. McKinley came to Westinghouse's East End "Solitude" mansion in early 1890 to confer on railroad safety issues. They would share a passion for industrial safety throughout their careers. Westinghouse would give him a ride on his Pullman car to McKinley's hometown of Canton, Ohio. They would immediately become friends, as Westinghouse discussed the new community he was developing at Wilmerding to support his air brake operation. McKinley had been a president of the YMCA in Canton and noted its value in communities. Westinghouse was a huge supporter of the YMCA. Maybe more importantly, they shared government support of business while rejecting trusts and a strong belief in "lunch pail" Republicanism. Another bond shared was their pride in being veterans of the Grand Army of the Republic. Both men would point to their military service as the highlight of their careers. It would be a friendship that would grow over the years. Westinghouse was never active in politics, but he was a Republican, going back to his abolitionist roots, and became a strong personal supporter of President William McKinley. McKinley, a devout Presbyterian, shared many of Westinghouse's core beliefs. Westinghouse was even a presidential elector for the McKinley election, as President McKinley was a house guest at all of Westinghouse's mansions. During the McKinley administration, Westinghouse was a personal advisor to the president and purchased a third mansion in Washington, D.C. known as Blaine Mansion (DuPont Circle). For a short time, Marguerite became involved in the social and political scene in Washington under the McKinley administration. Westinghouse's Washington ties became critical to his businesses. He was a regular guest of the McKinley White House.

The year 1897 was a time of relaxation for Westinghouse, and he spent more time than in previous years at his summer home "Erskine" in Berkshire Hills because his wife hated the increasing smoke of Pittsburgh's East End. Westinghouse put on Fourth of July fireworks displays and added a light show that included a profile of President McKinley.

In late September his old friend, President William McKinley, visited him and Mrs. West-inghouse at Erskine. McKinley visited Westinghouse a number of times as he loved to vacation in the Berkshire Hills area. He had also won over most of Pittsburgh's East End with his pro-industry, pro-American policies, and he made several visits to the East End. Carnegie (now in New York for many years) was his only detractor. Carnegie saw McKinley as responsible for the Spanish–American War, and Carnegie had become a pacifist in his retirement. He tried to distance himself from his capitalistic roots in later years as well.

McKinley proved to be one of America's most popular presidents as he presided over the golden era of American manufacturing. The decade of the 1890s represented the greatest period of economic growth and industrial expansion for America, and not just for the East Enders but for many in the surrounding mill towns. Statistics for the 1890 to 1900 decade were impressive no matter how they were presented and support the conclusion that prices came down, profits rose, capital investment went up, and wages held or slightly increased (real wages clearly rose). Average annual manufacturing income went from $425.00 a year and $1.44 a day in 1890 to $432.00 a year and $1.50 a day in 1900, while prices remained steady or declined. The average day in manufacturing remained around ten hours a day. Heavily protected industries such as steel fared slightly better with wages. Automated manufacturing drove consumer prices down on most products. The cost of living index fell during the decade from 91 to 84 or about 8 percent. The clothing cost of living dropped even more from 134 to 108 or 19 percent. Food stayed about the same, but the cost of protected sugar dropped around 25 percent. The bottom line is that real wage (adjusted for cost of living) index rose from $1.58 a day to $1.77 a day in 1900 or about a 12 percent increase.[1] In addition, millions of jobs were created. The success of this period of managed trade, trade reciprocity, and protective tariffs depended on government oversight, business cooperation, and labor support. Proper management and congressional oversight avoided the feared trade wars.

September 1901 brought disturbing news in the East End. President McKinley had been shot a week earlier at the Buffalo World's Fair and had died. The assassin, Leon Czolgosz, was a socialist and anarchist. (Anarchists were the terrorists of the time.) Leon Czolgosz had a link to Frick's past. Czolgosz's girlfriend, Emma Goldman, had been the earlier girlfriend of Frick's would-be assassin, Alexander Berkman. Emma Goldman had also been taken into custody. Henry Clay Frick, who was visually shaken, made a rare statement to the reporters on hearing of the McKinley shooting: "I hope that the president will live. His death would be a serious blow to the great commercial interests of this country, which have grown along such healthful lines during his term at the head of our government. The country cannot afford to lose him."[2] McKinley died on September 14, 1901, however, and lay in state briefly in Buffalo. Howard Heinz headed to Buffalo to view the body as did other young East Enders. In 1900, a young Howard Heinz (son of H. J.) had headed up the McKinley–Roosevelt grand parade in Pittsburgh, and Howard was one of

---

1 Albert Rees, *Real Wages in Manufacturing 1890-1914*, (Princeton: Princeton University Press, 1961)

2 *Daily Picayune*, September 13, 1901, page 7

McKinley's strongest supporters. When McKinley died, Howard, who owned one of the few automobiles in Pittsburgh, got his brother and drove to Buffalo. McKinley had been extremely popular among the youth of the East End (a John Kennedy of his time).

Frick and his East End neighbors had supported McKinley since his early days in congress. They never fully understood McKinley, but they shared a belief in American capitalism and exceptionalism. The McKinley assassination shook the nation as did John F. Kennedy's assassination. Frick and the Pennsylvania Railroad Board of Directors supplied a special funeral train for McKinley's body, cabinet, and family. The body of McKinley moved from Buffalo to the Capitol and then to his home of Canton, Ohio. As the funeral train passed the Frick's Pennsylvania coalmines, miners' torches lit the way. As a young lawyer, McKinley had represented striking miners who were being charged. The train was scheduled to slowly pass the Westinghouse plants where women workers stood on railcars. As the train with East Ender and Attorney General Philander Knox and McKinley's body passed by the mills of Braddock and Homestead, work was stopped for ten minutes as steelworkers lined the tracks holding their dinner pails high as a tribute to the "Napoleon of Protectionism."

The train passed slowly through the East End and on to Pittsburgh. The funeral train passed in view of the Monongahela House where presidents from Lincoln to McKinley had stayed. Pittsburgh was an important port of call in this industrial era, and McKinley had visited here often, twice as president. At Pittsburgh's Second Avenue, the train passed the exact location where the Westinghouse railroad air brake had been tested successfully, saving the life of a peddler. McKinley would pass legislation over the years which would make air brakes mandatory on American trains. Also in the crowd at the Pittsburgh station was M. M. Garland, who was president of the Amalgamated Association of Iron, Steel, and Tin Workers at the end of the Homestead Strike. Garland had become a McKinley supporter and was working with him for labor peace. Garland, like Samuel Gompers, had come to realize that prosperity meant union membership as well as corporate profits. Union membership quadrupled during the McKinley administration as industry rapidly expanded.

Most East Enders would attend the massive funeral of an extremely popular president in Canton, Ohio. They rode on a special train of the Pennsylvania Railroad. They would be among tens of thousands to do so; and United States Steel called for a holiday to allow steelworkers to travel by rail to Canton. Again special trains were assigned for that purpose. McKinley's full cabinet, most of Congress, all of the Supreme Court, and endless politicians descended on the small city of Canton. America's greatest industrialists also gathered in Canton. In addition to America's aristocracy, hundreds of steelworkers and miners came to Canton. Henry Clay Frick would always remember this gentle middle class president who was the political lion of capitalism. Frick could not fully understand McKinley's passionate defense of capitalism, since McKinley, unlike Frick, had gotten very little rewards from capitalism, lacking even the money to buy a new suit for his swearing-in ceremony. Furthermore, with McKinley gone and Teddy Roosevelt as president, Frick and his neighbors realized that capitalism would have a new competitor in progressivism.

Roosevelt was generally disliked by the capitalists. Even J. P. Morgan had little good to say about Roosevelt. Roosevelt would live up to their fears in the first year by breaking up Morgan's railroad trust and forcing a labor settlement in the Eastern anthracite coal fields by threatening to nationalize them. East Enders considered the Republican progressive more dangerous than any of the other anti-capitalists. Yet, Roosevelt would travel to Frick's East End home in 1902 to pay his respects to the East End. He also held East Ender Philander Knox in his cabinet after the McKinley death.

Shortly after McKinley's death, a McKinley Memorial in Niles, Ohio, was proposed. It is in Niles that an Ohio Pig Iron Aristocrat of the nineteenth century, Joseph Butler, built an architectural monument to a fallen friend and supporter of the industry — his beloved President William McKinley. Butler was having trouble getting the funds, and even the Carnegie fund rejected his library request. The financial support for such a project came from another admirer of McKinley and America's bad boy and East Ender — Henry Clay Frick. It is the bust of Henry Clay Frick that fills the prominent place of America's Jupiter at the Memorial. Frick, a Pittsburgher, has found no such honor in his hometown or in any American town. In the last October of his life, Henry Clay Frick visited this Niles Memorial, as he had done often in prior years, and was brought to tears. Those tears surely were not for McKinley alone but for golden times now past. It is in Niles, Ohio, that Frick finds such a place of honor. Frick's bronze bust is not alone; it is surrounded by East Enders: Andrew Mellon, Andrew Carnegie, Philander Knox, Benjamin Jones, and George Westinghouse. Out of 42 busts, no neighborhood is even close to being represented as well as Pittsburgh's East End. The memorial is a marble pantheon where America's greatest industrialists are honored. By honoring men filled with contradictions like Frick but bound together by a belief in capitalism, this pantheon was filled with bronze busts of the zenith of American capitalists during the McKinley administration. Its torch remains ready to be lit by some future generation. Interestingly, when Carnegie hesitated to make a donation to the Memorial, the Carnegie Foundation collected funds to assure that Carnegie's bust would be included. Built as a type of Alamo of America's great manufacturing past, it was a place that an older Frick visited often, weeping. Frick not only was the main supporter of the building and library, but in a rebuff of Carnegie, he filled the Presidential Library with books.

CHAPTER 16. THE END OF CAMELOT

The death of McKinley coupled with the death of the Carnegie partnership delineated the move into the new century for the East End Capitalists. A peak followed by a slow decline of Pittsburgh's neighborhood started in the early 1900s with the breakup of the Carnegie Empire and the formation of United States Steel's headquarters in New York. The end of Carnegie's steel empire created personal divisions and geographic divisions. It also created a massive amount of wealth as paper percentages into cash. United States Steel would be located in New York, which would take several East Enders away. The earlier dissolution of the great Carnegie partnership created over 30 millionaires, many of whom moved or upgraded in the East End. The distribution of the Carnegie's partner money would send others to retire in more exotic places. In general, New York money would draw many out of the neighborhood. National powers struggles would affect men like George Westinghouse. The iconic symbol of Pittsburgh, its sulfuric smoke, would drive out women like Mrs. Westinghouse and Mrs. Frick. Still the Mellon families, Jones Families, Heinz family, and the Frick family would remain at the foundation of the neighborhood.

In January 1899, an unprecedented meeting of East Enders took place at Carnegie's New York home. The meeting was led by four partners (only Schwab was not yet living in the East End) — Henry Clay Frick, Henry Phipps, Dod Lauder, and Charles Schwab. These partners had been negotiating and dealing together on their own for a possible sale or merger of Carnegie Steel. Such a possibility seemed impossible a few months earlier. Carnegie was open to the idea, as he got more involved in politics, social issues, and philanthropy. The others wanted the ability to take more cash out in stock. Carnegie's partner pact, known as the "Iron Clad Agreement," left partners rich on paper but cash poor compared to their style of living. The group represented both sides of the issue. Carnegie had sent mixed signals for years; at least now the discussion was brought into the open.

With the Chicago steel mills and its increasing competition, Carnegie faced pouring even more profits into capital spending versus partner dividends.

The time seemed perfect for Carnegie to become a stock company as profits for 1899 were expected to double to $21 million, but the future looked difficult. Federal Steel of Chicago, with J. P. Morgan money, was becoming too strong to take down. The National Steel tube-making trust of Chicago was looking at moving into steelmaking versus buying out Carnegie Steel. Partners came to the meeting with their own agenda. At the time Frick was dealing behind Carnegie's back with William Moore of National, who had put together trusts in steel tubes and steel plate. Frick hoped to achieve Carnegie's approval to sell or at least combine his H. C. Frick Company in Carnegie Steel to make a future sale easier. Carnegie still wanted to fight, but he could count and realized that most partners wanted to sell. The result was Frick was given the go-ahead to negotiate a sale at a price of at least $250 million. The deal for combining H. C. Frick Company was tabled as a concession to Carnegie. Dod Lauder, however, was suspicious of Frick and Phipps. Lauder probably realized there was more than Frick was telling.

Frick wasted little time to initiate his own campaign to sell or merge Carnegie Steel. Frick's first plan was to combine with Morgan and Judge Gary's Federal Steel. Frick met with Judge Gary in the early spring of 1899 to compare properties and the possibility of a merger.[1] One hang-up became the need for the combination to include the coke operations of H. C. Frick Company. A good supply of high-quality Connellsville coke was one item Federal Steel lacked. While negotiations failed because Frick would not assure support from the Carnegie organization, it was the beginning of an exchange that would ultimately lead to the formation of United States Steel. Partners were anxious to convert shares into cash for various reasons. Frick wanted more control; Phipps wanted to retire; and some, like Charles Schwab, wanted more money to spend.

Frick and Phipps continued to negotiate with Chicago steel man, William Moore, on a buyout. Both kept the potential buyer a secret from Carnegie, knowing he would have a problem with Moore because Carnegie disliked him. They also knew they only had to deal with Carnegie in the final details; if not, they would have to deal with Carnegie interference. Frick finally negotiated a very favorable deal with William Moore, particularly for Frick. Carnegie Steel would be purchased for $250 million and H. C. Frick Company for $70 million. Carnegie did not know the buyer but probably figured Rockefeller or Mellon were involved, although some believe that Carnegie had to know that it was Moore. Carnegie asked for $2 million as a retainer for the partnership in return for his power of attorney. As always, Frick proved his mastery of financial deals in handling Carnegie's requirement. Frick and Phipps were to give the partnership the $2 million by negotiating with Moore and the other Carnegie partners; they needed only $170,000 out of their own pockets. They realized the importance of speed once Carnegie was aware of the buyer. Carnegie was more hesitant, the more time he had to think about it. On May 4, 1899, Carn-

---

1 Tarbell, p. 107

egie was cabled in Scotland that $170,000 had been deposited and a deal was imminent. Carnegie handwrote his farewell to the business world in preparation of the sale.[1]

With all parties now assured of the deal, Providence stepped in and changed America's industrial history. Moore was having trouble raising the money. He intended to sell stock to the public to raise the cash; and when the word of the deal got out, Moore could not get the stock price. Frick and Phipps tried to save the deal by upping the price and asking for more time to complete the deal. Frick had hoped to bring his neighbor and best friend Andrew Mellon into the deal, but to the embarrassment of Frick, Moore refused to allow Mellon into the deal, fearing he would take control. Frick and Phipps realized they needed to close the deal or face the revenge of Carnegie, the senior partner, especially since Carnegie was now aware that Frick and Phipps stood to get a commission; and Carnegie would be in a position to turn the other partners against them if the deal failed. In June, both Phipps and Frick left for Skibo Castle, Scotland, to talk it over with Carnegie. The meeting at Skibo failed to convince Carnegie, and he was determined to pocket the $170,000 retainer which Frick had raised. While Phipps stayed on in Scotland at his own castle, Frick returned to Pittsburgh, realizing his days at Carnegie Steel were numbered, but he proceeded with a new type of reorganization plan to suit Carnegie.

The final break was near, and three months later the last dispute erupted. Frick remained Chairman of the Board for both Carnegie Steel and H. C. Frick Company. Carnegie remained the majority stockholder of both companies. Frick was in the weaker position but had developed an alliance with many partners in both companies. Now Frick's alliance at Carnegie Steel had been weakened by the proposed backdoor sale. It was probably clear to both men that there would be one last and final battle. In fact, Carnegie was probably looking for the right field of battle to put an end to Frick. It is interesting that both men saw Napoleon as their personal hero. Carnegie could be extremely vengeful, and Frick could make ice-cold business decisions. Frick probably realized his failure to close the merger deal meant he was done as a Carnegie partner.

In 1899, H. C. Frick Company had dominance in metallurgical coke greater than Carnegie Steel in steel. Carnegie knew that the best way to punish Frick was to attack "his" coke company; and Carnegie felt Frick needed to be put in his place. Twice before, Carnegie had pushed Frick to the limit by moving on coke issues behind Frick's back. While Carnegie was the majority stockholder in H. C. Frick Company, Frick resented any Carnegie involvement. Nothing pushed Frick's button more than Carnegie getting involved in H. C. Frick Company. Frick was Chairman of the Board of both companies and looked at H. C. Coke Company as his company, although Carnegie was the major shareholder. This arrangement had been awkward from the start. While Carnegie owned the coke company, Frick controlled the management. The president of H. C. Frick Coke Company, Thomas Lynch, was a strong Frick man as was most of the board.

The final showdown would come as it had begun over coke pricing. In the winter of 1898, Frick and Carnegie had come to a "verbal" agreement over the price of coke to

---

1 Wall, p. 725

Carnegie Steel. It was a loose arrangement with H. C. Frick Coke billing Carnegie Steel monthly. The Connellsville coke of H. C. Frick Company was the nation's metallurgical standard for steelmaking and could command a premium price on the market. In the fall of 1899, Carnegie was back in Pittsburgh looking over the books and attending board meetings. In reviewing the October minutes of the H. C. Frick Company, Carnegie saw the pricing and wrote on the minutes, "Declaration of War." Carnegie lined his supporters up to confront Frick at the November Board Meeting of Carnegie Steel. Carnegie was absent, allowing Charles Schwab and cousin Lauder to carry the message. Frick made comments about Carnegie and the stage was set. In reading the minutes, Carnegie took it as a major insult. Carnegie went on to write his partner and cousin Dod Lauder: "Frick goes out of the Chairmanship of Board next election or before. . . . He's too old-too infirm in health and mind."[1] Carnegie had started his campaign of the partners to get the necessary vote. Carnegie knew he could count on Schwab and Lauder, but most of the partners did not want to be forced into a decisive vote. Even though Schwab was anxious to get cash for his partnership shares, he feared Carnegie. Schwab had tried for a year to hold things together, but Carnegie was determined to oust Frick. Schwab wrote Frick telling him the situation and suggested Frick resign. Frick didn't hesitate and sent his resignation to the Board. Still, Frick held his huge partnership share control, which Carnegie had to address.

Frick's resignation from the Board of Carnegie Steel was only the beginning of one of America's first great corporate battles. It was a battle fought in many of the East End mansions. The neighborhood that had controlled much of America's industrial assets was now divided. Frick still had some assets; he had a six percent interest in Carnegie Steel and board control of H. C. Frick Company. Carnegie's first order of business was to replace enough board members in H. C. Frick Coke to take the control that he had in stock. The by-laws allowed for a new vote based on ownership. Frick was able to name two — Thomas Lynch and himself. Carnegie named five — Dod Lauder, Daniel Clemson, A. Moreland, James Gayley, and Thomas Morrison. Lauder and Morrison were Carnegie relatives. This was clearly a neighborhood feud splitting the East End partners. In January 1900, Carnegie took control of H. C. Frick Coke, and Frick and the position of Chairman were eliminated.

Carnegie was well aware that once you attack a king, you must kill a king. To that end, Carnegie started to plan to force Frick out of the partnership. Carnegie came to Frick's office on January 8, the day after the Carnegie Steel Board meeting. It would be the last face-to-face meeting for the two partners. Carnegie wanted Frick to back out of the partnership peacefully. The book value for Frick's 6 percent in Carnegie Steel was about $1.5 million while the market value was around $15 million. Carnegie planned to enforce the "Iron Clad Agreement," which required Frick to sell at book value. The "Iron Clad Agreement" had been a problem in the organization. Carnegie used it to keep the empire together, but older members wanted to take their money and retire. The young partners wanted more

---

1 Letter Andrew Carnegie to Dod Lauder, November 25, 1899, Volume 70, Andrew Carnegie Papers-Library of Congress

income, since Carnegie poured money into the mills versus dividend payouts to partners. The result was an explosion of Frick's temper. Frick yelled, "For years I have been convinced there is not an honest bone in your body. Now I know you are a god damned thief."[1] Carnegie left and called a special meeting of the Board of Carnegie Steel to remove Frick. Carnegie moved, and over two days got 32 partners out of 36 partners to sign off on the ouster of Frick. Many of the younger partners favored the breakup of the partnership but had learned to fear Carnegie's potential revenge. The four that did not sign off were Frick and his neighbors H. Curry (who was ill), Phipps, and Francis Lovejoy. For his part, Frick was off to see his lawyer. He would contest the sale of his share at partnership book value, and Frick was the better businessman and finance man.

Frick soon realized that he could turn this setback into an opportunity. If the Iron Clad Agreement was found illegal, it would force reorganization and the ultimate sale of the company. Carnegie was slow to realize the danger. Phipps joined the fight in the hope that reorganization could be forced legally. Most partners wanted this feud ended. The problem was that the court proceedings were public and the press followed it like a famous Hollywood divorce today. The Allegheny County Court of Common Pleas became the rallying point for the national press. The dollar amounts mesmerized the public. The timing coincided with attacks on "Big Business" from the press as trusts mushroomed in the late 1890s. For the Democrats in the upcoming election, it offered a way to break "Dinner Pail Republicanism" which had forged a weak alliance with labor and capitalists. Many believed this East End family feud would cost McKinley the presidential election. The neighborhood fight was becoming a major national problem. A scandal of "Big Business" would supply the ammunition needed to give the election to the Democrats.

Frick had some very damaging documents in his possession. Carnegie's own internal analysis during the potential sale to Moore showed the value to be $500 million. Phipps found additional documentation where Carnegie noted the value to be well beyond book value. In board meeting minutes of August 1898, a letter from Carnegie estimated the value of Carnegie Steel at a prophetic $300 million.[2] Dollar amounts in the hundred millions were extremely hard for the general public to imagine, remembering the average income was under $400 a year. The court battle and records worried even the Republican Party, with William McKinley facing reelection in 1900 against an anti-business populist. The press across the nation had taken on the "robber barons." In early 1900 rumors were everywhere, and it was clear that there would be no winners in a court case. Frick had the stronger case, but Carnegie could bring his millions and his lawyers to the fight. The bigger fear for the Republican Party was that Carnegie steel costs would become public knowledge. In particular, Carnegie steel rails were selling at $23.50 a ton, but costs were only $12.00 a ton.[3] This would hurt the tariff argument of the Republicans. It was more of a political

1 Hendrick Interview, February 16, 1928, Volume 239, Andrew Carnegie Papers-Library of Congress
2 Letter (minutes) Andrew Carnegie to Carnegie Steel board of managers, August 23, 1898, Andrew Carnegie Papers-Library of Congress
3 Holbrook, p. 256

issue or image problem since tariffs had, in reality, created thousands of jobs, producing steady income for steelworkers. Carnegie re-invested most of the profits in building more mills, which was the source of discontent among the partners. Republicans could count on Pittsburgh votes, but the issue could cost votes elsewhere in the nation. Again Pittsburgh's East End was the center of a national election, but this time it was about image more than money.

The local Republican machine and national delegates had many East End friends in Frick, Mellon, Westinghouse, Lovejoy, Phipps, Jones, and Peacock. George Westinghouse, a Frick neighbor and outside friend of both, tried to mediate a settlement to no avail. The Pittsburgh Republican machine wanted this settled quickly. Friends and neighbors such as Benjamin Jones could not end the feud. National Republican leaders came to Pittsburgh to help negotiate an East End agreement to save the presidential election. Neighbor George Westinghouse was chosen as a mediator. Westinghouse was one of President McKinley's biggest supporters as well. Frick was a big supporter of McKinley while Carnegie was not. Westinghouse had talked to his neighbor Frick with some success.[1] Westinghouse wrote Carnegie, but Carnegie was un-moved. He had never been a big McKinley supporter and had opposed McKinley's involvement in the Spanish–American War.

Frick and Carnegie were at the point they could not face each other. East Enders Schwab, Lovejoy, and Phipps forced a meeting with Carnegie but without Frick to settle this outside of the public eye in an ugly court battle. The meeting took place on neutral ground — actually a playground in Atlantic City, New Jersey. The issue was settled with Carnegie Steel to become a corporation at a value of $250 million and merge with H. C. Frick Coke at $70 million. That would mean Carnegie's value was $176 million, Phipps's share was $35 million, and Frick's share was $31.6 million. Frick's $15.5 million in stock and $16 million in 5 percent bonds was considerably better than the book value of $1.5 million of the "Iron Clad Agreement." Frick and Phipps would then have shares to sell or keep. Frick, however, was to be banned from active management. Frick's supporter, Francis Lovejoy, was eventually crushed by Carnegie for his role in helping Frick and died financially and mentally broken. Phipps sold most of his shares to fully enjoy his retirement in Scotland. He would be remembered by his gift of the Phipps Conservatory in 1893 to the neighborhood. Interestingly, Frick held on to most of his shares, probably realizing a takeover would drive prices up. He resigned from the board of the Carnegie Library and Art Institute, replaced by Charles Schwab. Carnegie and Frick would never meet again. The "Boys of Braddock" would shun Frick, remaining loyal to Carnegie. Years later Carnegie tried to patch things up, and Frick sent a note: "meet you in hell." The neighborhood of Carnegie partners would never be the same. It was torn socially and politically. While the wealth generated by the breakup of the partnership created a building surge in the East End, Carnegie realized that without the "Iron Clad Agreement," the days of the empire were over.

---

1 Les Standiford, *Meet You in Hell*, (New York: Random House, 2006), p. 271

The first effect of the East End of the Carnegie partnership breakup was a creation of many millionaires now able to get their money on the open market. For a two-year period the East End's millionaire row grew, prior to the sale of Carnegie Steel, to form United States Steel Corporation with New York headquarters. Charles Schwab now purchased a mansion, "Highmont," formerly owned by J. J. Vandergrift in the Squirrel Hill area (6200 Fifth Avenue at Shady Avenue) to reflect his newfound wealth. He only lived there briefly as he was made president of United States Steel in 1901, and New York became his headquarters. Francis Lovejoy purchased the mansion of local businessman Colonel Edward Allen (1830–1916) near Frick's "Clayton" in 1899. This area of Point Breeze was known as the "Carnegie-Frick" compound or "Frick's Manor." In 1899, Frick's mansion Clayton was on the top of a hill at Penn and Homewood Avenues that overlooked a couple blocks, which included mansions of Francis Lovejoy, George Lauder (cousin of Carnegie and partner), Lucy Coleman Carnegie (widow of Carnegie's brother Tom), and Alexander Peacock (Carnegie partner). On the border were H. J. Heinz's "Greenlawn," George Westinghouse's "Solitude," and the mansion of Tom Armstrong.

Carnegie's sales agent and vice president, Alexander Rolland Peacock (1861–1928), was an example of the peak of the East End. Peacock had been born in the same town as Andrew Carnegie but would only meet Carnegie in 1889 while selling linen to Mrs. Carnegie. Carnegie moved Peacock into the sales department, and he rose to vice president and partner. He and his wife had started in the East End in an old Victorian home on Penn and Lexington Avenue; they then moved to a mansion next to Frick. Receiving more money from the breakup of the Carnegie partnership, he designed a new mansion in the Highland Park area (Jackson and Wellesley Streets). This new mansion "Rowanlea" would dominate the Highland Park area of the East End. He had the biggest mansion in the area with forty employees, a huge conservatory and a garage full of cars. His high living created many legends, one of which was retold by James Van Trump: "Peacock rose from bed one morning and, clad still in his pajamas, ordered two seven-thousand-dollar motor cars sent to the house before noon. He hunted out many of his early associates and paid their debts. Another story tells that, being served a cold-storage egg for breakfast, he bought a farm in Allegheny County and spent sixty thousand dollars to insure a supply of fresh eggs and other farm products."[1]

Not to be out done, Francis Lovejoy planned an even greater mansion to be known as "Edgehill," but it would become better known as "Lovejoy's Folly." This was to be the area's great mansion of fifty rooms and three stories and a series of garages to house his fleet of 12 automobiles. Hanging gardens and expansive grounds, a three-story gymnasium, an electrical power plant, and a full machine shop to repair his cars were planned. The location was a piece of high ground on South Braddock Avenue not far from the intersection of Penn Avenue. It was to take five years to complete the full complex by 1905. In the meantime, Lovejoy made some risky mining investments which bankrupted him. He left

---

1 James D. Van Trump, *Life and Architecture in Pittsburgh*, (Pittsburgh: Pittsburgh History and Landmarks Foundation, 1983), p. 275

for Utah in 1904 to manage his failing mining company, with "Edgehill" incomplete and out of funds. He suffered a total breakdown and returned to the East End to die in a small apartment. Another effect of Carnegie was a breakdown of restrained and moral behavior by many Carnegie partners. Under Carnegie, a strict Scotch–Irish code of behavior was enforced; now they were free of moral scrutiny.

CHAPTER 17. THE MILLIONAIRE'S DINNER

The "Millionaire's Dinner" that augured the formation of United States Steel on January 9, 1901 would be held at the East End's Hotel Schenley. The dinner assembled over 89 millionaires in one room, something that had never occurred before in the history of the world. These millionaires were the result of Carnegie partners being paid for their shares. The company's party boy, Charles Schwab, had planned the great celebration. The future looked even brighter as the day before when Carnegie Steel had announced plans to invest $12 million in the world's largest steel tube mill to be built at Conneaut, Ohio. The Conneaut mill was a direct challenge to the newly formed "Chicago Steel Trust" of J. P. Morgan. Among the diners were East Enders Charles Schwab, Lawrence Phipps, William Singer, Alexander Peacock, S. Schoonmaker, Daniel Clemson, Charles Taylor, and Thomas Morrison as well as the down-the-road "Boys of Braddock." Schwab had just moved from his Braddock mansion, purchasing the East End home (6200 Fifth Avenue) of J. J. Vandergrift. Carnegie returned to Pittsburgh for this magnificent event to celebrate the amazing success of the old Carnegie partnership. He had to leave before the dinner, however, as rumors of a major business war between him and the Pennsylvania Railroad were breaking. He was a bit disapproving of such a party, writing to Schwab to take care of his health as "the dinner of Wednesday night may require you to lie up for a day or two."[1] The real rumor known to many at the dinner was the complex behind-the-scenes negotiations going on with Charles Schwab and J. P. Morgan to United States Steel.

The behind-the-scenes negotiations, suspense, and clandestine moves of J.P. Morgan, Charles Schwab, and Andrew Carnegie played like a modern day version of "A Lion in Winter." The first meeting of Charles Schwab and J. P. Morgan was a dinner in early December 1900 given by Vice-President Teddy Roosevelt in honor of J. P. Morgan. Morgan

---

1 Letter Andrew Carnegie to Charles Schwab, January 7, 1901, Andrew Carnegie Papers, Library of Congress

must have at least discussed the potential of a steel trust with the McKinley administration as well as with Henry Clay Frick, who best understood the possible combination. Frick had secretly suggested that Schwab was the key to Carnegie selling. Morgan used Schwab's New York poker buddy "Bet-a-Million" Gates (Gates had once bet a million on a single poker hand) to set the bait. Schwab was invited to speak at a dinner on December 12, 1900 at the New York's University Club. The dinner included some of America's greatest bankers and industrialists including Morgan, William Vanderbilt, Chauncey Depew, Jacob Schiff, George Baker of First National Bank, and H. H. Rogers of Standard Oil. Schwab, the guest speaker, was to talk on the future of the steel industry. Andrew Carnegie was there only briefly before leaving for another appointment. According to corporate mythology, the talk was the turning point for J. P. Morgan. The idea that Morgan had an epiphany seems to be more mythology than reality. Morgan had been briefed by Frick and others about a big merger. Some even believe that Carnegie engineered the dinner.[1] Morgan had studied the possibility of an expanded steel trust for some time. John "Bet-a-Million" Gates confirmed with Morgan that Schwab would be the key in getting Carnegie to sell. Gates is sometimes given credit for conceiving of the steel trust while shooting pool at the Waldorf-Astoria. It may be more likely that Morgan planned to win over the young Schwab to mediate between him and Carnegie from an earlier meeting with Frick. The history of the rest of the night has several versions. Most of the sources are from the Senate anti-trust testimony 12 years later. One version has Morgan and Schwab talking till early morning. Schwab biographer Hesson suggested Schwab talked for 45 minutes, and then Morgan held a side meeting with him for 30 minutes.[2]

Carnegie was aware of meetings but not the details. He had pushed Schwab to announce the Conneaut mill as a threat to Morgan. After the "Millionaire's Dinner," Schwab was called to Morgan's New York mansion at 219 Madison Avenue. A deal was set for Schwab to take to Carnegie. Schwab approached Carnegie at his New York home. Schwab went over the whole story with Mrs. Carnegie and then went off to meet Carnegie at his cottage for a cold game of golf. Schwab told Carnegie of the meetings and asked what price he needed. Carnegie asked for a night to think it over. Schwab returned the next morning and Carnegie wrote the number on a piece of paper. He wanted $480 million to be paid in $160 million in gold-backed bonds, $240 million in stock exchange in the new company, and $80 million in cash. Morgan accepted the price with the details to be worked out. Morgan and Carnegie did meet for fifteen minutes a few days later. Carnegie would not be a stockholder, but his stock exchange value would be paid in gold back bonds and some preferred stock.

Judge Gary was to be Chairman of the Board with a salary of $100,000, and Charles Schwab was to be president of the new corporation with a $100,000 salary and a 1 percent profit-sharing bonus. Because of Schwab's endless spending, it was rumored he made a million dollar salary. While Schwab was president, the real power and decision

---

1 Hesson, p. 114
2 Hesson, p. 116

making was held by the executive committee. Rockefeller was a major shareholder, and the Board of USS reflected this with John Rockefeller, John Rockefeller Jr., Judge Gary, Henry Clay Frick and Henry Rogers. Charles Schwab balked on hearing that Frick would be a board member, but Morgan promised that Frick would not attend meetings. Other board directors included Elbert Gary, Charles Schwab, Robert Bacon (Morgan's partner), Marshall Field, James Reed (Carnegie Steel lawyer and East Ender), William Moore (National Steel), Edmund Converse (National Tube), Francis Peabody, Charles Steele, Norman Ream, Peter Widener, William Edenborn (American Steel and Wire), Daniel Reid (American Tin Plate), Alford Clifford (American Steel and Wire), Clement Griscom, William Dodge, Nathaniel Thayer, Percival Roberts (American Bridge), George Baker (First National Bank), and Abram Hewitt. Frick's $61 million of stock became $88 million in a few days as prices of the new company stock rose from $38 per share to $55 per share. Carnegie's old (but many young) 35 partners became instant multimillionaires. The structure of USS was based on the model of Frick and Rockefeller who believed in committee infrastructure versus a powerful autocrat. The committee structure continued with an executive committee consisting of Elbert Gary (chairman), Daniel Reid, William Edenborn, E. Converse, Percival Roberts, and Charles Steele. The executive committee was the real power in the new corporation. President Schwab needed to clear major decisions through the executive committee. In addition, Schwab and the "Boys of Braddock" and some old partners remained in executive positions. Carnegie Steel became a major division and was ruled by the "Boys of Braddock." The East End would have been in control except for the Frick/Schwab split, which would eventually lead to the power center going to New York, and the ultimate decline of the world's richest neighborhood.

Initially, Henry Clay Frick took a back seat on the United States Steel Board to pursue other interests. H. J. Heinz, Henry Clay Frick, and other East Enders had become active in the commercial development of Pittsburgh's East End and Oakland area with entrepreneur Franklin Nicola, who believed in the future of Oakland as a cultural center for the Pittsburgh area. Nicola formed Bellefield Company to develop the Oakland area. The focus was to be on the lands formerly owned by Pittsburgh's first great capitalist, James O'Hara, and his granddaughter, Mary Schenley. The Bellefield Company had grown out of Duquesne Club luncheons. Nicola was able to enlist Heinz as an investor as well as Andrew Carnegie, George Westinghouse, and Andrew Mellon. The first project was a first class hotel — the Hotel Schenley — which would become known as the "Waldorf of Pittsburgh." The hotel was built on Schenley Farms next to Frick Acres, both of which were pastureland. Even on the day of the "Millionaire's Dinner," cows could be seen grazing across the street. The Hotel Schenley became the hotel of great corporations and meetings including Westinghouse Electric, Jones and Laughlin Steel, H. J. Heinz, Westinghouse Air Brake, and Carnegie Steel. H. J. Heinz would move his annual company meeting to the Hotel Schenley. Built in 1898, the Hotel Schenley would have guests such as William Howard Taft and Teddy Roosevelt. The register included Babe Ruth, Ty Cobb, and Roger Hornsby. Today the Hotel Schenley is part of the University of Pittsburgh (William Pitt Union).

Bellefield Company is considered to be the first real estate development company. In 1909 Bellefield Company developed Forbes Field, the home of the Pittsburgh Pirates. That same year the University of Pittsburgh moved from the North side to the East End. Bellefield Company was behind most of the campus development, which East Enders poured donations into it as well. Bellefield also was responsible for Soldiers and Sailors Hall, Carnegie Institute of Technology, the Carnegie Museum and Library, Forbes Field, the Pittsburgh Athletic Association, and the Masonic Temple.

After the formation of United States Steel, Frick expanded into many commercial interests such as banking and real estate. In 1900, Frick was one of the largest real estate owners in Pittsburgh and one of the wealthiest in the East End. The Duquesne Club luncheons of Frick and Mellon turned more to real estate after the formation of United States Steel. Frick, in particular, had additional free time between 1900 and 1905 before taking a more active role in the management of United States Steel. In 1899, Frick purchased the old St. Peter's Episcopal Church at the corner of Grant and Diamond Street in the city of Pittsburgh for $180,000 to build the future Frick Building. It would stand next to and overshadow the Carnegie Building of 1893, which was known as the city's first skyscraper. Frick planned a 24-story skyscraper at 265 feet to cast a shadow on Carnegie's 15-story building. The building was a steel frame with carved stone of classical Doric design. Each office had two 47-inch by 62-inch mirror windows. The interior had rich Italian marble, Honduras mahogany, and bronze metalwork and doors. The primary tenant was to be Frick's Union Savings Bank, which Mellon and Frick controlled. Another tenant was the infamous Equitable Life Company of which Frick was a board member. Frick maintained his own personal office there as well until his death. The top floor was reserved for the Union Club, and the basement had the Union Restaurant paneled in Flemish Renaissance oak. The Union Club and Union Restaurant had two refrigerating plants to produce ice. Also in the basement was the largest nickel steel plate vault in the world, which weighed 17 tons. The whole building had a central vacuum system for cleaning. The next year Frick built Pittsburgh's William Penn Hotel. The William Penn was to be the second largest hotel in the United States at the time. He would also continue to invest in land around the Oakland section. By 1904, Frick was the largest owner of real estate in the city of Pittsburgh followed by the Mellon family.

CHAPTER 18. A TALE OF TWO CITIES

East End capitalists were different, regardless of the reasons. Their rivals on New York's Fifth Avenue found no place on the social register for them. They failed to make the famous "400" for party invitations. For their part, they showed little respect for the inherited wealth of these New Yorkers. East Enders like Carnegie who moved to New York were often changed by their desire to fit in. Carnegie with all his wealth could fully join the American aristocracy of New York; he was knighted in Europe. Others who moved there, like Charles Schwab, were corrupted by the quest to gain acceptance. Some who moved to New York for business, like Frick, isolated themselves in limestone mansions. Those who stayed in the East End formed a type of fortified monastic community governed by Scotch-Irish morals and ethics. They kept to themselves except for philanthropic excursions. The press was not welcome. Many of their mansions, such as Frick's Clayton, were also real homes. East Enders had no problem in dealing with the less blessed of society and could often relate to them. Many East Enders were deeply religious, such as H. J. Heinz. He and George Westinghouse, and others, not only paid their employees well but also actually respected them. Many donated not only their money to the poor but also their time. Most had known poverty in their lives. Heinz and Westinghouse had known bankruptcy and personal setbacks. In general, they hated and feared inherited wealth as a source of weak morals and laziness. They enjoyed a family picnic and vacation, but they preferred business clubs to social clubs. They were not ashamed of their patriotism, civic pride, and nationalism.

This was in stark contrast to New York's Fifth Avenue which loved publicity. They even encouraged press coverage of their weeklong parties and social excesses. They promoted the society page of the *New York Times*. The money spent was noted to the press as a badge of prestige. For them it was the quest of showing what money could buy. Their weddings were front-page spectacles. Like today's billionaires, they bought paintings for prestige and their mansions took excess to new levels. They often opened their mansions for people to tour while they were in Europe or at their summer homes. Their mansions were castles more than homes. They presented themselves as a new type of aristocracy and even set "membership" requirements. Inherited wealth was prized over new money. Scandals seemed to be accepted as more publicity and a testimony to their role of royalty. There was no moral code to be broken. They were more focused on European culture than American values. While it might be argued that East Enders had lost touch with the workingman, New York's Fifth Avenue had lost touch with reality. Their wealth came more from exchanging capital than creating it. They could not possibly conceive of the world of a steelworker. Their commuting to Europe took them past no factories, and on their return they found reporters waiting to report on their latest Paris fashions. At least the East Ender had to pass through the industrial ghetto of Braddock on their rail trip to New York to give them perspective.

East End capitalists were extremely generous to the community. One could not fault their giving and community involvement. They were patriotic and nationalistic. Unlike New York capitalists, they generally stayed inside the law. They even followed a type of ethical code, although ruthless and cold at times. They had a strong moral code in most cases, and at least they knew right from wrong. They were family men, good fathers, and good neighbors. For the most part, they deplored divorce. Yet they were acquisitive, ambitious, and aggressive. Their brains were all business. In the financial arena, their quest for success knew no bounds. They were financial gladiators who would fight to the death. They believed in social Darwinism and its survival of the fitness. The only mortal wound was financial failure. While laws and even ethics bounded the arena, friendship and loyalty had no place in the contest. They were pure capitalists. Making money could approach that of an obsession and addiction for many of them.

In trying to understand the heart and soul of Pittsburgh's East End, it becomes illustrative to compare the East End to the core rich of Fifth Avenue and other cities. It was in cities like Pittsburgh, New York, and Chicago that the economic landscape of America was being designed. In New York, there was an American aristocracy forming after many generations of wealth. The inherited wealth dominated New York's Fifth Avenue. The parties and balls exceeded those of Louis XVI, whom they openly tried to emulate. The press reinforced them with wide coverage. The public followed it as a soap opera of today. New York wealth was English based. The important religion was Anglican and Episcopalian. Their universities were Harvard and Yale. The source of their wealth tended to be banking and financial investment versus making or inventing things. Their "factories" were the banks. They were elitist and saw class distinction as important. They even established a line of royalty. They looked down on the "nouveau riche." They were truly the leisure class and found work vulgar. It was difficult for "working" members such as banker J. P. Morgan to gain full acceptance.

The "400" wealthiest including the New York bluebloods such as the Astors, Vanderbilts, Roosevelts, Hydes, and Goulds made up the top of the list. Even the Vanderbilts did not gain acceptance until they were in the second generation. It loosely included Andrew

Carnegie, who moved to New York early on to be part of this aristocracy. Carnegie had been accepted probably because he was the richest American; and Carnegie truly wanted to be part of this leisure class. The term "Four Hundred" came from the Astor family guest lists, which indicated they believed there were only four hundred people in America worth inviting. Some say it was the most Mrs. Astor could comfortably seat in the ballroom in 1882. It was a socially elite group, which initially rejected Vanderbilt as a "businessman" and nouveau riche. East Enders were clearly not considered for "membership." Charles Schwab tried to build his way into the "400" by building a block-long mansion and hosting extravagant parties, but as a Catholic and first generation wealth, he could never hope to be accepted. Even Frick, whose art collection was superior to those of most of the New Yorkers, could not gain full acceptance. Frick maintained homes in New York, Boston, and Pittsburgh; while he was loosely part of the 400, with one of the nation's highest incomes, he never was a "dues paying member." Frick cared little for their famous costume balls. Transplanted East Enders in New York had their own social circle, which instead of costume balls brought artists, scientists, and businessmen together at smaller dinners.

Frick also built a summer home at Eagle Rock on Boston's North Shore (Pride's Crossing-mailing address). Neighbors included William Taft, Henry Cabot Lodge, Louis Comfort Tiffany, Theodore Roosevelt, Justice Oliver Wendell Holmes, and Pittsburgh East Ender Philander Knox (summer home). The North Shore crowd was characteristically a mix of the East End and Fifth Avenue. Still, the mix seemed to work best on an informal and summer level. Frick's daughter, Helen, however, preferred Clayton to these other homes, which seemed to pull the family back to Pittsburgh. Even Frick's heart (some would say cold) was always in Pittsburgh where he planned to be buried beside his daughter, Martha. Frick's Eagle Rock home was not far from President Taft's summer home, and Taft and Frick became good friends. Both Frick and Taft were conservative Republicans opposed to Roosevelt's progressive wing. East End conservatives never mixed well with New York progressives. Taft and Frick also shared a friend and golf partner in department store king, John Wanamaker, who was also a very close friend of H. J. Heinz. They were members of the exclusive Myopia Hunt Club. The Myopia had the nation's first polo field for Childs Frick to learn the game, and one of the most famous golf courses, having hosted the U.S. Open in 1898, 1901, 1905, and 1908. Frick would golf with Taft and take part in his famous "automobile parties." They also competed in the Myopia Club's horse shows in which Frick often won medals for his horses. At Eagle Rock, one of Frick's first visitors was George Westinghouse and his wife, who had a summer home in the Berkshires.

Eagle Rock was an area where the 400 "mixed" with capitalists such as East Enders. One example of the mindset difference between New York and Pittsburgh capitalists is seen in Helen Clay's twenty-fifth birthday party at Eagle Rock after Frick had moved to New York. The party of 500 guests was to feature dancing and John Philip Sousa's band. Frick, probably with the encouragement of Helen, invited most of the North Shore townspeople, not realizing the uproar it would cause. North Shore Society refused to mingle with mere townspeople. The uproar made both the New York and the Pittsburgh papers.

Many balked at attending, and the response required Frick to split the party into two separate groups. Frick himself made no public statement about the well-publicized party, but it was clear he had not integrated into New York society. Helen Frick would always long for the East End, caring little for New York society.

J. Ingham best defined the East Enders:

> Like the Mellons, many of them were Scotch–Irish Presbyterians (or Scottish immigrants) and many lived in the East End, the most fashionable neighborhood in town, where the Shady Side Academy provided for the exclusive early education of their sons. These were men devoted to making money; they accumulated wealth and advantage over generations; they despised leisure and even idleness; and they had little appreciation of culture or the arts. Increasingly, they formed a self-sufficient and exclusive coterie with a strong sense of their own moral rectitude and superiority — at least in Pittsburgh. For they had little to do, either socially or financially, with the East Coast elites of Boston, New York, and Philadelphia, whose condescension at their parochialism, their unremitting devotion to work, and their lack of refinement was resented. As a result, they sent their sons to the Western University of Pennsylvania or to no university of all. Harvard and Yale and Princeton and Columbia were not [yet] for them."[1]

Andrew Mellon and Henry Clay Frick truly loved art, while New York collectors such as J. P. Morgan invested in art. Morgan bought and sold while Frick and Mellon lived with their art. Most the East Enders were fairly new wealth; the Mellon family was an exception.

Interestingly, these differences may account for the two factions of the Republican Party which exist to this day. The Republican Party had been formed in Pittsburgh, but its heart was in Ohio with conservative leaders such as James Garfield, William McKinley, and Howard Taft. The Pittsburgh capitalists supported the McKinley conservative wing of the Republican Party, which was rooted in manufacturing, versus the blueblood Republicans of the East Coast. McKinley Republicanism was based on nationalistic tariffs and manufacturing expansion. Blueblood Republicans such as Roosevelt and Lodge had made fun of McKinley's middle class background and values.

In particular, five blueblood Republicans fathered the progressive movement: John Hay, Henry Cabot Lodge, Teddy Roosevelt, Alfred Mahan, and Elihu Root. John Hay had been an advisor to Republican presidents going back to Lincoln. He would be Ambassador to Great Britain and Secretary of State under McKinley. Henry Cabot Lodge was a Republican blueblood and powerful Senator from Massachusetts. Teddy Roosevelt was McKinley's first Assistant Secretary of the Navy. Future Vice-president, Elihu Root, a blueblood with strong ties to the bankers and capitalists, would become Secretary of War under McKinley. Alfred Mahan was a navy strategist who was behind the growth of American naval power. Mahan's book, *The Influence of Sea Power upon History*, was a source book for the nation and for Republican presidents. These economic progressives would

---

1 J. N. Ingham, *Iron Barons: A social analysis*, (Westport, Conn., 1978), pp. 6-7

father the anti-trust movement of the Republican Party. Other than Carnegie, in later life, the East Enders hated the progressive movement. Progressives often aggressively attacked industrial wealth while tacitly supporting the wealthy elite of Wall Street.

The progressive Republicans were considered no better than the Democratic progressives such as Woodrow Wilson. East Enders like Westinghouse and Frick had little time for the progressive wing of the Republican Party. The old McKinley wing of the Republican Party had formed a powerful alliance of management and labor which had established a 60-year protective tariff policy. The progressive wing of the Republican Party had its roots in New York. The progressive movement split the New York and East End Republicans, who supported the Howard Taft Ohio Republicans and drove the progressives out. Henry Clay Frick, in particular, saw Teddy Roosevelt as America's worst president. He supported him financially as a Republican because he was a marginal improvement over Democrats. East Enders were strong supporters of a long line of Ohio Republicans such as Garfield, McKinley, Harding, and Taft. New York elite cared more for their ability to control Republican politicians. J. P. Morgan had even tacitly supported his friend, Democrat Glover Cleveland, since he controlled him.

Another significant difference between Fifth Avenue, New York, and Penn Avenue, Pittsburgh, was religion. East Enders were predominantly Presbyterian. A study of 1900 residents of Shadyside showed 56 percent Presbyterian and 16 percent Episcopalian with a Scotch-Irish heritage.[1] The Fifth Avenue elite were primarily of English extraction, Congregationalist and Episcopalian with a Puritan heritage. Roman Catholics were non-existent in both neighborhoods with the exception of possibly Charles Schwab. The same study showed that between 1880 and 1920, 42 percent of Shadyside were self-made and 38 percent were inherited wealth (although most of this was second generation). Fifth Avenue was mostly inherited wealth, and some of it was two to five generations old. As already noted, newcomers were frowned upon by these wealthy New Yorkers. Maybe more enlightening in the Shadyside study was the fact that over 90 percent of the source of the money was industrial, while Fifth Avenue sources were banking and financial.

Socially liberal Protestant values versus Scotch-Irish Presbyterian might explain a lot of the differences. These Scotch-Irish tended to be theologically liberal and socially conservative. The old "Puritan" New Yorkers tended to be socially liberal and dogmatically conservative, at least on the surface. The Scotch-Irish were clannish and close knit. One social historian called them "different," stating: "There was something about Pittsburgh which made its wealthiest and most prominent citizens, those who were becoming cosmopolitan in nearly every other respect, retain a strong local orientation in their marriage patterns, and most notably in their social contacts." Pittsburgh industrialists tended to use Pittsburgh bankers or no bankers at all. They preferred to do business at the Duquesne Club versus the financial district in New York. They married local girls in most cases and stayed with them. Even the international playboy, Charles Schwab, never divorced

---

1 Renee Reitman, "The Elite Community in Shadyside, 1880-1920," Seminar Paper, Department of History, University of Pittsburgh, 1964, pp. 2-3

his Braddock sweetheart. When Schwab's gambling and carousing in Monte Carlo made the front pages during the time that he was president of United States Steel, his biggest fear was not explaining to his current bosses, Judge Gary and J. P. Morgan, but to his old Pittsburgh boss, Andrew Carnegie! New York living had affected Charles Schwab and the other "Boys of Braddock" who had moved.

Schwab had gone on a public spending spree after becoming president of United States Steel including mansions, parties, trips, mistresses, and gambling. Schwab sold his East End mansion "Highmont" to Carnegie partner Daniel Clemson (now vice-president of Carnegie Steel Company — USS) in 1903 to build a super mansion in New York. Schwab's New York $3 million mansion was said to make Carnegie's house look like a cottage. It was four stories with a 116-foot lookout tower, 90 bedrooms, an Olympic size pool, bowling alley, wine cellar, gymnasium, a network of phones connecting all the bedrooms, and a coal-powered electric plant. He installed a $100,000 pipe organ and added a two-story art gallery. The full block mansion known as "Riverside" was the most lavish ever built in New York; but Schwab could not make the "400." Men like Carnegie, Frick, and J. P. Morgan could accept huge mansions, but it was Schwab's partying that worried all. His gambling was making bigger headlines than Carnegie's giving. Schwab's gambling at Monte Carlo literally made headlines as did his socializing without his wife and his late night poker games and afternoon billiard games with John "Bet-a-Million" Gates at the Waldorf-Astoria. Judge Gary, the president of United States Steel, had deep Methodist roots and was opposed to any form of gambling. Gary wanted Schwab out. Morgan believed such things should be kept as quiet as his girlfriends were concealed from the public. Schwab's affair and birth of a daughter had also become public knowledge. Carnegie was embarrassed by Schwab's behavior and wrote Morgan about it. It would cost Schwab the presidency. In Pittsburgh's East End and the Pittsburgh Golf Club, Schwab's goings-on were well known, but the Pittsburgh press downplayed it. While New Yorkers loved to follow the parties and escapades, Pittsburghers and Presbyterian East Enders found such things appalling.

Schwab was not alone as William Corey, another of the "Boys of Braddock," became president of the United States Steel. William Corey was the son of Judge Mellon's old coal partner, Carnegie Steel executive, and in 1905 became president of United States Steel. Corey had moved from Pittsburgh to New York to head up United States Steel and quickly joined the party crowd. In Corey's case, it was wine and women on a public level. While his wife remained in Pittsburgh, Corey made headlines with his partying and girlfriends. His affair with a New York chorus girl, Mabelle Gilman, made the paper almost daily, even in Pittsburgh. Workers at Homestead called the works "Marybelle Gilman Works"; and it is rumored that Corey wanted it changed officially.[1] The affair resulted in Mrs. Corey, accompanied by her Braddock friend, Mrs. Charles Schwab, going to Reno to file for a divorce and a $3 million dollar settlement from William Corey. The vice-president of USS and another of the "Boys of Braddock," James Gayley, was involved in a divorce as well,

---

1 Holbrook, p. 280

but Gayley decided to resign quietly while Corey decided to stay. For Judge Gary, CEO of United States Steel, this was another nightmare. An informal meeting was held at the Duquesne Club in Pittsburgh with Frick, J. P. Morgan, and H. Rogers on what should be done about the "Corey problem." Pittsburgh East End society was shocked by the behavior of Corey and Schwab. Both, however, became known as Braddock boys, unrelated to the Pittsburgh aristocrats of the East End. There was little that could be done. Corey would make matters worse in late 1908 when headlines detailed his extravagant wedding (costing over a half million dollars, $5 million plus today). This did not compare to his first wedding in Braddock, which cost five dollars in total. The lack of taste was enough to persuade Judge Gary and Director Henry Clay Frick to force Corey to resign while he was on his honeymoon.

The East End had its sex scandal and national crime case in third-generation East Ender Harry Kendall Thaw, one of the ten sons of William Thaw, scion of an old Pig Iron Aristocrat family. Benjamin Thaw and William Thaw had been good friends of Henry Clay Frick. Harry had not managed his inherited wealth well but moved to New York to live a voluptuous life. He was a notorious playboy known for destroying cafes and riding a horse up the steps of the exclusive New York Club while drunk. In 1905 he married a chorus girl, Evelyn Nesbit, at East End's Third Presbyterian Church. She was known nationwide as the "girl on the velvet swing". Evelyn Nesbit had been in relationships with architect Stanford White and actor John Barrymore. The New York press loved the story. Harry took his wife to the New York Theater in 1906, and seeing her old boyfriend there, he casually went over and shot him. What followed was one of the most sensational trials ever held in America. Thaw's mother hired America's most famous lawyer, Michael Delmas, for $100,000. The case turned into a racy scandal. The trial evolved into stories of immorality, sex parties, torture, child molestation, and drugs on a scale never heard of in America. It shocked the Scotch–Irish roots of the East Side, and the Pittsburgh press could not avoid covering the sensational story as much as the Thaw family tried to suppress it.

Henry Clay Frick was commuting on the "Pittsburgher" between the East End and New York. Frick, the press's bad boy, was no partygoer. In fact, he saw this excessive partying and carrying-on as bad for business. He hated the social page of the *New York Times*. He was torn between his home in the East End and a possible mansion in New York. His New York mansion was more art museum than home, but it served his purposes. It housed his beloved art for the future, and it located him at corporate headquarters. He knew that in the end he would be buried with his beloved daughter Martha in the East End Homewood Cemetery, which was in sight of his East End home. Neither did his daughter Helen have any doubts; her home was in the East End. Years later, after her father's death, she moved back to the East End and died in 1986 at Clayton. Henry Clay's biggest problem would, however, come from the party he never attended.

On January 31, 1905, the greatest ball of the Gilded Age was held in New York. It was the infamous ball of James Hazen Hyde at New York's Sherry's Hotel (where Frick had an apartment from 1900 to 1905). James Hazen Hyde was the young heir of an insurance fortune. The twenty-eight-year-old James Hazen had become the major stockholder and director of the Equitable Life Assurance Society, on whose board Henry Clay Frick served. Hyde's father was a friend of George Westinghouse and had served on the board of Westinghouse Electric. The Equitable Life Assurance Society at the time was one of America's largest insurance companies with over 300,000 policyholders and over one billion dollars in assets. At the time, insurance companies were the major investors in Wall Street, and Equitable was a major holder of railroad stocks. Equitable Life had a significant number of offices in Pittsburgh's Frick Building. Frick sat on the board, but he rarely attended meetings, seeing it as an honorary position. Young James Hyde lacked any real business sense or even the work ethic of his father. Hazen was interested in socializing. Frick had never been much interested in Equitable, but the Hyde Ball, with over 600 costumed guests covering all of Astor's "400," would soon change all of that. Hazen encouraged full press coverage.

The guests were predominantly America's "old money" such as the Astors, Belmonts, Depews, and Vanderbilts. A young Franklin D. Roosevelt represented one old New York family. Frick and most of the Pittsburgh capitalists were not there. J. P. Morgan preferred to relax behind closed apartment doors. The Hyde Ball lasted from 6 p.m to 7 a.m. and three meals were served. The menu was French, and the French entertainment was brought in by special ship. The total bill was around $200,000. It was considered the greatest ball of the Gilded Age.[1] It was clearly over the top. Several stories quickly started to circulate that Hyde had used Equitable money for the party. The scandal rocked Wall Street and Washington and put fear into millions of small policyholders. The great scandal commanded 115 front-page articles in the *New York Times* and 122 in *The World* in a single year.[2] It tarnished New York's highest society and disturbed the normalcy of business in Morgan's library.

There was an uproar at the Equitable Board meeting. The Board of Directors selected Henry Clay Frick to head up an investigatory committee. Initially, some policyholders feared that the issue might be covered up. The result showed the character of Frick as a tough and ethical businessman. Frick dug deep into the whole issue of corporate affairs, going over cash balances, salaries, and compensation back to 1900. Frick found a long list of instances of mismanagement and misuse of corporate funds. The recommendation was to fire Hyde and ask for some payback as well as to demand a state investigation. The report highlighted corruption as well as Frick's dislike for business entertainment and other indirect expenses.

When the board hesitated on the implementation of the report, Frick walked out, stating: "I will no longer sit on the same board with that young man."[3] Frick dropped off the boards of Franklin National Bank and Commercial Trust so he would not be on boards with Hyde. Hyde did resign, as the state announced an investigation, and he took a thirty-five year vacation to France. The newspaper reports in his home state reached the desk of President Teddy Roosevelt, who launched a federal investigation. Roosevelt was going after Big Business, and conspicuous parties and scandals were opportunities to point out

---

1 Patricia Beard, *After the Ball*, (New York: Harper Collins, 2003), p. 178
2 Patricia Beard, *After the Ball*, (New York: Perennial, 2003), 5
3 Schreiner, p. 34

problems. These investigations supported Frick's conclusion. Frick and President Roosevelt agreed that Frick's neighbor and friend, George Westinghouse, should be put on the new Board to restore public confidence in the insurance industry.

Many believed that J. P. Morgan and his rival insurance company, New York Life, were waiting to take over forming an insurance trust. Frick, of course, was tied to Morgan in the ownership of United States Steel and could not have further involvement. A congressional investigation opened up many political ties as the scandal spun out of control. The stock drop had taken Equitable to the edge of bankruptcy, and the politicians both nationally and in the state of New York needed a way out.

Roosevelt selected men who could quickly rebuild public confidence. It was a troika of former President Grover Cleveland, former Supreme Court Justice Morgan O'Brien, a presiding appellate judge, and George Westinghouse. Westinghouse had the only organizational management experience, but it was a major strength. Some considered Westinghouse a flawed candidate, since James Hyde's father, Henry, had been a director on the board of Westinghouse Electric. While James had technically inherited the director seat, he never used it. Westinghouse and Henry had gone back to 1885, when a Westinghouse steam engine powered an elevator for the Equitable Building. The elevator allowed the Equitable Building to be the largest in the world at seven stories. Westinghouse, already overloaded with his companies, needed convincing by his friend and New York lawyer, Paul Cravath. Once Westinghouse accepted, the policy owners received ballots and returned total support to the committee of three. J. P. Morgan cared little for Westinghouse, since Westinghouse had refused to form an electrical trust with him; and Morgan had been targeting Westinghouse for years. Westinghouse, however, was "Mr. Clean," and this scandal needed his stature.

The troika was given unrestricted authority to reorganize the company. They set out to bring in new and competent managers. Within a year they reformed the company and headed off what had been called the "Rich Men's Panic." Westinghouse was showered with praise as Morgan fumed at Westinghouse's success. The scandal actually drew Morgan, Frick, and Belmont closer, which would be a future problem for Westinghouse. The *New York Sun* hailed Westinghouse as the "world's greatest engineer," "an architect of America's Golden Age," and a "truly fine, kindly and lovable human being." Westinghouse was hailed as the greatest American capitalist and manager. He was probably the only major capitalist of the time that was not tarnished by the scandal, but whose image improved from it. Unfortunately, within months Morgan would destroy Westinghouse and his image of a great businessman.

CHAPTER 19. PANIC OF 1907

With the encouragement of J. P. Morgan, Henry Clay Frick took on a more active role on the board of United States Steel in 1905. The infamous Hyde party and failure of Equitable Insurance had created a financial crisis in New York banking circles, but it had been contained. By early 1907, the great expansion and prosperity that had started with the McKinley administration had run its natural course. The Panic of 1907 began in the summer with a financial crisis in New York. That very summer Frick had been in Paris on an automobile tour of Europe. He returned to find a shaky stock market in August. In addition, financial scandals had rocked a number of important insurance and financial companies. In October, the stock market slumped again. It was falling rapidly, and the Dow Jones average would lose 25 percent by month's end. The situation had reached crisis stage with little hope of stabilization. While the New York exchanges struggled, regional markets such as Pittsburgh closed for lack of liquidity. Before the Federal Reserve, these "panics" had to take their course. Interest rates were spiraling out of control as stock prices plummeted day after day. It would also be much different than the great "Panic of 1893." This time the currency problem had international roots. Currency problems in Europe had already started a wave of gold hoarding. Even world markets such as Japan had a currency shortage. At the time, few Americans realized what was taking place in the world's financial centers, and the people on Main Street had no idea of the coming crash. Soon insurance, bank, and trust companies found themselves unable to get credit. Without credit, financial operations froze, and insiders at the stock exchange drove stock prices down. The Pittsburgh steel mills were still running flat out, the Pittsburgh smoke was thick with prosperity, and overtime was available to any worker. To the Pittsburgh steelworkers, things seemed normal. The New York bankers were starting to worry, however. The word was getting out in New York and lines were forming outside banks.

October 13 was considered a lucky day by J. P. Morgan; he was clearly preparing for the opportunities that might arise from a financial panic. Morgan, who was in England earlier in the year on an art collecting trip, may have consulted with the Archbishop of Canterbury, as he often did, for "mystical" signs. On October 13, Morgan was at a church convention in Virginia, and President Teddy Roosevelt was hunting bear in Louisiana. Andrew Mellon was in Paris and quickly arranged to return to Pittsburgh. Frick had been in touch with Morgan, realizing the problem was mounting, and he left Pittsburgh for New York. Frick was one of several called to Morgan's library at Thirty-Sixth Street and Madison Avenue to take the helm as Morgan returned. Then a run started on Knickerbocker Trust Company which could not be stopped. Depositors withdrew over eight million dollars in less than four hours. On Friday, October 18, all backers pulled out, thereby assuring its failure. J. P. Morgan had his own interests and allowed his competitor to fail. The stock market saw a number of companies go under that Friday. The weekend added to the tension as stories of bank failures hit the nation's press.

In Pittsburgh, the stock market closed, and rumors spread that Westinghouse Electric could not meet a call on its loans. This was amazing, as Westinghouse was highly profitable and had just reported record profits. But the debt was over $40 million for Westinghouse Electric alone. It was a short-term issue which would not be a problem with today's Federal Reserve. The immediate danger then was that the banks would call in short-term money market loans, which was typical of financial panics before the Federal Reserve. Four million dollars in cash would be needed by midweek just to keep the financial markets from freezing up. Thursday was payday in the Turtle Creek Valley; and Westinghouse Electric met it, but Westinghouse would have to reduce the payroll by Monday to get all the cash possible. George Westinghouse had left for New York to look for help from the New York banks after Mellon Bank had refused to help. Westinghouse was a go-it-alone manufacturer who avoided bankers as much as possible. In New York, Westinghouse's primary banker, August Belmont, refused, and Morgan controlled the others. Morgan controlled General Electric, Westinghouse Electric's biggest competitor, and Morgan was happy to see loans called on Westinghouse.

On Monday morning, October 21, the city of Pittsburgh braced for the arrival of the New York financial tidal wave. With Frick and Westinghouse in New York, the East End braced for a banking panic, but the general fear had not fully reached the worker neighborhoods. At the mills, there were only rumors of some problem in New York, but by afternoon, word had hit the city that payrolls around town would be affected, including those of the booming mills of Carnegie Steel Division of USS. Ernest Heinrichs, Westinghouse's public relations man described the mood in the Westinghouse Building on October 21: "an atmosphere of ominous oppression pervading the offices. Conversations were carried on in whispers. Everybody seemed to have a feeling of fearful expectancy, as if some dangerous catastrophe was about to descend on the factories of Pittsburgh. Although nobody appeared to have any idea what was going to happen." The same feeling existed at Carnegie Steel Headquarters. Cash calls would quickly become cancelled orders and layoffs for Pittsburgh's industries. All morning, Carnegie Steel had been taking order cancellations, and problems lived up to the term "panic." The monthly profits of USS reflected the plunge in orders — profits in October were $17.05 million, $10.47 million in November, and $5 million in December. Again, America's banker, J. P. Morgan, stood on the sidelines, except to assure cash for USS operations in which he had the controlling stake. Only Morgan was in a position to decide the course of this panic.

Interestingly, J. P. Morgan's refusal to aid Knickerbocker on October 22 caused the panic to proceed, but now Morgan could direct its path. He had a few plums in mind. Morgan wanted Westinghouse Electric, his main competitor, to fail. Westinghouse was again the target of press articles, claiming poor management. Morgan, of course, had great influence in the press. Edison Electric was part of the Morgan electrical trust and had everything to gain from Westinghouse's problems. The Panic provided another opportunity for Morgan to see a competitor in Westinghouse Electric fail. Westinghouse could find no help in the local papers, either. With Morgan's takeover of Carnegie Steel in 1901, Pittsburgh's press followed the lead of the Morgan-controlled New York press. Besides, Westinghouse was an outsider to the Scotch–Irish bankers who controlled the city's financiers such as Andrew Mellon. They met briefly with East End Judge Reed of Mellon Bank at the Duquesne Club, hoping that he might act as a bridge. Reed had been Carnegie's chief lawyer and had worked with Morgan to negotiate the formation of United States Steel. Westinghouse's old friend and now Mellon Bank lawyer, Judge Reed, would try heroically to pull together Pittsburgh bankers to help. On October 23, the Pittsburgh stock exchange was forced to close, which crippled Pittsburgh's banks. It's not clear whether Frick realized his neighbor's company was about to fail. It does seem likely that Frick knew Mellon would not help, and Morgan wanted Westinghouse Electric to fail. Westinghouse had always been vocal about his dislike of bankers. Frick was in a tough spot, but business required him to watch his friend go down. Strangely, both Westinghouse and Frick seemed to accept this as the law of the financial jungle.

By now J. P. Morgan was in his library directing events. Morgan's library was the nerve center of the crisis, and Henry Clay Frick was with him most of the time. The panic had hit the streets, with bank depositors pulling their money, since in those days there was no protection of bank savings. The Panic of 1907 was different because of its speed. Some creative individuals earned as much as $10 a day to wait in bank lines as depositors tried to salvage other parts of their life savings. The draw down on bank reserves caused banks to call in loans from big and small companies. In Pittsburgh, retailers had "panic prices" to help generate cash. Morgan held day and night meetings in his library as he moved to take control of the panic. Morgan even forced the banks to issue scrip in lieu of cash to keep the banking system floating. Lacking any government regulation, the public and the government looked to Morgan as their savior. It was an image promoted by the *New York Times*, as Morgan controlled most of their debt. The president of the United States at the time had no way to influence financial markets. Even Teddy Roosevelt had no choice but to ally himself with Morgan. Europe was also near collapse, and the renowned banker Lord Rothschild called Morgan, the world's greatest financier. Morgan was informally in charge of the nation's money supply; Roosevelt and Congress could only watch as the nation spiraled into depression. Morgan controlled not only the nation's press and banks, but most of its major corporations. The crisis would not be wasted by Morgan. J. P. Morgan & Company officers served as directors in 114 corporations with a capitalization of $22.5 billion compared to the total capitalization of $26.5 billion for all of the New York Stock Exchange. New York bankers were said to be coming and going from Morgan's library. Morgan was able to stall the panic in October by forming a bank alliance to save the market. Still, many companies remained days away from collapse, and Morgan was the only one who could save them. More importantly, Morgan could pick and choose the winners such as his steel trust of United States Steel.

Morgan had no interest in saving Westinghouse. He could now strengthen his many trusts. This was the overall strategic approach of Morgan, which awaited only the opportunity to activate. Furthermore, Westinghouse had soundly defeated Morgan, Edison, and General Electric in the "war of the currents." Westinghouse Electric was thus left to fail. It is interesting that there is no record of Frick's efforts, if any, to help his friend, Westinghouse. Morgan and the New York banks, however, had a deep dislike of Westinghouse who often rebuffed them in good times. In Pittsburgh, the Mellon family was holding its customers above water. President Roosevelt sent his Secretary of the Treasury to Morgan to ask for help to prevent a full collapse of the American economy. The meeting with Frick and others on the situation went all through the night, which was typical of Morgan's "Library meetings." The Morgan meetings moved to stabilize the nation's banks while also picking some industrial plums as part of the harvest. Frick and the United States Steel Company moved to purchase Tennessee Coal and Iron which would further their great steel monopoly.

In 1907, TC&I accounted for a mere one percent of steel production. TC&I served a niche in the southern rail business, which could be a major plus for Morgan's United States Steel. Frick had studied the possibility of taking over TC&I but felt it to be inefficient and overcapitalized. In addition, TC&I was producing rails about $3 a ton more than USS plants, even though they were using cheap black labor and free state convict labor. TC&I was rich in mineral rights, including massive southern iron ore reverses. United States Steel was dependent on Lake Superior ore. Many believed the Lake Superior iron ore was running out, although Frick didn't believe it. Morgan continued to push for a deal, while the USS Financial Committee hesitated. As TC&I stock continued to decline along with their New York brokerage house, Moore & Schley, the opportunity arose for a financial deal that would deliver TC&I at a cheap price. Moore & Schley creditors were holding TC&I stock as collateral for Moore & Schley loans. In addition, if Moore & Schley were to fail, the market would tank again. It was Saturday, and the rumors were that the market would crash Monday if Morgan didn't jump in with aid. Morgan got the USS finance committee to agree, but the concern was that President Roosevelt would file an anti-trust case if they moved forward. Morgan knew he was holding all the cards, but he sent Frick and the president of United States Steel, Judge Gary, to meet with the president.

Late Sunday, Frick got the Pennsylvania railroad to prepare a locomotive and his Pullman car, the *Westmoreland*. As a director of the Pennsylvania railroad, Frick could pull the necessary strings. They got to Washington by 8 a.m. and met the president over breakfast. Roosevelt had little choice, believing the nation's markets near collapse. Frick and Gary got Roosevelt's approval to move ahead. Years later in his autobiography Roosevelt used the following justification: "It was necessary for me to decide on the instant, before the Stock exchange opened, for the situation in New York was such that every hour might be vital . . . From the best information at my disposal, I believe that the addition of the Tennessee Coal and Iron property would only increase the proportion of the Steel Company's holdings by about four percent . . . It offered the only chance for arresting the panic, and it did arrest the panic."[1] Morgan had won. In addition, Morgan's saving of the brokerages was hailed in the popular press as a miracle, and Morgan was a savior. The panic did not spare Pittsburgh. Within six months, the steel industry was hit hard, with 175 out of 314 blast furnaces closing by 1908. Over 50,000 Pittsburgh steelworkers would lose their jobs. Tennessee Coal and Iron (TC&I) was insignificant in terms of nation production.

In fact, most populists and Republicans of the time suspected that Morgan had caused the panic to destroy competing companies such as Westinghouse Electric. Wisconsin's populist Senator Robert La Follette stated in 1907 that Morgan and his associates "deliberately brought on the late panic, to serve their own ends."[2] John Moody charged that Morgan and associates stopped the panic by "taking a few dollars out of one pocket and putting millions into another. Upton Sinclair used the panic as a basis for his novel, *The Money Changers*, to illustrate Morgan's ruthlessness. In the novel, a Morgan-like character orchestrates a financial crisis for private gain while destroying ordinary people across the nation.[3] The Senate committee investigating the panic for years concluded Morgan had taken advantage of the situation.

At the end of November, Frick tried to push Roosevelt for more favors. In particular, Frick wanted the anti-trust case against Standard Oil to be dropped, but this time Roosevelt refused.[4] Frick was extremely upset with Roosevelt over this and his anti-trust policies in general. Later the next month, however, Frick and his wife were special guests at a White House dinner. Still, he never believed that Roosevelt was a typical Republican but lamented the passing of the McKinley administration. Frick, however, wanted to purge the Republican Party of the liberals and progressives like Roosevelt. Frick continued to work in the party to elect more conservative Republicans. Frick and Morgan would support William Taft in 1912, which forced Roosevelt out of the party, but put the Democrat Woodrow Wilson in the White House. Morgan cared little about who was president as long as they could be bought. He had controlled Democrat Grover Cleveland as he had Roosevelt. In retrospect, too much was made of the anti-trust issues. USS's market share declined and competition increased. While Westinghouse Electric failed, Morgan never

1   Theodore Roosevelt, *The Autobiography of Theodore Roosevelt*, (New York: Charles Scribner's Sons, 1958), p. 245
2   Jean Strouse, *Morgan: American Financier*, (New York: Harper Perennial, 2000), p 589
Harvey, p. 309
3   Jean Strouse, *Morgan: American Financier*, (New York: Harper Perennial, 2000), p 589
4   Harvey, p. 309

got direct control of it. Morgan, however, now could add Westinghouse to the list of East End capitalists he had defeated. Another result of the investigations into the House of Morgan's role in 1907 was the signing of the Federal Reserve Act by Democratic president Woodrow Wilson in an effort to free the government from the House of Morgan in financial emergencies.

In late October of 1907, Westinghouse was on a train to New York once again, this time to discuss receivership with the bankers. He rode separately in his car from the Pittsburgh bankers who were invited to the meeting. He was never comfortable traveling, preferring an evening at home, and this day was even more trying. The train passed the Air Brake Works and the town of Wilmerding, which he had built. From the train, Wilmerding looked like a great industrial castle surrounded by well-planned rows of houses. It had only been a few weeks earlier that Westinghouse had signed the order for thousands of turkeys to be distributed in Wilmerding for Thanksgiving. The tradition went back to 1870, when in the early years he had invited all his workers to Thanksgiving dinner at a Pittsburgh hotel. As he opened the morning paper, the train rolled by his huge complex of Westinghouse Electric and Machine companies in Wilmerding and East Pittsburgh. Westinghouse had always enjoyed the support of the local press, and it hurt deeply to have it turn on him. He noted to his associate, "I suppose all those great works built themselves." The fact was Morgan controlled and was favored by the press nationally, which assured many more difficult mornings for George in the months to come. Papers that had once hailed the kindness and character of Westinghouse now portrayed him as a fool at every chance. It was tough medicine, but it was part of the image building of Morgan, the corporate white knight. In a few years J.P.M. would be answering to Congress about how he "saved" the country or whether he created the problem.

A jealous former East End neighbor, Andrew Carnegie, made the hardest and most unfair criticism of Westinghouse. Carnegie was returning from Europe when the press caught up with him. Carnegie's remaining investments and friends were protected from the Panic by the hand of Morgan. Feeling a bit superior and lacking details, he was his usual gregarious self on the deck of the ship. Carnegie quotes made the newspapers and the following quote was typical, "I feel very, very sorry that George Westinghouse should have trouble and I want to see him out of the woods. Fine fellow, George, George is — splendid fellow. And a great genius. But he is a poor businessman. A genius and a businessman are seldom found in one individual. Now Westinghouse is of too much value to the world, in originating ideas and developing them, to have one whit of energy wasted in business work and worries. You see, all of his business activity would never get him individually a noticeable success, whereas his genius, at play, would keep home an outstanding figure in the world. He should have a good business man, so that he never would have to bother about business details."[1] Carnegie was just plain wrong. Westinghouse had done things Carnegie had never done as a businessman or human being. Westinghouse started over thirty companies from scratch and built them into multi-million dollar

---

1 Greater Pittsburgh Chamber of Commerce, printed by Robert Forsythe Company, 1928

international companies. Neighbors such as Henry Clay Frick and Andrew Mellon also deserted Westinghouse.

In New York, Westinghouse would sit down with conservative lawyer Robert Mather, who had been appointed interim chairman. Westinghouse was to remain on as company president. The new board represented bankers from New York, Pittsburgh, Chicago, and Boston. He returned to Pittsburgh to talk things over with his wife, Marguerite. Westinghouse had been the lion of industry for years and had ruled the electrical industry for most of its existence. Marguerite had been in the shadow of her husband. Now he needed his wife's support at the age of sixty, as his dreams seemed to ending. He could have no better friend and wife than Marguerite. Their marriage had been full and loving through the best and worst of times. She sold all her gifts of stock to assure that her husband would know no embarrassment in this short-term money crisis. His marriage was something Morgan lacked, for Morgan's marriage was merely a front for his business, as he went from affair to affair behind closed doors while paying off the press. Westinghouse had built many companies and advanced engineering, again something that Morgan had never done.

Westinghouse was hurt, depressed, and disillusioned. For Westinghouse, the company was his family and his dream, making the loss paramount. He had started to believe the editorials which blamed him for the company's demise. That very day, the editorial had been titled, "The Dynamo is stilled." The next two years would be a personal hell. Westinghouse battled against a boardroom bully, usually coming out on the short end. He was suffering from a type of depression known well to men of achievement. Without Marguerite, he would have given in to it, but her support kept him in the fight. Westinghouse stayed on as company president, but he was restricted from any financial decisions. The bankers now wanted Westinghouse out; they had hoped that he would leave as a gentleman. Morgan modeled his takeovers after Napoleon, his hero, allowing local control but requiring strategic loyalty. Morganization was usually a long process. Organizations and cultures survived as long as money flowed to the stockholders. Some smaller East End bankers and brokerage houses also courageously helped out as a personal favor to Westinghouse. The big bankers realized that the Westinghouse name was a key component to the company success, so that their victory was not complete. The company retained its name, a concession that the bankers had not even given Thomas Edison when they took down Edison Electric in 1891. Westinghouse never fully accepted these bankers in charge of "his" company.

Though Westinghouse was too big a name for the bankers to publicly force out, he felt compelled to hold on to what little he could — not for himself, for he was crushed mentally, but because he felt obligated to his employees. Morganization meant the Westinghouse workplace advances would be repealed. His pride was wounded and his need for control assaulted, but he stayed. Westinghouse surely wanted to resign, but he felt an obligation to the stockholders and employees. It was extremely hard on him, but he fought through his personal depression. Westinghouse was able to entrench his employee-oriented policies. The bankers surrounded and isolated him and made his life hell. They vetoed the money for many of his projects. The strategy was typical of Morgan and the big bankers of New York. It was a strategy of slow internal revolution. It had taken almost ten years for Morgan to route the Carnegie men out of United States Steel after the buyout of Carnegie Steel in 1900.

In the summer of 1911, the Westinghouse Electric directors forced a proxy fight for the company president. Thousands of workers in Pittsburgh were disappointed at the loss of their beloved boss. Marguerite and George soon came to the same conclusion; it was time to break from Westinghouse Electric. He was too old to battle twelve bankers every day. He needed to accept the fact the company was lost. Now he would take that long vacation to his summer home in Lenox, Massachusetts. Lenox was where Westinghouse had built his "recreation house." He would go there every summer with Marguerite, whose health demanded she leave the hot sulfuric air of Pittsburgh. At Lenox, George Westinghouse passed the time hunting, fishing, gardening, and bowling on his built-in lanes. He seemed comfortable at Lenox away from the press and the business world of the East End. He would never be the lion of old, but neither could he retire from his passion for work and innovation. He had made the decision to work through his depression because he could not bring himself to accept the defeat of retirement. Few East Enders ever retired, and they never fell on their swords. The defeat cut deep, however, and Westinghouse never fully mentally recovered. He still owned many companies including Westinghouse Air Brake; but his baby had been Westinghouse Electric, which retained his name.

CHAPTER 20. DEATH OF THE LIONS

In particular, five East End neighbors had transformed the industrial world. Carnegie, Frick, Mellon, Westinghouse, and Heinz were these lions. Judge Thomas Mellon died in 1909. Westinghouse died in 1913, and Heinz, Carnegie, and Frick all passed in 1919. Andrew Mellon would live until 1937. No single neighborhood block had ever controlled so much money and industrial assets. It's hard to find a similar group of genius neighbors. There was the Lunar Club in Manchester, England that included Wedgwood and Watt. In London there were the "Honest Whigs" who included Priestley and Ben Franklin. There were, of course, many other greats who had been East End neighbors before, during, and after this quintet, such as B. F. Jones, Charles Schwab, Thomas Scott, Thomas Bakewell, Charles Lockhart, and James O'Hara. Their legacy is more than money; it was electrical power distribution, electrical generation, canned baked beans, steel making, coal mining, coke production, steel railroad rails, the railroad air brake, aluminum, glass packaging, the science of marketing, employee pensions, employee health care, and the AC motor. These were men who made things. They built factories, railroads, and mills. Money was their measure of success, not their quest. These were men who would be unhappy becoming lottery millionaires because such money would not reflect their efforts. They gave their money back in most cases through their lives and at death. Many believed that in various ways they were but stewards of money. Almost all believed money would corrupt their offspring.

Many look at 1909 as the peak of the City of Pittsburgh as well as its East End. On November 18, 1907, the City of Pittsburgh annexed the City of Allegheny (today's North side). The merger joined 150,000 people in Pittsburgh with 62,000 from the City of Allegheny. It became the seventh largest city in the United States, its highest rank. Allegheny's rich had been moving to the East End since the 1860s. The East End's Oakland district had become the area's culture side. In 1909, the Pittsburgh Pirates moved from their old Allegheny

City stadium to the Oakland. Forbes Field was named after the first commander of Fort Pitt — General Forbes. In 1909 the Pittsburgh Pirates won the World Series over Detroit. The three games at Forbes Field had over 80,000 fans to watch their hero, Honus Wagner, face Detroit's Ty Cobb. It was revenge, though, for Pittsburgh's 1903 World Series lost to Detroit.

The year 1909 brought new scandals to the East End. This time it was Andrew Mellon and his wife, a friend of Henry Clay Frick. In fact, Frick had introduced Andrew to his future wife, Nora McMullen. McMullen was the British heiress of the Guinness Brewery. They married in 1900. By 1909, however, Nora was having an open affair. She promised to scandalize the East End and rock the East Liberty Presbyterian Church. Mellon had 13 listening devices installed in his East End mansion to assure success in suing for divorce. Mellon even got Scotland Yard involved. The story made headlines in New York, Philadelphia, and Europe but was completely suppressed in Pittsburgh. Mellon even had out-of-town papers suppressed in Pittsburgh. Pittsburgh police confiscated papers at the railroad station. With famous East Ender Judge Reed, Mellon negotiated a respectable East End divorce. Nora would be paid well over a million dollars, but she had to leave for Europe so that the basis would be desertion. Part of the money required her to stay unmarried and out of the newspapers. The couple would have joint custody of the children. Amazingly, the deal broke down and Mellon again moved to control proceedings. Nora wanted a jury trial which would allow for press coverage. Mellon enlisted the political ties of neighbors such as Henry Clay Frick and Philander Knox, who passed a special bill through the state legislature to prevent a jury trial. Mellon won the fight and Nora was blocked from taking the children outside of Pennsylvania.

The East End reflected the phases of growth of Pittsburgh and American industrial capitalism. Its initial phase began with Scotch–Irish and German settlers which included men like Judge Wilkins, James O'Hara, Thomas Mellon, and Alexander Negley. It followed by a wave reflecting the industrial surge of Pittsburgh and the nation. The East End became the suburb of the wealthy industrialists and capitalists of Pittsburgh. The biggest influx and the building of the great mansion mainly occurred in this period between 1878 and 1900. These were the golden and final years of the Carnegie Brothers partnership; the peak of the Pittsburgh oil industry; the peak of Westinghouse Electric, Westinghouse Air Brake, and H. J. Heinz Company; the beginning of the Mellon banking empire; and the start of the aluminum industry. The suburban Eden started with the wealthy Pittsburgh manufacturers moving from downtown Penn Avenue to Shadyside, which accounted for 15 percent of the East End population in 1907, followed by an *en masse* influx of the Pig Iron Aristocrats from Allegheny City (Pittsburgh's North side), which accounted for 25 percent of the population. The largest were established wealth coming from all over the Pittsburgh area. Less than 5 percent came from outside the Pittsburgh district. One sociologist noted: "What was being created in Shadyside and the East End in the late nineteenth century was a melting pot of older and newer money. All the wealthy residents were similar in ethnic and religious orientation, and all their families had been in America for some time with at least middle-class status, but this new suburban environment was one instrument used to create a new metropolitan aristocracy."[1]

The East End continued to be the home of the wealthy industrialists, as many millionaires were created by the breakup of the Carnegie partnership and formation of United States Steel. Still, things were changing between 1900 and 1920. The old industrial lions had left. Henry Clay Frick moved to New York in 1905, but he maintained "Clayton" for business trips and his daughter, Helen, who never lost her attachment for her children's home. George Westinghouse was living mostly at his mansion in the Berkshires; H. J. Heinz never left but he traveled a great deal in later years; Charles Schwab left for New York in 1902 to work as president at the New York headquarters of United States Steel; and many of the Pig Iron Aristocrats had passed the torch to second and third generations. The Mellon family was still the lord of the east, but the new and old wealth were moving to the new rich Pittsburgh environs of Sewickley and Sewickley Heights as well as New York's Fifth Avenue. Locally, the East End would continue for decades to represent Pittsburgh's elite, but its national dominance was past.

Henry Clay Frick had cheated death in 1911. Frick had been with J. P. Morgan on a major art collecting trip. J. P. Morgan was also on a collecting and business trip in Europe, and they would meet briefly. The tour included Rome, the Vatican, and Pompeii. For Frick, it was almost an annual event to tour Europe and collect. Often Andrew Mellon, another of the world's great collectors, would travel with Frick. The trip home had been booked on the *Titanic*, but Frick canceled. Two reasons have been given; one was that Mrs. Frick sprained her ankle and delayed the party.[2] The other is that Helen feared the ship's eventual sinking.[3] The suite of rooms (B-52, B-54, and B-56) was transferred to J. P. Morgan, who also cancelled. The Hardings took over the suites, but they too cancelled. Eventually, the shipping line's director, J. Bruce Ismay, took the suite and would perish in the sinking. It wasn't death, however, that many East Enders feared the most.

The East End's national dominance passed because of what the old lions feared most, the corruption of old money. Money took away the motivation so critical to the advance of capitalism, innovation, and creativity. Carnegie feared it so much that he refused to pass his millions to the next generation of the family. Frick and Westinghouse tried to limit the corruption of money in their families as well. Benjamin Thaw's passing of millions in the family showed how money could corrupt future generations. The Mellons used a military-type training for their young sons to mold them to be responsible with the family fortune. It was a family application of survival of the fitness, which they had applied in business. Heinz used a similar approach, restricting allowances and forcing sons to work on farms and at low-level factory jobs. The Heinz and Mellon approach was successful (if you don't count the breakdown of his oldest son, who couldn't handle the military approach). Their approach gave rise to a dominant survivor of several siblings to take over the family busi-

---

1   Renee Reitman, "The Elite Community in Shadyside, 1880-1920," Seminar paper, University of Pittsburgh, 1964
2   *Chicago Record-Herald*, Friday, February 19, 1912, p. 3
3   Sanger, *Helen Clay Frick*, p. 83

ness. For Frick, the approach resulted in his daughter Helen being the heir to the main fortune rather than his fun-loving son.

There were other shifts in the demographics. The Presbyterian dominance gave way to the Episcopalian, and with it passed the spirit of the frontier to the social establishment. The sons of most of the old lions were sent to Yale, Princeton, and Harvard versus the University of Pittsburgh and Carnegie Institute of Technology. Childs Frick went to Princeton, and Howard Heinz and George Westinghouse III went to Yale. Andrew Carnegie and Henry Clay Frick gave millions to Presbyterian-based Princeton. Frick built Princeton's Colonial Club for $100,000 and then left Princeton $7.2 million in his will. Younger sons and third generation saw a shift at the secondary schools such as Shadyside Academy to eastern prep schools. This educational shift eroded the core of Scotch–Irish enlightenment and *McGuffey Reader* principles. With these changes came an Astor-like obsession with the social register versus the stock quotations in the paper. The nationalism of their fathers turned to internationalism with tastes as well as business. The pride of the dark daytime skies of Pittsburgh turned to hatred. It became fashionable to hide their Pittsburgh heritage, where once their fathers flaunted it. Second and third generation sons found little time for business as more pressing social engagements interfered.

Like the Pig Iron Aristocrats before them, the East End Elite established a type of upper society. The old money no longer built mills, founded new industries, created new technology, or employed millions. The change was not at first seen in the neighborhood mansions but in its spirit. It is the spirit of the neighborhood that is lamented much more than its physical decline. It is the loss of its spirit that reflected America best. There were notable exceptions such as Howard Heinz (son of H. J.), who took H. J. Heinz Company to new heights. Frick's daughter, Helen, who never lost her love of the old neighborhood, preferred to live out her life there versus living with the east coast elite. The Mellon family, however, managed to continue the growth of the great banking empire and their love of the Pittsburgh area.

On the first Friday in December of 1917, a quiet yet momentous reunion took place in the East End at the Phipps mansion. It was the sixteenth annual meeting of the Carnegie Veterans Association. The Association was a society of ex-Carnegie Steel managers. Initially it consisted of forty-nine members with honorary members being Mrs. Andrew Carnegie, Mrs. Margaret Carnegie Miller, and Mrs. Charles Schwab. Many of the members such as Schwab, Corey, Dickson, and Dinkey were the "Boys of Braddock" from the "class of 1879." Almost all had started in low positions at Edgar Thomson Works and Homestead Works. Mrs. Carnegie, who often hosted the group, called them "her boys."

For the first sixteen years, the Carnegie Veterans Association had met at Carnegie's New York home. In 1917 it moved for one year to the East End where most of the members lived or had lived prior to 1917. From 1917 to 1936, they would meet at Charles Schwab's New York mansion "Riverside." This 1917 meeting brought together not only former Carnegie partners but also some of the nation's most powerful executives. Charles Schwab was president of Bethlehem Steel; William Corey was president of Midvale Steel (the nation's third largest steel company); Charles Baker was now vice-president of American

Zinc; Torstein Berg was now vice-consul to Sweden; William Dickson was vice-president of Midvale Steel; Alva Dinkey was a vice-president of Midvale Steel; Robert Franks was president of Home Trust; Ambrose Monell was president of International Nickel; William Palmer was a director of USS and Cleveland Trust; Lawrence Phipps would shortly become a U.S. senator; Judge Reed was now president of Consolidated Gas; Emil Swenson was president of the Society of Engineers; Charles Taylor was president of the Carnegie Hero Fund and Carnegie Relief Fund; and Fred Wood was vice-president of International Nickel. The following veterans were key United States Steel executives: David Kerr (first vice-president USS); Homer Williams (president of Carnegie Steel — USS); William Blackburn; Henry Bope; John Campbell; William Clyde; and John McLeod. The following lived in the East End in 1917: John Campbell, Henry Bope, George Lauder, John McLeod, David Packer, Alexander Peacock, Lawrence Phipps, Judge Reed, and Homer Williams. The meeting was social and a night of remembrance for the neighborhood and friends who had created so much of America's wealth. While many were still powerful executives, they were in the twilight of their careers.

While spread across the eastern United States, the old capitalistic Pittsburgh lions continued to play a huge role nationally into the 1930s. Many presidents visited the East End and many were made in the East End such as William Harrison, William McKinley, William Taft and Warren Harding. One of Henry Clay Frick's final imprints on the nation was his alleged involvement in the selection of Warren Harding as the Republican candidate for president in 1920. Frick had first met Senator Harding at a Pittsburgh Chamber of Commerce meeting in 1916 and had noted, 'he looks like fine presidential timber.'[1] Frick's opposition to Woodrow Wilson's League of Nations had taken on an unusual vigor for a political issue, and Harding was in Frick's camp against the League. Many businessmen were supporting the Democratic pro-League view. These businessmen saw it as a way to increase their foreign trade, but the League would be backed financially by the United States. Frick held a private dinner in 1919 that included George Perkins (USS and J. P. Morgan Company); Dan Hanna (son of Senator Mark Hanna); Ambrose Monell of International Nickel; George Whelan (head of United Cigar); Henry Sinclair (Sinclair Oil); A. A. Sprague (Chicago wholesaler); George Harvey; and others.[2] The dinner was the source of a major fund to defeat the League of Nations, and many believed the diners picked Warren Harding as the Republican candidate. Sinclair was assigned the job of building a campaign chest to defeat the League. The fund was believed to be over $3 million dollars. Frick was considered the largest contributor, but the list was long including Charles Schwab, George Westinghouse, Herman H. Westinghouse, John Rockefeller, Andrew Mellon, Walter Chrysler, Harry Sinclair, and many others. Harding won a landslide victory in 1920. President Harding would ultimately name Andrew Mellon as his Secretary of Treasury and George Harvey as Ambassador to Great Britain, further supporting the link to Frick. Andrew Mellon would remain secretary throughout the decade.

1 Hartley, p. 363
2 Ferdinand Lundberg, *America's Sixty Families*, (New York: Citadel Press, 1938)

CHAPTER 21. THE CITY ON THE HILL — EAST END PHILANTHROPY

East End philanthropy defies most traditional labels such as paternal or welfare capitalism. Neither was it "liberal capitalism," but a unique vision rooted in industrial Western Pennsylvania. East End philanthropy was deeply rooted in Scotch–Irish Presbyterian beliefs. It focused on community but differed in how the result was achieved. East Enders H. J. Heinz and George Westinghouse were the most progressive employers in the nation, if not in the world. While United States Steel was taking the headlines, Westinghouse Electric, Air Brake, and other Westinghouse companies were creating a new type of workplace. H. J. Heinz had already established a new workplace and employee-oriented factory. The East Enders were very diverse in their approaches to giving back. Westinghouse was generous but resisted the pure charity of other industrialists; he preferred to spend money on personal, educational, and community improvement. He actually deplored straight, indiscriminate philanthropy, believing a high-paying job was the best philanthropy. He viewed himself as an industrial leader, not a trustee of the society's money. Westinghouse pioneered mutual insurance and disability insurance plans. As early as 1884, Westinghouse Machine formed the Westinghouse Machine Company Mutual Aid Society. The company funded this separate organization in large part. Membership was voluntary for the employee, requiring 50 cents a month. In the case of disability due to sickness, the worker was entitled to $5.00 a week for six months, and $7.00 a week for disability due to injury. The death benefit was $100.00 from natural causes and $150.00 from accidental death. The company contributed one-third of the injury benefit and one-third of the accidental death benefit.[1]

---

1 Crystal Eastman, *Work Accidents and the Law*, (New York: Charities Publication, 1910), 158

Company health, disability, and pension benefits were a pioneering concept of George Westinghouse, but as always with Westinghouse, it was a mutual benefit. In 1903 Westinghouse established the "Relief Department" at Air Brake to help employees. The *Wilmerding News* described the department mission in 1904 as: "To insure a certain income to the employees who might become unfitted for work through illness or injury and in the event of death to pay the beneficiary a stipulated sum. Any employee under 50 years of age is entitled to membership, subject to successful physical examination, but membership is not compulsory. Members contribute according to the class in which they belong, there being five, the class being determined by the wages received, varying from $35 to $95 or over per month, the contribution ranging from 50 cents to $1.50 per week. A member may receive benefits for 39 consecutive weeks, in event of disability extending so long a period. The air brake company is the custodian of the funds, but being such does not benefit the company peculiarly, as it pays four per cent interest on monthly balances to the credit of the relief fund. The company goes further and guarantees payment of all benefits, and if the money received from the monthly contributions be insufficient to meet the requirements the company makes good such deficit."[1]

By 1888, Westinghouse was planning a move for Westinghouse Air Brake from Pittsburgh to a new location to the east of Pittsburgh. Westinghouse dreamed of a worker republic and utopia. He hired architects to help locate a site that could support both the works and a planned community. Westinghouse's East End friend and Pennsylvanian Railroad executive, Robert Pitcairn, recommended the Turtle Creek Valley near a small railroad flag station. Pitcairn was an executive of the Pennsylvania Railroad and a board member of Westinghouse Electric Company. The Turtle Creek Valley offered water, railroad connections, a river port, and availability. It would also allow Westinghouse to commute from his personal Pennsylvania Railroad station to his string of new factories in the Turtle Creek Valley. The factory and community would be integrated. The factory was designed to be a safe environment with good lighting and ventilation. A clean and well-planned community would be built into the surrounding hills. Of particular interest to Westinghouse was the use of parks and greens to achieve a campus-like atmosphere. The planned employee houses were to have an emphasis on lawns and trees. Westinghouse's plan would go further than even communist/socialist Robert Owen's New Lanark in Scotland, in that his plan would include all phases of the community. Yet it would be unique from the American societal imitations of New Lanark (such as Economy, Pennsylvania; Zoar, Ohio; and Harmony, Indiana) in that it would have political and religious freedom. Westinghouse had actually started to offer low cost "cottages" to his workers at Union Switch and Signal in Swissvale around 1886.[2] Many East Enders such as Frick and Mellon saw it as socialism. Westinghouse, however, believed in employee home ownership, not rentals.

---

1 *Wilmerding News*, November 23, 1904
2 "Building Intelligence," *Manufacturer and Builder*, May, 1887

Westinghouse's approach to employee housing was much different than that of other industrialists. For example, Frick had supplied (rented) company housing for employees, but Westinghouse focused on home ownership. Westinghouse had experimented with low-cost employee houses in Swissvale. These Swissvale "cottages" were six-room homes costing around $1,200 to $2,000, but they were very high quality. Westinghouse wanted to build a still better house for his Wilmerding project. The company supplied low-cost loans to support the higher-cost housing. Initially in the 1890s, Westinghouse Air Brake purchased the land and built individual houses. The houses were then sold to the employees at cost. The mortgages were adjusted to the employee income and allowed for payments over fifteen years. Frick and Carnegie also experimented with mortgage help for their employees. The houses were also covered by a type of mutual insurance that protected the owner in times of unemployment, disability, and death. Westinghouse did use company resources to clean streets and plant flowers. Prizes were offered to homeowners for yard care and flower gardens. This stood in stark contrast to the Frick and Carnegie mining towns in which, when a death occurred, the company quickly foreclosed on the house. Furthermore, Air Brake's maintenance department would help repair utilities and appliances as well as some major repairs. In general, the company assured that all houses were maintained in a state of excellent repair.

Westinghouse planned a safe and comfortable workplace. He paid special attention to restrooms, lunchrooms, and rest areas. Like Heinz, Westinghouse was a major employer of women in labor-short Western Pennsylvania. Women employees had special lunchrooms with tablecloths, which was the same as H. J. Heinz's factory. Artesian wells were dug to supply safe drinking water for the employees, which was uncommon thinking for the time. The cleanliness of the plant was emphasized and maintained to strict standards. Lighting was also state of the art throughout the plant. Health care was supplied to workers and their families. A number of these features were directly related to experiences at his father's New England manufacturing plant. Westinghouse Air Brake headquarters was a beautiful castle modeled after one in Scotland. The original central building, however, was a wooden frame house that served as a community club with a library, bowling alley, and swimming pool. It was very similar in scope to Carnegie's first library in Braddock a few miles away, with its bowling alleys and swimming pool built about the same time. One big difference was that the Westinghouse employees had time to enjoy it, while Carnegie's steelworkers were working 12-hour shifts with a day off every few weeks. Westinghouse had pioneered the Saturday off for his employees and the company picnic.

For years the main role of the Westinghouse-supported Wilmerding YMCA was to integrate foreigners into American society. Westinghouse merged paternal capitalism with the American principles of self-reliance. New immigrants in Wilmerding were sent notices of meetings for citizenship, which were conducted by lawyers. Beginning emphasis was on English classes in which the association worked with the public schools. In addition, the association worked with the Daughters of the American Revolution to present extensive American history programs prepared in seven languages. This foreign program became the model for the whole United States. Westinghouse had shared this vision with his friend, President William McKinley. The YMCA shared facilities of the Westinghouse castle until 1907. In 1907, Westinghouse completed the "Welfare Building" for use by the YMCA, and shortly after, he built a building for the women (YWCA). These had world-class swimming pools and gymnasiums. The Wilmerding YMCA became the second largest in Pennsylvania by 1910. It was available to all residents in Turtle Creek Valley. In general, the YMCA was the type of community self-help organization that was popular with East Enders.

At the castle, further educational opportunities were offered. These included basic math, electricity, grammar, typewriting, and machine design among others. One specific course focused on the construction and operation of the railroad air brake. Machining and technical training was essential to Air Brake because the available immigrant workforce consisted mainly of unskilled European peasants. Westinghouse and East Ender Charles Schwab supported a type of manual training for all boys, which evolved into a state law in the 1900s. Boy apprentices were paid an hourly rate as they attended night school courses. The night school became known as the Casino Night School. The Casino Building erected near the plant offered recreational and educational opportunities for East Pittsburgh employees. The Casino functioned as a corporation school or night college offering general courses in English, shop practice, mathematics, and science. Westinghouse Electric funded 70 percent of the budget, but students were charged $2.00 per month. Students who performed well might receive company scholarships to attend college. Graduates of the school tended to have a fast track in the company, and most of the plant managers were graduates. Besides the courses, there were a wide variety of special lectures and talks. Westinghouse managers were expected to be instructors and lecturers. The physical programs offered would rival today's health clubs. Special classes were offered in tennis, wrestling, and fencing, all favorites of George Westinghouse. In addition, the association hired a prominent expert in "physical culture institution." Services were also held on Sundays, and evening Bible schools were offered. Even his plant managers spent time in the training rooms. Many clubs were organized including chess and checkers. Young immigrant women and daughters were taught an array of skills for the home.

Similarly, Heinz had an employee-driven focus. There were reading rooms and libraries at the Heinz factory. Heinz's approach stressed healthy employees. There was a gymnasium and a swimming pool. There was also a small hospital with full-time doctors. Finally, a large auditorium with massive stained glass windows was used for free lectures and many topics. Musical events were common for Heinz employees at lunchtime. Heinz built an employee library and offered sewing classes and home economic classes for employees. The Heinz factory had garden rooftops for relaxation. Dances were scheduled for his mainly young women workforce. Uniforms were also supplied to his workforce, which reduced clothing costs. Heinz also employed a type of housemother to generally help with employee problems. Heinz, like Westinghouse, often intervened in employee financial problems with a helping hand. Both Heinz and Westinghouse had traveled to and studied the German paternal factory system, but modified it with basic Scotch–Irish principles of self-reliance. Westinghouse, however, went a step further with employee insurance and home ownership.

Westinghouse companies were self-insurers for mutual benefits, using the company financial resources as collateral. The company and the program were independent, except that the company bore the expense of administration. Participation in the program was voluntary; the disability benefits covered about three-fourths of the Westinghouse employees. Of course, Westinghouse plants were safety oriented and had a significantly lower accident rate than the steel mills of the area. In addition, Westinghouse plants had doctors and nurses available to employees daily at the plant. Westinghouse employees who were "disabled" to a lesser degree were often given light work assignments to keep them employed. In fairness, the Carnegie and Frick coal mines had an informal program of keeping disabled employees working and earning money. Westinghouse programs were never socialistic but remained capitalistic in structure. In many ways, the Westinghouse programs fostered a competition for the best labor in the Pittsburgh area. Frick initially opposed the approach because he always avoided formal contractual agreements. In New York, J. P. Morgan fiercely opposed the programs of Westinghouse and Heinz. New York capitalists, lacking the operating experience of the East Enders, never understood the relationship of these benefits to motivated employees. New York financiers saw it as an expense item on the income sheet. Eventually in 1908, even the Morgan-controlled Carnegie Steel was forced to offer some disability insurance.

By 1913, two years before the Workmen's Compensation Act in Pennsylvania, Westinghouse Air Brake started to fully fund a workmen's compensation program. The fund was totally maintained by Air Brake with no payments by the worker, and all workers were covered. Again, Westinghouse pioneered the way for what would become state law. Even with the law, Air Brake payments were much more generous; and payment began immediately while the state allowed for a ten-day waiting period. Interestingly, other than H. J. Heinz (and later Carnegie), most East Enders did not support this type of "factory philanthropy;" but with the successes, many started to convert to the approach although it was consistent with early Scotch–Irish principles. Similarly, Westinghouse had one of the first pension plans for his employees. There is much evidence that Westinghouse had an informal pension plan in the 1890s based on the discrimination of the board of trustees. The plan required no employee payment and was based solely on years of service and was not at the discretion of management. Pensions did exist at Carnegie Steel in the area but were based on a demonstration of need after "long and creditable service." Carnegie become impressed with the Westinghouse plan in the early 1900s, and in 1907 gave money to start a plan at the Carnegie Steel Division of United States Steel. The Carnegie Steel plan, known as the Carnegie Relief Fund, was actually a gift of Andrew Carnegie in his retirement to his old company and was a trust of four million dollars to be administered by Carnegie Steel. Carnegie's boyhood friend, East End neighbor, founder of Pittsburgh Plate Glass, railroad executive, and Westinghouse Air Brake director, Robert Pitcairn, was named by Carnegie as administrator. The Carnegie plan was not financed by the company but functioned from Carnegie's gift.

Westinghouse Electric at East Pittsburgh (in Turtle Creek Valley) was a major new plant built to supply generators at Niagara Falls. Westinghouse proved every bit as creative in employee friendly and ergonomic workplace design as his neighbor, H. J. Heinz. The factory design took the individual worker into account as he had in his Wilmerding Air Brake plant. Washrooms and toilets were designed with the same creativity as electrical devices. Dining rooms were built and Westinghouse subsidized meals to assure reasonable rates (a similar practice to his neighbor, H. J. Heinz). The plant was the precursor of ergonomic design with skylights to maximize daylight, which was estimated at 70 percent of outdoors. Overall lighting was the best available including vapor lamps. Sports activities were promoted like the paternal factories of Germany which had been studied by both Westinghouse and Heinz. Both men saw a direct link to health and worker productivity. There was an auditorium for movies, shows, and lectures (again like the Heinz plant of the late 1888s). A library was added as well with popular books and magazines. There were a number of conference rooms for the many employee clubs and organizations. One employee club, The Electric Club, would become world famous, rivaling the greatest technical societies of the time. The club offered two lectures a week on technical and popular topics. It also printed a monthly newsletter which quickly evolved into a technical journal of international distinction. Westinghouse often allowed community organizations to use the conference rooms. In 1902, a large assembly hall built for the employee Electric Club was open to all Westinghouse company employees and even included some non-Westinghouse area engineers. Every two weeks the Electric Club had a social event planned from a committee of members' wives. One Christian group offered a Thursday Bible study; another Christian group, Christian Endeavor, was also given access to the rooms. Christian Endeavor was a national evangelical movement of the period. Westinghouse built special boarding houses for his single employees.

Westinghouse believed in fraternity and community as foundational to productivity, and the East Pittsburgh plant had other clubs related to the plant which were supported by the company. Again Westinghouse merged German paternal practices with Scotch-Irish principles. There was a Foremen's Association comprised of 200 to 300 middle managers, which included foremen, chief clerks, and inspectors. The association was both social and professional as was characteristic of Westinghouse organizations. Here again, we see a fundamental belief of Westinghouse about charity that employees should pay for education. Another organization was the "East Pittsburgh Club" designed for comfortable dining for the engineering and sales staff. This practice was so successful that much of Pittsburgh's heavy industry adopted these management approaches.

Westinghouse employees became known nationally as the most provided for and best paid. East Pittsburgh and Wilmerding earned the interest of many traveling criminals of the time as well with the large Westinghouse paydays. A group of "con men" and "street men" rode the rails to prey on workers. These traveling con men set up gambling wheels and games by the plant on paydays. Four plants were rated as the "best works in the country in which to make a pitch." These works had large payrolls and were located on the major railroad junctions. They included "The Baldwin Locomotive Works in Phila-delphia, the Union Iron Works in San Francisco, the Pullman Car Shops in Chicago, and the Westinghouse plants of East Pittsburgh."[1] Wilmerding factory, which was a closed community, was able to control the problem, but the massive East Pittsburgh complex could not. Like a carnival, the games were "legal." The traveling con men targeted the big holidays in many cases. In fact, other than angry wives, the immigrant workers seemed to enjoy the gambling. The prosperity of the plant seemed to foster an acceptance. East Pittsburgh was, in fact, one of America's highest paying plants for piecework and a very successful one as well.

At Westinghouse's Union Switch and Signal in the early 1900s Westinghouse pio-neered an employee stock program. This experiment was clearly visionary but consistent with Westinghouse's idea of employee ownership. The plan allowed employees to buy stock but was not a matching program. This was at a time when the mechanics of the stock market and capital requirements limited the ability of the worker to buy a small amount of stock. The plan allowed for small installments and gave a small bonus after five years. The money would be taken directly out of the paycheck, or the local savings & loans were brought into the purchasing program. This type of automatic plan was at least fifty years ahead of its time. The employee stock plan overall was one of the example in which Westinghouse followed his neighboring industrial giant — Carnegie Steel. Carn-egie had promoted stock ownership with his management as early as 1878. The Carnegie plan, however, was limited to partners and key managers. The Carnegie employee stock plan saw little success because the lower pay of the steelworkers prevented investment. Stock ownership was also one of the few employee programs that bankers such as J.P. Morgan found acceptable. In fact, it was George Perkins, a Morgan partner on the Carn-egie Steel Board, who devised one of the first stock programs in 1901 with the support of Henry Clay Frick. The collective wisdom at the time was that it offered an effective deterrent to unionization. The idea was that ownership would replace union protection as well; the loss of dividends by strikes would make workers hesitant to strike. In theory, it made sense, but even today the amount of stock ownership available rarely translates into a feeling of ownership.

The Heinz and Westinghouse employee programs started to become more popular after the famous *Pittsburgh Social Survey* of 1907 painted a vivid picture of worker suffering. The *Survey* did wake the conscience of many industrialists including Frick. Three steel executives that Heinz had worked with on civic committees were particularly touched. They were William Dickson, then first vice-president of United States Steel, William Corey, and Alva Dinkey, the plant manager of the vast Homestead Steel Work, which came under heavy criticism. Dickson was clearly moved by the *Survey*, professing that it changed his life and likened it to Abe Lincoln seeing the abuse of slaves as a youth and resolving to destroy slavery. Dickson moved to improve hours and working conditions

---

1 Wage Earning Pittsburgh, Survey, 1914

throughout United States Steel Corporation and continued the quest throughout the steel industry for 30 years. Dickson would become a passionate labor reformer and an admirer of H. J. Heinz for the rest of his life. The *Survey* touched another steel executive, Charles Schwab, who implemented reforms at Bethlehem Steel. Even the retired Andrew Carnegie was moved while reading it and established a fund for workers' pensions and insurance for his old employees.

These "Boys of Braddock" even formed a new steel company based on employee ownership and improved working conditions. Midvale Steel was formed in 1917 as "an experiment of industrial democracy." William Corey, William Dickson, and Alva Dinkey were all former Carnegie and United States Steel executives. Dickson had been known as "Carnegie's Conscience." Dickson had designed a safety program for Schwab and Frick at Homestead Works. Midvale was the third largest steel company and it was devoted to employee participation. It was to be a worker utopia and democracy pushing the eight-hour day, collective bargaining, employee representation, employee insurance, and improved bonus systems. It proved to be too much democracy for an industrial organization. Midvale Steel failed, but it pushed Morgan, Gary, and Frick to accept the eight-hour day at United States Steel and improved employee benefits by Charles Schwab at Bethlehem Steel.

One of the problems of understanding East End philanthropy is getting past the philanthropy of Andrew Carnegie. East End philanthropy had a long history going back to East Enders James O'Hara, William Safe, and Alexander King, who gave huge amounts of their fortunes to Pittsburgh's poor. This early East End philanthropy developed as New York capitalists were building family dynasties. For these early East End capitalists, there was no honor in money alone. Carnegie's view of philanthropy came out of the tradition of Pittsburgh Scotch–Irish, but it also gave one a unique mark of Carnegie's worldview. Some call it "welfare capitalism" but Pittsburgh social historians coined a better term, "constructive philanthropy," defining it as "attempting to define the basis for harmony, authority, and contemporize society."[1] But Carnegie's approach was really a blend of his Scotch–Irish responsibility and an adopted Puritan obligation to direct society. Clearly, Carnegie's New York friends had influenced him. Typical East End philanthropy was more anonymous and aimed at helping versus directing. Most of the hospitals of nineteenth century Western Pennsylvania were the result of East End philanthropy. East End industrialists routinely gave many lesser donations such as X-ray machines, clinics, gardens, organs, and musical instruments to communities. Lacking any government support, all social aid and welfare organizations in the area were dependent on gifts of the East Enders.

East End philanthropy was complex and diverse, and it eluded economic labels such as welfare capitalism or paternal capitalism, although it had many elements of both. The roots of the approach were, however, that of East End pioneer capitalists, James O'Hara and Jeffery Scaife. Communal capitalism focused on the community. Some like Carne-

---

1 Hays, p. 311

gie, Frick, Lockhart, and even Mellon focused directly on community building. Others like Heinz and Westinghouse preferred to build community from the bottom up with employee benefits. Often with Frick and Carnegie, it was a response to disasters. The Mammoth Mine cave-in of 1891 killed over a hundred, and Frick set up a $25,000 fund. A mine explosion in 1904 killed over 180 workers, and Carnegie donated over $40,000 and established a major trust fund known today as the Carnegie Hero Fund. The roots were clearly Scotch-Irish with the focus on community, even though many East Enders were German. Scotch-Irish values had become the region's standard. To understand East End philanthropy, one must first understand the common beliefs and traditions of the area. The earliest Scotch-Irish communities built social services and schools. It was considered a personal obligation and was promoted in the *McGuffey Readers* of their schools.

One common characteristic of the East Ender was freemasonry. It had been the home of the famous Lodge 45, which fathered some of the East End's greatest capitalists. The bonds of freemasonry seem to have been stronger than any social ties. The bonds of free-masonry and Pittsburgh capitalism go back to the founding families. In 1895, a National Masonic Convention was held in the East End at Phipps Conservatory. The East Enders were not really as social as the wealthy of New York. Their party topics were business. It was said that the Mellons only broke dinner table silence to speak business. The social bonds seemed to be more Scotch-Irish ancestry, Presbyterianism, and freemasonry. This freemasonry bond can be seen in a letter of Carnegie to Judge Mellon, neither of which was close. Carnegie noted: " 'I often think of you.' There is freemasonry between charac-ters that commonplace people cannot enter. You are always in that circle in my thoughts."[1] The freemasonry link was not so much a conspiracy link, but one of networking. It was one of the few places (other than church) where many of these diverse capitalists gathered for conversation.

It is not easy to generalize the nature of East Enders because so many of them were independent. Nationality was a somewhat common factor. Almost all were Scotch-Irish, Scotch, or German with a few English. The Scotch-Irish, Scotch, and Germans had natural frontier affinity. In Western Pennsylvania, they had formed schools together out of neces-sity. Often German immigrants followed the trail of the Scotch-Irish across the frontier. They shared conservative and protestant values, which often led to mixed marriages of the two. The Germans and Scotch-Irish cross-pollinated each other. The Scotch-Irish did maintain superiority in the community and in Western Pennsylvania; the Scotch-Irish had nearly 60 percent of the population for most of the 1800s. The Scotch-Irish controlled the money throughout the 1800s. Germans tended to come into power through special crafts initially. Even among the Scotch-Irish, there were significant differences as was seen in their political division during the Whiskey Rebellion. Judge Mellon was on one extreme. He was tough and hard driving. He disliked the English and Catholics as might be expected from his Ulster background. He believed in accumulating money for family

1 Cannadine, p. 125

and friends. The Germans had a similar outlier in H. J. Heinz, who believed in temperance and was a Methodist.

So what was basic to all? They all valued education. Education was at the heart of their capitalism. Free and equal education justified an initial steep distribution of wealth. Schools, universities, libraries, and cultural organizations all benefited. They believed it a duty to help the poor. Capitalism was another root. They all believed strongly in property rights and the right to prosper. They disliked any display of that wealth in public outside their neighborhood. They believed in conservative family values. They mostly held inherited wealth in low esteem with the exception of old Judge Mellon. They all opposed unions because they related them to socialism. They cared little for politicians but that didn't stop them from buying them off or for pragmatic alliances. They were extremely patriotic and nationalistic. With the exception of Judge Wilkins, they were Whigs and Republicans with anti-slavery, pro-tariff and small government beliefs. They generally were not opposed to taxes for defense and a strong military. Carnegie in his later years was the exception, taking on the goal of world peace. Frick had even supported special war taxes and the 1 percent income tax of the top 1 percent, although Frick correctly predicted that once government got the right to tax income, they would not be stopped. Men like Frick often showed resistant on tariffs. They believed in unrestricted trusts but believed in ethical behavior.

The East Ender was trained in one-room schoolhouses to be philanthropic in nature. Their Presbyterian roots, Masonic views, and education augmented that view. In addition, the founding capitalists of the area set an example going back to colonial times. This was in stark contrast to that of New York's Fifth Avenue capitalists, who often looked at philanthropy as feeding the birds. They tended to support social causes versus pure giving. New York millionaires like Vanderbilt even opposed philanthropy and thought of it as being destructive to society. For Vanderbilt, one excursion into philanthropy was Vanderbilt University; but even here, it was an endowment fund that required the money be invested in Vanderbilt's railroads. With the exception of Mellon and Carnegie, East Enders tended to give quietly and often anonymously.

The early East End capitalists set a tradition of philanthropy, taking care of the less fortunate and improving the arts. It was a tradition with deep Scotch–Irish and German roots. The Scotch–Irish were aggressive capitalists, but their Presbyterianism preached a duty to give to the less fortunate. Their Masonic membership also promoted a sharing and helping. It was an example readily adopted by their German brothers who were educated in frontier Scotch–Irish schools. Frontier Scotch–Irish pioneers established the first community houses for the poor. Care of the poor was deeply rooted in their belief system. It was typical of the Scotch–Irish to have poor guests at their Sunday dinner. East Enders were the country's greatest philanthropists due, in part, to their Presbyterianism and to help them feel better about their quest to accumulate money. Schools and libraries were considered the responsibility of the wealthy. The Scotch–Irish believed in a type of survival of the fittest in business; but on a personal basis, they were obligated to take care of the less fortunate. In addition, the Scotch–Irish and Germans believed that basic education was a basic right of all, and this funneled large donations to schools. Their support of education could be found in their rejection of the European class system.

Interestingly, East Enders Bakewell, Eichbaum, and Page established two of the earliest Pittsburgh social institutions. These institutions were the Pittsburgh Permanent Library Association and the Pittsburgh Humane Society. Benjamin Bakewell founded the Pittsburgh Humane Society in 1813 with a mission to: "alleviate the distresses of the poor — to supply the wants of the hungry, the naked and aged — to administer comfort to the widow, the orphan, and the sick."[1] The Humane Society asked for dues of $2.00 a year to fund their efforts. The Presbyterian minister of the First Presbyterian Church was also a key founder of the Humane Society, which was so fundamental to the frontier Presbyterian beliefs of helping the less fortunate. The Humane Society would be the taproot of East End philanthropy. Frick donated and supported orphanages and children's homes. Heinz similarly built houses for children and the homeless.

The early libraries were consistent with the frontier belief in education. Education was a shared belief of the region's Germans and Scotch–Irish. The Scotch–Irish considered good education a basic right. William Bakewell, Benjamin Page, and Peter William Eichbaum founded the Pittsburgh Permanent Library Association in 1813. Presbyterian Rev. Francis Herron was elected president with Bakewell and Page as officers. The Library required a $10.00 fee and dues of $5.00 a year, which limited it to the upper class. Wealthy patrons were encouraged to donate books as well. The Library was open on Saturday nights and allowed members to borrow books. In 1816, the Pittsburgh Permanent Library had over 2,000 books, making it one of the nation's largest non-university libraries. After membership in the Masonic Lodge, membership in the Library Association was considered the most prestigious. Still, it was amazing that a frontier town such as Pittsburgh had one of the first public libraries, an event not lost on Andrew Carnegie years later.

Free education and extensive education was a core value of East End capitalists going back to frontier days of the Scotch–Irish. The Scotch–Irish saw the limiting of education as the true oppression of the aristocracy. As the Scotch–Irish fled British oppression to America in the 1700s, they brought a love and culture of elementary and high level education. The Scottish enlightenment was a true revolution. The Scots believed that education was the main defense against the tyranny of the aristocratic class. They believed that capitalism could only be justified where all had access to education. For the Scotch and Scotch–Irish, education was a leveling factor and a basic human right. In Scotland, the literacy rate was an amazing 80 to 85 percent in the 1700s. The Scotch–Irish Presbyterian school system came with them to the American colony, and brought its enlightenment with it. By the American Revolution, America's literacy rate was the highest in the world

---

1 Joseph Rishel, *Founding Families of Pittsburgh*, (Pittsburgh: University of Pittsburgh Press, 1990), p. 59

(second only to Scotland) at 70 to 75 percent, while England's rate was only 50 to 60 percent. France and Italy were under 40 percent. York County's Presbyterian schools were popular with the Germans as well as the Scotch because of their high standards. Presbyterians made up the majority of roving "subscription" teachers. The Pittsburgh frontier, where Scotch–Irish William Holmes McGuffey would be born, had an amazing literacy rate of 65 percent.[1]

The high literacy rate, coupled with the high average wealth, allowed Americans to read and buy books at an amazing rate. Pittsburgh had even formed the Adelphi Society in 1812 by wealthy manufacturers to offer free schooling to the poor. This literacy rate turned the Western frontier of Pennsylvania and Ohio into the seed of the American empire and the foundation of capitalism. One common denominator of the East End capitalists was their common school background and use of the popular *McGuffey Readers*. East Enders such as Henry Clay Frick, the Mellons, the Carnegies, George Westinghouse, H. J. Heinz and many others got their values and ethics from these Readers. McGuffey preached property rights, competition, and charity. One of McGuffey's most powerful stories is found in the *Second Reader's* "*Emulation without Envy.*" This is a story of two competing students, one the son of a wealthy farmer, the other a son of a poor widow. The two boys are competing for top honors. They competed week after week with the widow's son taking the lead just before the holiday break. "When they met again, the widow's son did not appear, and the farmer's son being next in excellence, could now have been at the head of the class." Instead the farmer's son went to the widow's home, only to find the widow could not pay for books and tuition. The rich farmer's son took money out of his pocket to pay for the poor boy's books and tuition. He would lose out to his rival, but note: "people of strong minds are never envious; that weak minds are ones filled with envy." This was typical of McGuffey's moral education. *McGuffey Readers* promoted fair competition, high rewards, and charity. Many McGuffey stories warned that there would be corruption with financial success and many abuse of privileges.

The *McGuffey Readers*, which first appeared in the 1840s, were really an expression of the core beliefs of frontier Presbyterianism and Scotch–Irish heritage. Pittsburghers like James O'Hara, Benjamin Page, Thomas Bakewell, and others had expressed the social link between capitalism and philanthropy decades before McGuffey. The *McGuffey Readers* were said to teach a strange mixture of competitive success and a responsibility for the less fortunate. In fact, Henry Clay Frick's only education was five semesters of *McGuffey Readers*. Henry Clay Frick often noted this humble education, and many have pointed him out as capitalistic evil generated by McGuffey. Frick, of course, is best remembered for his role in the bloody steel strike at Homestead in 1892. Henry Clay Frick, with all his love of money and art, had been touched about the need for charity. He gave quietly to hospitals, children homes, and parks. The real point, however, shows that charity was put above all other virtues and was hailed in the earliest stories. In the end, Frick gave over 70 million

---

1 Joseph Ellis, *After the Revolution*, (New York, W. W. Norton, 1979)

mostly anonymously to the poor and needy. Similarly, lesser capitalists such as Charles Schwab built high schools and churches without much acclaim.

The tradition of giving did have the Scotch–Irish roots of James O'Hara. O'Hara gave generously to area churches of all dominations including the often ignored Irish Catholics. Years later Charles Schwab, like O'Hara, donated churches to his Irish Catholic workers. There is no doubt that the East End capitalists often had a strange mix of profit making with a philanthropic vein. Frick, Mellon, and Carnegie all fit this mold, yet it would be impossible to generalize. Frick represented the biggest dichotomy with his giving and almost ruthless business practices; yet Frick's giving was also in many aspects the purest, given anonymously with no requirements or naming rights. Carnegie's giving was very targeted in an effort to enlighten the worker. Carnegie had buildings by the hundreds named after him. Mellon found a way to incorporate his hobby of art collecting into a philanthropic endeavor. On the other hand, there were H. J. Heinz and George Westinghouse who believed in a type of enlightened treatment of workers and building community. Westinghouse, while well known for his fair treatment of employees, was often noted for his smaller philanthropic efforts compared to Carnegie. Westinghouse's response was the best philanthropy was a good paying job. Westinghouse did give deeply to community organizations such as the YMCA. H. J. Heinz's was similar but he did gave freely to religious endeavors such as Sunday Schools. None of them had the heart of Dickens's Scrooge, which was a characterization of British capitalists.

Carnegie is probably the best-known philanthropist, but his giving was very focused on his own interests. Probably the most unique thing about Carnegie was that his will left enough money to allow his heirs to live out their life in wealth. He did not want to have wealth passed on in the family because it might destroy them. Carnegie's view of philanthropy was a reflection of his capitalism. He believed in a type of destiny (not being a religious man) in which he had been assigned to improve the human race. This destiny would allow him to justify paying low wages. In his own words: "wealth, passing through the hands of a few, can be made a much more potent force for the elevation of our race than if distributed in small sums to the people themselves."[1] By small sums, Carnegie meant wages, which he felt would be wasted on "appetite" if too large. Carnegie believed in a Calvin doctrine where he was chosen to improve the lot of the human race. Carnegie's touch mark was the giving of over 300 libraries, most of which had his name. He gave the buildings, requiring the community to furnish the books. He built a natural history and art museum in Pittsburgh's East End and a full university in the Carnegie Institute of Technology. He gave 7,689 organs to churches at a cost of over $6 million. He also gave millions in educational funds, peace funds, and special institutes and funds such as the Carnegie Hero Fund. Carnegie found a unified philosophy in his money making and giving. Carnegie is said to have made and given away over $360 million. Carnegie argued that leaving $150 million to one heir disgraced the great New York capitalist John Astor. Most Pittsburgh workers gave Carnegie's worldview very little thought.

---

1 Peter Krass, *Carnegie*, (New York: John Wiley & Sons, 2002), p. 242

Frick's giving approached that of Carnegie but was far different than that of Carnegie. Frick was the quintessential capitalist seeing no destiny in his wealth or giving; however, Frick, the East End's most hated capitalist, was also the most giving. He was both a pure capitalist and a pure philanthropist. Frick was a strange study of man who believed in an American right to earn as much as possible. Known as the "butcher of Homestead" and the country's union breaker, his anonymous giving to the nation's needy seems strange. Yet on a percentage basis, he was close to Carnegie; but it was mostly anonymous giving without any strings attached. He opposed the use of his name on any of his giving. During his life, Frick gave to many charities, particularly those for poor children as well as hospitals. He often gave small amounts to needy charities or families of injured managers. He quietly gave money to the coal mining Catholic churches and x-ray machines to hospitals. He gave much to the American war effort and veteran groups. He gave the funds to build the McKinley Presidential Library and Memorial, requiring his name not be used. Frick's estimated giving during his life was just as amazing, consisting of $70 million, very little of which was publicly marked or attributed to Frick![1] It's hard to find a capitalist that gave so much with so little fanfare.

Henry Clay Frick represents historical extremes and contradictions, but he is more typical of East End charity. Recently the view of Henry Clay Frick has become one of representing the true evil of capitalism. Frick's role in the Homestead Strike of 1892 seemed to have marked him for history, yet his views on unions were no different than his saintly neighbors, H. J. Heinz and George Westinghouse. Frick, a lovingly husband and father, is more often pictured as a brute willing to break the poor immigrant worker at any cost. Yet Frick often helped poor children of these very workers without much fanfare, giving millions to children's organizations and hospitals. He formed a national organization to help retarded children.[2] He created a Pittsburgh educational fund to improve grade school education. In December of 1915 when the bankruptcy of Pittsburgh Savings caused 40,000 schoolchildren to lose $130,000 (about $1.5 million today) of their school's dime savings plan, Frick repaid them all in time for Christmas, wiring the money from New York. He often spoke privately of his distaste for the wild spending of the young New York millionaires. While he went to the very limits of the law, he hated the unethical gain of money and left the boards of such companies. Frick was not the Nero of the Gilded Age promoting wild parties of excess, but a good father and family man. The fact is Frick was neither a saint nor a devil, but a complex product of a struggling America. In the end, Frick gave much to the city who disowned him. No man can really judge Frick in the end. It would be a task of a true god to sit in the judgment seat of a Henry Clay Frick.

Frick's net worth at his death was estimated to be $143 million.[3] The actual number was later reduced to $77,230,392 with the paintings appraised at $13,000,000.[4] Frick left an amazing five-sixths of it to charity. The estate taxes of $10,000,000 set a new record.

---

1 Lorant, p. 558
2 *New York Times*, October 4, 1915
3 *New York Times*, December 3, 1919, p. 1
4 *New York Times*, February 3, 1922

His daughter was the main benefactor and received around $5 million direct in cash and stocks. Adelaide, his wife, received about $6 million. Helen, however, received $12 million in Pittsburgh real estate and another $1 million for maintenance. Other related real estate shares to Helen were valued at $6 million. Helen also gained control of $2.5 million for her charities. Childs Frick, his son, and his wife got about $1,000,000 with a life interest of $2,000,000. Nephews, nieces, and cousins received $50,000 each. The art collection was assessed at $13 million in 1920 and was finally settled at $30 million in 1931. The estimated value in 1948 was $50 million.

Frick's residual estate was divided into shares and varied with market price. In 1923 prices,[1] the amounts included $7,200,000 to Princeton, $2,400,000 to Harvard and Massachusetts Institute of Technology respectively. The Pittsburgh Educational Commission, begun by Frick, received $2,400,000. The bequest to the City of Pittsburgh for Frick Park was $2,000,000. Mercy Hospital in Pittsburgh got $1,500,000. The Lying-In Hospital in New York received $720,000. The following are Pittsburgh hospitals and organizations that received $240,000: Children's Hospital, Allegheny General, Home for the Friendless, Pittsburgh Free Hospital, Pittsburgh Newsboy Home, Kinsley House, Western Pennsylvania Hospital, YWCA, Uniontown Hospital, Braddock Hospital, Cottages State Hospital, Mount Pleasant Hospital, Westmoreland Hospital, and Homestead Hospital. He left no special funds using his name.

The East Enders were the most giving people among the nation's wealthy. Their views on philanthropy took different directions. Only Judge Mellon seemed to be the exception with many reservations about philanthropy. Mellon's banking disposition seemed to go to his heart. He was a "scrooge," believing that inequality actually was necessary for the good of society. Even in the face of the Johnstown Flood, it was Mellon's name that was missing among the many rich and poor that donated. Judge Mellon believed that his obligation was to family and friends. He particularly despised Carnegie's ostentatious style of giving. The Judge was obsessed with building a family empire. The family women, however, in the mode of New York millionaire wives, were involved in the YMCA, YWCA, hospitals, children's aid organizations, and Presbyterian Church activities. The Judge's sons — Andrew and Dick — fell more in line with the neighborhood tradition of giving after the Judge died. Later in life, Andrew would make a major donation of land and money totaling $1.6 million to the University of Pittsburgh. The donated land known as "Frick Acres" is the present location of University of Pittsburgh's Cathedral of Learning.

The East Enders built colleges, schools, social houses, and social institutions. Of course, Pennsylvania universities and colleges were highly endowed by the East Enders, as were Princeton, Yale, and MIT. Charles Schwab built a state-of-the-art technical high school. Westinghouse offered free education to his employees and families. The YMCA received tens of millions from East Enders. Community homes and homes for East Enders almost exclusively supported the homeless in the nineteenth century. Heinz and West-

---

1 *New York Times*, March 3, 1923

inghouse offered free classes in English and citizenship for workers and their families as well as housekeeping, sewing, and cooking classes for young female employees.

The East End capitalists were involved in many civic improvements that helped their image. Pittsburgh mills and factories faced the results of a major social analysis known as the "Pittsburgh Survey," which had been funded and supported by the Chamber of Commerce and Pittsburgh's new Democrat reform mayor, George Guthrie. It was a major project of outside social scientists, which was a great risk for its wealthy supporters. East End neighbors H. J. Heinz and Frick's close friend, Benjamin Thaw, helped fund the project. As a major real estate holder and Pittsburgh social donor, Frick supported the survey as well. The results were eye opening. The survey's director noted: "Pittsburgh is not merely a scapegoat city. It is capital of a district representative of the untrammeled industrial development, but a district which, for richer, for poorer, in sickness and in health, for vigor, waste, and optimism, is rampantly American."[1] The horrific report was made public in 1909 and profiled water pollution, air pollution, living conditions, industrial accidents, and wage issues for Pittsburgh's 1.6 million immigrants. USS steel executives were clearly moved by the facts. Alva Dinkey, who was manager of Homestead Works, said the report was an epiphany similar to Lincoln seeing the abuse of the slaves in his youth. USS executives including Frick became important partners in finding solutions to the city's problems. Even Carnegie, while living in Scotland, aided in programs to improve the lives of his old employees.

Another reaction to the Pittsburgh Survey was the further development of cultural and educational institutions, adding to the beauty of the area. Most of this was in the development of the Oakland section of the city by real estate developers such as Frank Nikola and Henry Clay Frick. Frick and Nikola would propose the Pittsburgh Athletic Association to 40 Duquesne Club members in 1908; by the end of the year, it had 1,500 members. While aimed at the wealthy, it was an attempt to combine sound mind and body as part of the Oakland cultural district. The Pittsburgh Athletic Association was part of a huge expansion of the Oakland cultural district including three large city parks — Schenley, Frick, and Highland. Nikola and Frick now owned all the land in Oakland upon which the University of Pittsburgh stands. With its expansive parks, clubs, Forbes Field Baseball Park, Carnegie Museum, University of Pittsburgh, Carnegie Institute of Technology, theaters, art galleries, and beautiful architecture, Oakland was a center for all Pittsburghers. After Nikola, Frick was the major real estate holder in the Oakland district.

Most fellow East Enders were out of the Frick mold. They were competitive businessmen. They felt more blessed from Providence than destiny; and, therefore, saw it as a responsibility to give back in the Scotch–Irish tradition. They had no real philosophy of the nature of capitalism and giving such as Carnegie. A few merely accumulated money for their families and gave according to their religious beliefs. Most gave generously to the community including hospitals and welfare organizations. East Ender Christopher Magee gave the city the Highland Park Zoo. Henry Phipps built a public Conservatory in

---

1   Roy Lubove, *Twentieth Century Pittsburgh*, (New York: John Wiley, 1969), p. 9

Oakland. Thaw and Frick opened up the Allegheny Observatory to the children of the city. East Enders supported most hospitals and churches. Schwab donated community fire departments and equipment. Of course, the argument of the socialist was that individuals should not accumulate such wealth. The living conditions of Pittsburgh workers often offered too great a contrast for even the average viewer. But even with these contrasts, class struggle was never a real issue in Pittsburgh. The wealthy East Enders were not generally seen as oppressors. Men like Heinz and Westinghouse even had a very positive view among Pittsburgh workers. This was related to upward mobility or at least the perception of it. The East End capitalists were not aristocrats like those of New York's Fifth Avenue, but first generation rags-to-riches stories. There were no weeklong balls and parties as seen in New York. East Enders tended to go about their lives, quietly preferring a low profile. There was even a type of civic pride in the accomplishments of Pittsburgh's manufacturing. Press coverage in Pittsburgh was generally favorable.

Not all of East End philanthropy was about massive donations of money, however. Examples abound of Westinghouse, Heinz, Frick, and others giving directly to needy people and families. Westinghouse was well known for helping older employees; Heinz for helping single, homeless women; and Frick for helping children. Heinz often invited street bums to have a free lunch at his employee dining hall. These capitalists also gave of their time to civic projects. The plague of Pittsburgh for over one hundred years had been typhoid fever and cholera from the polluted water supplies. Typhoid respected no class distinctions. H. J. Heinz's wife and his brother had died from it as well as Tom Carnegie. East Enders such as Henry Clay Frick, Captain Alfred Hunt, Andrew Carnegie, and Charles Hall had almost died from it. Pittsburgh alone had the highest incidence of typhoid fever because of its polluted water; and its sewage system was no better than a medieval village. Often typhoid fever in Pittsburgh was a death sentence leading to air-related illnesses such as pneumonia. Pittsburgh's death rate from typhoid was an unbelievable 10 percent. It would be three East Enders — Captain Hunt, William Holland, and H. J. Heinz — who would defeat this disease, not with money but with their time and energy.

The great aluminum pioneer and owner of Pittsburgh Testing Laboratory did some of the earliest studies of Pittsburgh water after his son, Roy, nearly died from typhoid fever. Hunt's study proved the suspected link between Pittsburgh's water and the disease. In 1893, Hunt was director of Engineers' Society of Western Pennsylvania. He formed a joint committee of the Engineers Society and the Allegheny County Medical Society. Hunt took a trip to Europe on his own expense to study water filtration systems. In 1896, Hunt was part of a city-formed committee known as the Pittsburgh Filtration Committee. East Ender and Director of the Carnegie Institute William Holland joined him. Holland also took his own trips to Europe to study filtration systems. He wrote the final 1899 report demanding a filtration system for Pittsburgh's water. For the next six years, Holland and Hunt were involved in a huge political battle over a filtration plant.

Nothing happened until the Great Flood of 1907 had crippled the city for weeks, and losses mounted to an unbelievable $30 million. Typhoid hit all sections of Pittsburgh. H. J. Heinz would lead the reform in Pittsburgh through his membership in three civic groups

— the Civic Club, Chamber of Commerce, and the Civic Commission. As a director and committee member of the Commerce of Commerce, Heinz had taken a leadership role in addressing these problems. He had joined the Chamber in 1903 and rose to vice-president. He also was assigned and later became president of the Pittsburgh Flood Commission.

H. J. Heinz took on impure water which had been a constant source of typhoid fever for over a hundred years in Pittsburgh and had won. For H. J. Heinz, it was personal because his wife died from the complications of typhoid. The fight for sewage and flood control was a long and difficult battle for Heinz and his fellow reformers. H. J. lacked the support of many allies in other areas; even his own local Republican Party opposed it. Pittsburgh of the early 1900s was far different than the one today. A Republican machine controlled the city. Heinz had been a staunch and major supporter of the Republican Party at the national level, but years of one party control had corrupted the local government. Two men, Christopher Magee and William Flinn, ran the city; but in 1906, reform Democrat Mayor George Guthrie took office. Heinz worked behind the scenes but then surfaced as vice-president of the Pittsburgh Civic Commission and a member of the Committee on City Planning. The fight for sewage control and water purification came first. Heinz's friend and East End engineer, Fredrick Law Olmsted Jr., was assigned to evaluate the problems. The Olmsted report of the problems would be a blueprint for years to come. Heinz enlisted East End capitalists Frick and Mellon and formed an alliance with Democrat Mayor George Guthrie. Heinz proved a great civic leader. He and the other city capitalists got filtration plants built. By 1908 all Pittsburgh water was filtered. Men like Heinz and Alfred Hunt always looked on Pittsburgh water filtration as one of their greatest accomplishments.

In World War I, the East End led the nation in "victory bond" sales. Frick was said to have purchased over $20 million alone. He proved to be a patriot in giving and business. Frick and the United States Steel Finance Committee invested in a 110-inch mill at Homestead to produce armor. Frick encouraged United States Steel to expand at Gary and to increase its overall shipbuilding capacity. Frick stood against many calls to nationalize the industry, and he proved that the company could put country ahead of company. The company out produced the whole country of Germany, supplying the government steel below market value. USS purchased $124 million in Liberty Bonds, and Frick personally purchased over $20 million. He made the largest Liberty bond purchase of $1.5 million in the name of the city of Pittsburgh. He gave generously to a number of charities for wounded soldiers including $300,000 to the Belgian Relief Fund. H. J. Heinz, similarly, invested in war bonds and developed special programs for veterans. Frick donated land and a house for soldiers and sailors to relax on Pittsburgh's Fifth Avenue. As a pure capitalist, Frick was willing to pay taxes for the war but noted his dislike for income-based tax. We can see this in a letter to friend, Senator Philander Knox: "I thoroughly believe that those of us who stay at home and take our ease should willingly pay any taxes that may be assessed to carry on the war, although, I have to confess that the present disposition seems to be to impose unfairly upon those who are supposed to have large incomes."[1]

When Frick heard the Mayor of New York had refused to build a viewing stand for disabled veterans to see a military parade, Frick built a covered viewing stand for 500 disabled soldiers and fed them. He personally donated a number of fully armored trucks and cars after reading that U.S. troops lacked armor. The full record is not complete, but biographer George Harvey reported a substantial reduction in Frick's net worth during the war. Frick gave his personal time as well, speaking to and thanking employees in the service. He was just as active in assuring that the company recognized its veterans. Frick's die-hard capitalism was always pro-American in his mind. Personally, Frick demonstrated disapproval for German goods, refusing to buy German. He supported many ethnic opposition groups such as the Italian Roman Legion of America. His daughter Helen spent months at the front lines distributing food and medicine, and Frick gave millions more to her many Red Cross projects. Other East Enders gave more directly. William Thaw served as a pilot in the famous Lafayette Escadrille. Howard Heinz was named as United States Food Administrator for Pennsylvania and became a member of the War Industries Board under future President Herbert Hoover.

---

1 Harvey, p. 318

EPILOGUE

East End capitalism has passed into history as has much of the once great neigh-borhood. Westinghouse's "Solitude," and Heinz's "Greenlawn" are forever gone. Frick's "Clayton" is all that remains of the golden delta of industrial wealth. Many of the lesser mansions remain in various stages of disrepair. Few, even in Pittsburgh, are aware of the East End's heritage and role in American industrialization and capitalism. The Mellon and Heinz families remain active in the Pittsburgh area. Some of the related companies such as Heinz Company and Westinghouse Electric still exist, but the families have long since left a managing role. Braddock's Edgar Thomson Works is the last remaining steel mill from Carnegie's steel empire. A Pittsburgh mall has replaced Homestead Works. With the possible exception of the Mellons, none have formed an American-style aristocracy. The great pillars and columns of the Oakland district and its educational and cultural buildings survive. Carnegie's museums, universities, and libraries are still there, but even some of Carnegie's libraries have been lost. Phipps Conservatory, however, is still an ac-tive cultural organization. East End capitalism has changed for the good and the bad. The spirit of American philanthropy exists, but to a lesser degree. Government now has the responsibility for social safety nets and most social institutions. The great fear of the East End capitalists that the factories would be owned and run by the financial districts of New York has, to a large degree, taken place. Bankers, not operators, run manufacturing firms. The unions, however, did not develop into a socialist movement as feared by the East Enders but cut out a uniquely American role in management-labor relations.

Many memorials to the East Enders are gone. The Westinghouse Memorial in Schen-ley Park built by employees in 1930s remains, but roads and parking have isolated the beautiful pond and memorial to visitors. A few company and building busts of others are scattered without much notoriety. Probably the only gathering of bronze busts of the old neighbors is at the McKinley Memorial in Niles, Ohio. It is there that East End "bad boy"

221

capitalist Henry Clay Frick's bust is prominently displayed, which does not occur in Pittsburgh. In Niles, we find a true tribute to East End capitalism, but even this monument is lost to most Americans.

The greatest statement of their beliefs survives in Oakland's Carnegie Institute. It is here that most pass by a series of murals, commissioned by Andrew Carnegie in 1905. Artist John Alexander (originally of Pittsburgh) received $175,000 to paint a series of murals covering several floors of the institute. The meaning of the murals remains conflicted as are the very beliefs that Carnegie wanted reflected. The dual title of the work *The Crowning of Labor* and *The Apotheosis of Pittsburgh* reflects this ambiguity.[1]

But what of their spirit and legacy? Many of the East Enders have survived the great fortunes of the last 100 years to remain on the top 30 wealthiest Americans of all time. Andrew Mellon is fourth behind Rockefeller, Vanderbilt, and Astor. Andrew Carnegie is sixth following Bill Gates, and Henry Clay Frick is 26. Even those who disagree with their belief in industrial capitalism cannot deny their lasting impact on American culture, arts, religion, and education. Their cultural institutions still offer a path to the upward mobility they believed in. Frick, Carnegie, Heinz, Phipps, Westinghouse and other East Enders built museums, Carnegie–Mellon University, the University of Pittsburgh, observatories, conservatories, high schools, grade schools, and cultural organizations. Out-of-state colleges benefited as well with Carnegie's and Frick's millions going to Princeton, MIT, and Yale. Heinz gave to Adrian College and Kansas City University. Their numerous scholarships, funds, and foundations continue to give and improve society. Carnegie funds have supported unique educational experiences such as "Sesame Street." Most of Western Pennsylvanian hospitals have benefited by their funds. Their many welfare and social programs continue to function today.

Family dynasties were never the goal of most of the old line East Enders. The majority of the wealthy heirs of many of the East Enders live in quiet society around the East Coast today. Some have even found new roles in the American middle class. Of the East End capitalists, only two families truly engaged in dynasty building — Heinz and Mellon. Members of the Heinz family continued in active management of the company into the 1980s. Remnants of the Heinz family remain active today in Pittsburgh philanthropy. The family is probably best known by the marriage of widowed Theresa Heinz to Senator John Kerry. The Mellon family also remains a factor in Pittsburgh to this day, and may be the only true line of East End aristocracy. The line began with old Judge Thomas Mellon and his two sons — Andrew W. and Richard B. Mellon. Richard B. Mellon's son, Richard King, was the product of the alliance of the old capitalist Pittsburgh family of Alexander King. Richard King Mellon had been raised in his father's 65-room mansion at 6500 Penn Avenue. Richard Mellon's sister, Sarah, married into one of the old East End families, that of Alan Scaife. The Mellon–Negley–King–Scaife line is truly aristocratic.

Of course, the spirit of the old lions remains to this day, not in family dynasties but in the educational, cultural, and recreational institutions they created. In most cases these

---

1 Rina Youngner, *Industry in Art*, (Pittsburgh: University of Pittsburgh Press, 2006), p. 131

institutions have far outlasted the mills and factories; and it is in these institutions that the seeds of a new generation of industrialists yet to be seen are preserved. Their spirit has lifted millions in education and social mobility, making doctors, lawyers, and scientists of the children and grandchildren of the immigrant steelworkers they brought to Pittsburgh. Carnegie left over 300 libraries across the country, and his greatest was in Pittsburgh's East End. The Mellon family art collection became the core of the National Gallery of Art in Washington, D.C. Frick's art is spread between Pittsburgh and New York in galleries. Frick, Heinz, Westinghouse, and Carnegie left a legacy of hospitals and social institutions. Charles Schwab left churches and schools. Carnegie, Phipps, Thaw, Frick, Mellon, and other East Enders left observatories, conservatories, museums, zoos, parks, churches, libraries, and college departments. Major colleges were the biggest beneficiaries such as Carnegie–Mellon University, University of Pittsburgh, and Princeton. These institutions and the East End remain a testimony and pantheon to these East End capitalists.

BIBLIOGRAPHY

Adams, Henry. *The Education of Henry Adams.* New York: Library of America, 1968

Adams, Henry. *Letters of John Hay,* ed. Henry Adams. Washington: 1908

Adams, James. *The Epic of America.* New York: Triangle Books, 1931.

Alberts, Robert. *The Good Provider.* Boston: Houghton Mifflin, 1973

Allen, Frederick Lewis. *The Great Pierpont Morgan.* New York: Harper and Brothers, 1949.

Barron, C. W. *They Told Barron.* New York: Harper, 1930.

Beard, Patricia. *After the Ball.* New York: Harper Collins, 2003

Berkman, Alexander. *Prison Memoirs of an Anarchist.* New York: Schocken Books, 1970.

Bridenbaugh, Carl. *The Colonial Craftsman,* New York: Dover Publications, 1990.

Bridge, James. *The Inside History of the Carnegie Steel Company.* New York: Aldine Book Company, 1903.

Brody, David. *Steelworkers in America: The Nonunion Era.* New York: Harper Torchbooks, 1960.

Burgoyne, A. G. *The Homestead Strike of 1892.* Pittsburgh: Rawsthorne, 1893

Burnley, J. *Millionaires and Kings of Enterprise.* Philadelphia: Lippincott, 1901.

Butler, Joseph. *Fifty Years of Iron and Steel.* Cleveland: Penton Press, 1917.

Byington, M. *Homestead: The Households of a Milltown, Pittsburgh Survey.* New York: Russell Sage Foundation, 1910.

Calhoun, Charles. *Benjamin Harrison.* New York: Times Books, 2005.

Cannadine, David. *Mellon: An American Life.* New York: Alfred A. Knopf, 2006.

Carnegie, Andrew. *The Autobiography of Andrew Carnegie.* Boston: Northeastern University Press, 1986.

Casson, Herbert. *The Romance of Steel: The Story of a Thousand Millionaires,* New York: A.S. Barnes & Company, 1907.

Carosso, Vincent. *The Morgans: Private International Bankers.* Cambridge: Harvard University Press, 1987.

Chernow, Ron. *The House of Morgan.* New York: Grove Press, 1990.

Chernow, Ron. *Titan: The Life of John D. Rockefeller.* New York, Vintage Books, 2004

Cochran, Thomas and William Miller. *The Age of Enterprise,* New York: Harper & Row, 1942.

Corey, J. B., *Memoir of J. B. Corey.* Pittsburgh: Pittsburgh Printing Company, 1914

Cotter, Arundel, *The Authentic History of The United States Steel Corporation,* (New York: Moody Magazine, 1916

Doherty, Donald. *Pittsburgh's Shadyside.* Chicago: Arcadia Publishing, 2008

DiCiccio, Carmen. *Coal and Coke in Pennsylvania.* Harrisburg: Pennsylvania Historical and Museum Commission, 1996.

Eggert, Gerald. *Steelmasters and Labor Reform.* Pittsburgh: University of Press, 1981

Evans, Henry Oliver. *Iron Pioneer: Henry W. Oliver.* New York: E. P. Dutton & Co., 1942.

Fisher, Douglas. *Steel Serves the Nation,* Pittsburgh: United States Steel, 1951.

Foner, Eric. *Free Soil, Free Labor, Free Men.* Oxford: Oxford University Press, 1995.

Garraty, J. *Right Hand Man: The Life of George Perkins.* New York: Harper, 1957.

Goldman, Emma. *Living My Life.* New York: Dover Publications, 1970.

Harvey, George. *Henry Clay Frick: The Man,* Privately printed, 1938.

Havighurst, Walter. *Vein of Iron.* Cleveland: World Publishing Company, 1958.

Hart, Lane. *Annual Report of the Secretary of Internal Affairs.* Harrisburg: State of Pennsylvania, 1884

Hays, Samuel, ed., *City at the Point: Essays on the Social History of Pittsburgh,* Pittsburgh: University of Pittsburgh, 1989

Hersh, Burton. *The Mellon Family.* New York: William Morrow & Co., 1978.

Holbrook, Stewart. *Iron Brew.* New York: Macmillan Company, 1939.

Kessner, Thomas. *Capital City.* New York: Simon & Schuster, 2003

Krause, Paul. *The Battle for Homestead 1880–1892.* Pittsburgh: University of Pittsburgh Press, 1992

Lundberg, Ferdinand. *America's Sixty Families.* New York: Citadel Press, 1938.

O'Hara, Mary. "My Father, Henry Clay Frick by Helen Clay Frick." *Pittsburgh Press,* August, 1959.

Mancke, Richard. "Iron Ore and Steel: A Case Study of the Economic Causes and Consequences of Vertical Integration," *The Journal of Industrial Economics,* Vol. 20, No. 3, July, 1972.

Meader, Jay. "Henry Clay Frick American Sepulchral," *New York Daily News,* February 25, 1999

Miner, Curtis. *Homestead,* Pittsburgh: Historical Society of Western Pennsylvania, 1989

McCollester, Charles. *The Point of Pittsburgh.* Pittsburgh: Battle of Homestead Foundation, 2008

McCullough, David. *Johnstown Flood.* New York: Touchstone, 1968

Meade, Edward. "The Genesis of the United States Steel Corporation," *Journal of Economics*, August, 1901, Volume 15, No. 4

Mellon, Thomas. *Thomas Mellon and His Times*. (Pittsburgh: University of Pittsburgh Press, 1994).

Miles, Lisa. *Remembering Allegheny City*. Pittsburgh: Pennsylvania Historical Commission, 2007

Miner, Curtis. *Homestead: The Story of a Steel Town*. Pittsburgh: Western Pennsylvania Historical Society, 1989.

Montgomery, David. *Beyond Equality: Labor and the Radical Republicans*, Urbana: University of Illinois Press, 1981.

Montgomery, David. *The Fall of the House of Labor*. Cambridge: Cambridge University Press, 1987.

Morgan, H. Wayne. *William McKinley and His America*. Syracuse: Syracuse University Press. 1962

Morgan, H. Wayne. *From Hayes to McKinley: National Party Politics*. Syracuse: Syracuse University Press. 1969

Mumford, Lewis. *Technics and Civilization*. New York: Harvest Book, 1962

Nasaw, David. *Andrew Carnegie*. New York: Penguin Press, 2006.

Nelson, Ralph. *Merger Movements in American Industry 1895-1956*. Princeton: Princeton University Press, 1959

The Pittsburgh Survey, Paul Kellogg, editor, New York: Survey Associates, 1908-1914, six volumes

Rayback, Joseph. *The History of American Labor*. New York: Macmillan Company, 1961

Reitano, Joanne. *The Tariff Question in the Gilded Age*. University Park: Pennsylvania State University Press, 1994.

Reitman, Renee. "The Elite Community in Shadyside, 1880-1920," Seminar Paper, Department of History, University of Pittsburgh, 1964

Report on Conditions of Employment in the Iron and Steel Industry, U.S. Bureau of Labor, Washington: 1911, Volume III

Ripley, W. *Trusts, Pools, and Corporations*. New York: Ginn and Company, 1905.

Roosevelt, Theodore. *The Autobiography of Theodore Roosevelt*. New York: Charles Scribner's Sons, 1958.

Root, Waverly and Richard de Rochemont. *Eating in America: A History*. New York: Echo, 1981.

Sanger, Martha Frick Symington. *Henry Clay Frick: An Intimate Portrait*, New York: Abbeville Press, 1998

Sanger Martha Frick Symington. *Helen Clay Frick*. Pittsburgh: University of Pittsburgh Press, 2008.

Scoville, Warren. *Revolution in Glassmaking*. Cambridge: Harvard University Press, 1948

Schlereth, Thomas. *Victorian America*. New York: Harper Perennial, 1991

Schreiner, Samuel, A. Jr. *Henry Clay Frick: The Gospel of Greed*. New York: St. Martin's Press, 1995.

Sheppard, Richard. "Homestead Steel Strike of 1892," *Susquehanna*, February, 1988

Sheppard, Murial, *Cloud by Day*. Pittsburgh: University of Pittsburgh Press, 1991.

Skrabec, Quentin. *Michael Owens and the Glass Industry*. Pelican Books, 2007

Skrabec, Quentin. *Metallurgic Age*. Jefferson: McFarland & Co., 2006

Skrabec, Quentin. *William McKinley: Apostle of Protectionism*. New York: Algora Publishing, 2008.

Skrabec, Quentin. *George Westinghouse: Gentle Genius*. New York: Algora Publishing, 2007

Slavishak, Edward. *Bodies of Work: Civic Display and Labor in Industrial*. Durham: Duke University Press, 2008

Standiford, Les. *Meet You in Hell: Andrew Carnegie, Henry Clay Frick, and the Bitter Partnership that Transformed America*. New York: Crown Publishers. 2003

Stefan, Lorant. *Pittsburgh — The Story of an American City*. Garden City: Doubleday, 1964.

Mark Summers. *Party Games*. Chapel Hill: University of North Carolina Press, 2004

Taft, Philip. *Organized Labor in American History*, New York: Harper and Row, 1964

Tarbell, Ida. *The Life of Elbert H. Gary*. New York: D. Appleton, 1925.

Timmons, Bascom. *Portrait of an American: Charles G. Dawes*. New York: Henry Holt and Company, 1963.

Wade, Richard. *The Urban Frontier*. Urbana: University of Illinois Press, 1996.

Wall, Joseph. *Andrew Carnegie*. New York: Oxford University Press, 1970

Warne, Colston. *The Steel Strike of 1919*. Lexington: D. C. Heath and Company, 1963.

Warren, Kenneth. *Triumphant Capitalism*. Pittsburgh: University of Pittsburgh Press, 1996.

Watkins, Elizabeth, "Heinz Varieties on Six Continents," *Western Pennsylvania History*, 1999, vol. 82

Welch, Robert. *The Presidencies of Grover Cleveland*. Lawrence: University of Kansas Press, 1988.

Winkler, John. *Morgan the Magnificent*. Babson Park: Spear & Staff, 1950.

Wiley, Harvey. *An Autobiography*. Indianapolis: Bobbs-Merrill, 1930

Wright, Carroll. "National Amalgamated Association of Iron, Steel, and Tin Workers." *The Quarterly Journal of Economics*, November 1901.

Youngner, Rina. *Industry in Art*. Pittsburgh: University of Pittsburgh Press, 2006.

Zieger, Robert. *Republicans and Labor*. Lexington: University of Kentucky Press, 1969

INDEX

A

Abbott, William, 124-125
ALCOA, 9, 11, 113, 135, 146, 150, 152-153, 155
Allegheny City (Pittsburgh's north side), 32, 46-47, 54, 56, 61, 65-67, 69, 74, 76, 87, 124, 129, 137, 151, 176, 195-196
Allegheny County Light Company, 18
Allegheny County Observatory, 44, 63, 151, 217
Amalgamated Association of Miners, 162
Amalgamated Association of Iron and Steel, 132, 162, 228
American Museum of Natural History, 20, 213
American Steel and Wire Company, 175
American System, 24, 45, 51, 53
Armor production, 15, 47, 60, 150, 158, 218-219
Armstrong, Thomas, 11
Astor's invitation list of 400, 179, 184
Automobiles, 10, 14, 16, 18-19, 83, 121, 136, 162, 171, 179, 187

B

Bacon, Robert, 175
Baker, George, 174-175
Bakewell, Thomas, 11, 16, 45, 53-55, 195, 212
Baltimore and Ohio Railroad, 74
Beehive ovens, 100-101
Bellefield Company, 14, 175-176
Berkman, Alexander, 130, 161, 225

Bessemer, Henry, 102, 125
Bessemer Process, 63, 102-103, 125, 152
Bethlehem Steel Corporation, 198, 208
Bigelow, Edward, 82, 120-122
Bope, Henry, 125, 199
Boys of Braddock, 104, 170, 173, 175, 182, 198, 208
Bradley, Alexander, 11, 43
Braun, Arthur, 11
Bridge, James, 225
Bryan, William Jennings, 157
Buhl, Henry, 54, 63
Butler, Joseph, 163, 225

C

Caldwell, John, 90, 113
Calvary Episcopal Church, 20, 124
Carnegie, Andrew, 1, 3, 5-6, 9-14, 19-21, 24, 26, 29-31, 33, 40, 44, 48, 54, 56, 58-60, 62-63, 67, 69-74, 76-79, 82, 88, 93, 97-98, 101-108, 111-118, 121-133, 135-136, 138, 140-141, 148, 152, 157-158, 161, 163, 165-177, 179, 181-182, 188-189, 192, 194-199, 203, 205, 207-211, 213-217, 221-223, 225, 227-228
Carnegie, Tom, 10-11, 30, 62, 70, 73-74, 97-98, 102, 104-108, 112, 125, 171, 217
Carnegie Institute of Technology, 6, 14, 176, 198, 213, 216
Carnegie Museum, 20, 105, 121-123, 136, 176, 216
Carnegie Veterans Association, 198
Charcoal furnaces, 34, 43, 77, 103